Nothing
but the
Best!

Nothing but the Best!

A Collection of Recipes from The University of Alabama Family

Library of Congress Catalog Card Number
ISBN 0-9654540-0-2

First Edition

Printed by

Wimmer Brothers
Memphis

Printed in the USA by
WIMMER
The Wimmer Companies, Inc.
Memphis

To order copies of *Nothing but the Best!* write:

College of Human Environmental Sciences
Box 870158
The University of Alabama
Tuscaloosa, Alabama 35487-0158

Proceeds from *Nothing but the Best!* will be used
for endowments to support academic programs in
the College of Human Environmental Sciences.

Constructed between 1839 and 1841, the
President's Mansion serves as the home of the
President and his family. The President's Mansion
is one of only four buildings that survived the
Civil War.

Officially Licensed Product of
The University of Alabama

DEDICATION

We proudly dedicate this book to our students—past, present, and future.

ACKNOWLEDGMENTS

The recipes in *Nothing but the Best!* were selected from more than 1,000 submitted by The University of Alabama family. We do not claim that these recipes are all original but they are favorites of the faculty, staff, students, alumni, and friends who submitted them. Hopefully, they will be your favorites, too.

Nothing but the Best! Cookbook Committee
MarLa Sayers–Honorary Chair
Beth Gibbs–Chair
Kathy Morrow–Co-Chair
Jan Brakefield–Marketing
Milla Boschung–Marketing
Lisa Parker–Finance
Dot Martin–Finance
Jo Bonner–Consultant

Photography
Chip Cooper, Alice Wilson, Kent Gidley, and Ricky Yanaura

Editing, Proofreading, and Technical Assistance
Gail Davis, Amy Gilchrist, Suzanne Henson, Susanna Kelley, Ralph Lane, Kristin Morris, Kathleen Stitt, Mildred Switzer, Tammy Ward, and Henry Wideman

Alumni Advisory Committee
Cherry Bryant, Angie Webb, Angela Fulmer, and Suzanne Harris

General Support
The faculty and staff in the College of Human Environmental Sciences.

*C*oming up with the name for this, the first official cookbook for The University of Alabama, was the easy part. After all, whether it's a memory of your first walk around the quad, the excitement of a Bama win in the closing seconds of the big game, or a lasting relationship which was forged years—or decades ago—the Alabama experience truly represents *Nothing but the Best!*

Selecting the recipes, on the other hand, proved more challenging than any of us imagined. Over 1,000 recipes were submitted. Due to space limitations, many wonderful recipes could not be included. Nevertheless, we deeply appreciate all the recipes that were shared.

First and foremost, this is a cookbook designed to be easy to read and fun to use. As you thumb through these pages, you will notice some recipes which are as old as the Druid Oaks lining University Boulevard. Others, quite frankly, are making their debut in this cookbook. All, however, have come to us from members of the extended group of faculty, staff, students, alumni, and friends that make up The University of Alabama family.

Proceeds from the sales of this cookbook will be used to create an endowment to support academic programs and new initiatives in the College of Human Environmental Sciences. Through this endowed fund, your purchase of the cookbook will benefit the academic experience of young people for generations to come.

In an undertaking such as this, it is dangerous to single out certain individuals for thanks and praise at the risk of leaving out others. Many people have played a major role in making this book a reality. Yet, we owe special thanks to MarLa Sayers, who served as honorary chair. And, to Chip Cooper, Alice Wilson, Kent Gidley, and Ricky Yanaura, who captured the beauty of the campus with their photography.

Over the course of time, we hope *Nothing but the Best!* becomes the first choice for your favorite recipes. Thanks for your continued support of The University of Alabama.

And, in the words of your favorite pachyderm, ROLL TIDE!

Judy Bonner

Judith L. Bonner, Ph.D.
Dean, College of Human Environmental Sciences

In 1818, one year before Alabama became a state, the Congress of the United States set aside land for a "seminary of learning." The state subsequently granted additional land and chartered The University of Alabama in 1820. The University received its first students in 1831. As Alabama's first university, The University of Alabama has a long and rich history.

Award winning photographers Chip Cooper, Alice Wilson, Kent Gidley, and Ricky Yanaura captured the beauty of The University of Alabama campus on the cover and in the pages that follow.

Denny Chimes was built on the quad as a monument to honor beloved University of Alabama President George Denny. The tower is built of Alabama limestone and brick from President Denny's native Virginia. A new carillon containing 25 bells was installed in the tower in 1986 from the generous contributions of University of Alabama alumni. The bells chime every fifteen minutes and play medleys, including the Alma Mater, each evening.

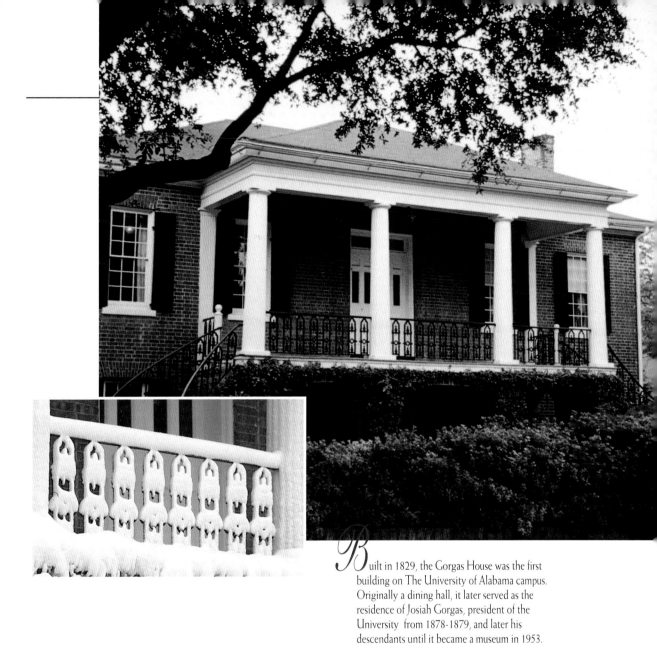

Built in 1829, the Gorgas House was the first building on The University of Alabama campus. Originally a dining hall, it later served as the residence of Josiah Gorgas, president of the University from 1878-1879, and later his descendants until it became a museum in 1953.

Named in honor of Amelia Gayle Gorgas, the main library is centrally located on the quadrangle.

$\mathcal{D}$edicated in 1930 as a memorial to all former
University of Alabama students who have borne
arms in defense of their state or their country,
Reese Phifer Hall initially served as the Student
Union Building. The building was renovated for
use by the College of Communication in 1980
and named Reese Phifer Hall in 1992.

MARY HEWELL ALSTON HALL

amed after Dean Lee Bidgood, Bidgood Hall was built in 1928 and is used today for classrooms and research and service centers in the College of Commerce and Business Administration.

Mary Hewell Alston Hall was completed in 1991 under a major building program designed to expand and modernize teaching and research facilities in the College of Commerce and Business Administration.

The Angelo Bruno Business Library and the Sloan Bashinsky Computer Center were occupied in 1994, completing the building program for the College of Commerce and Business Administration.

$\mathcal{B}$ibb Graves Hall was dedicated in 1929 and named in honor of Governor Bibb Graves. Etched in the stone attic is the inscription "Religion, morality, and knowledge being necessary to good government and the happiness of mankind, schools and the means of education shall forever be encouraged." Graves Hall provides offices and classrooms for the College of Education.

The School of Law was completed in 1978 on the southeastern part of campus and contains classrooms, seminar and conference rooms, faculty offices, a courtroom, and a law library.

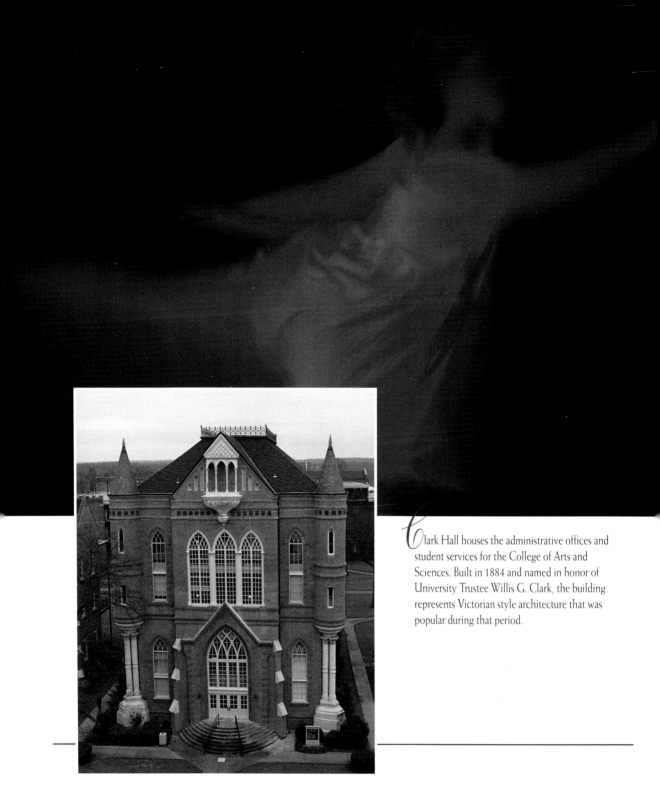

Clark Hall houses the administrative offices and student services for the College of Arts and Sciences. Built in 1884 and named in honor of University Trustee Willis G. Clark, the building represents Victorian style architecture that was popular during that period.

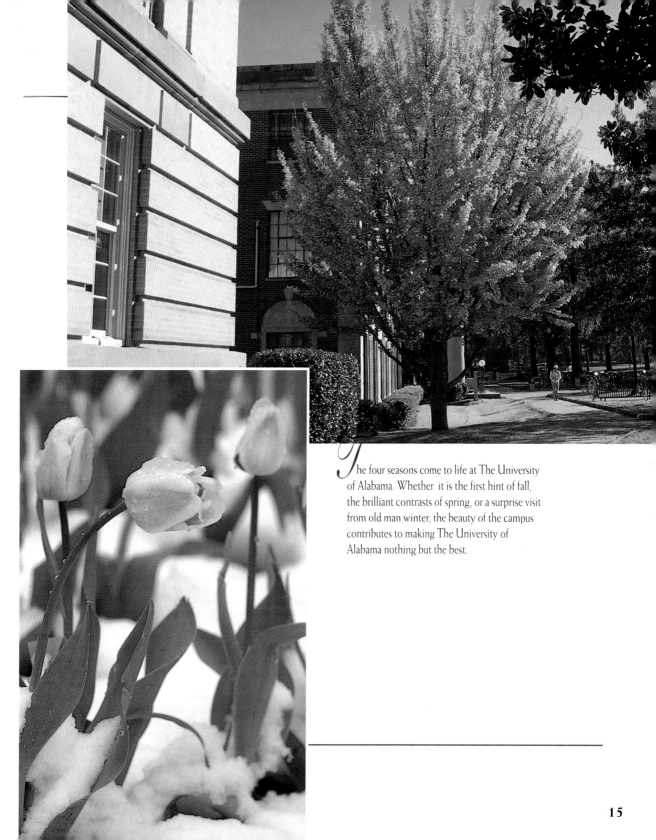

he four seasons come to life at The University of Alabama. Whether it is the first hint of fall, the brilliant contrasts of spring, or a surprise visit from old man winter, the beauty of the campus contributes to making The University of Alabama nothing but the best.

15

As the capstone of higher education, The University of Alabama has a rich tradition of producing champions that, with time, become legends on the field, in the classroom, and beyond.

Table of Contents

Appetizers & Beverages

Appetizers and Beverages

Nothing but the Best!

Crab Bacon Rolls

¼ cup tomato juice
1 well-beaten egg
1 (7½-ounce) can (1 cup) crab meat, flaked,
    cartilage removed
½ cup fine dry bread crumbs
1 tablespoon snipped parsley
1 tablespoon lemon juice
¼ teaspoon salt
¼ teaspoon Worcestershire sauce
dash of pepper
9 slices bacon, cut in half

- Mix tomato juice and egg. Add remaining ingredients, except bacon; mix thoroughly.
- Roll into 18 fingers 2 inches long. Wrap each roll with bacon and secure with wooden picks.
- Broil 5 inches from heat 10 minutes, turning often to brown evenly. Serve hot.
- **Yield: 18 rolls.**

Jenelle Marsh
Assistant Dean for Student/Academic Affairs, Dean's Office
School of Law
Gene Marsh
Professor of Law, School of Law

Marinated Shrimp

10 pounds raw shrimp, peeled and deveined
1 (5-ounce) bottle soy sauce
1 (16-ounce) bottle Wishbone Italian
    dressing

- Marinate shrimp overnight in mixture of soy sauce and Italian dressing.
- When ready to serve, spread shrimp on cookie sheet and cook in 350° oven 15 minutes.
- Serve on platter over warmer, if possible. May be prepared a day ahead.
- **Yield: Serves 40.**

Ann S. Fulmer
Secretary, Department of Human Nutrition
and Hospitality Management
College of Human Environmental Sciences

Annie Moore's Asparagus Roll-Ups

3 ounces blue cheese
1 (8-ounce) package cream cheese
1 egg
20 slices bread
20 asparagus spears
½ pound butter, melted

- Blend cheeses and egg.
- Trim crust from bread and flatten with rolling pin. Spread with cheese mixture.
- Place asparagus on bread, roll up jellyroll-style, and secure with toothpicks. Brush with melted butter and chill for 1 hour.
- Cut into thirds, wrap, and freeze.
- When ready to serve, bake at 400° for 15 minutes until lightly toasted.

Elise F. Bagwell
Selma Regional Office

Low Cal Artichoke Chili Potatoes

6 baking potatoes
3 ounces low-fat cheddar cheese, grated
½ cup chopped mild green chili peppers
½ cup coarsely chopped artichoke hearts
¼ cup low-fat sour cream
¼ cup salsa

- Bake potatoes at 450° for 1 hour, or until soft. Split in half. Remove most of pulp with spoon, leaving enough to keep skin intact.
- In bowl, combine potato pulp, cheese, peppers, and artichoke hearts. Fill potato skins with mixture.
- Reduce oven to 350° and bake an additional 10 minutes.
- Top with sour cream and salsa just before serving.

Sandra Perkins '84
Academic Advisor, External Degree Program
New College

Stuffed Mushrooms

cream cheese
bacon, fried crisp and crumbled
mushroom caps, cleaned

- Combine cream cheese and bacon.
- Pipe into mushroom caps.
- Bake in 350° oven until bubbly.

Jeannie Englebert
Program Assistant, Center for Business
and Economic Research
College of Commerce and Business Administration

Nothing but the Best!

Low-Fat Ham Roll-Ups

10 medium flour tortillas
1 (8-ounce) package low-fat or fat-free
    cream cheese, softened
1 package low-fat ham slices
small head lettuce

- Spread each tortilla with 1 teaspoon cream cheese. Top with ham and lettuce leaf. Roll up and chill. Cut each tortilla into five pieces before serving.
- **Yield: 50 roll-ups.**

Kathy Godfrey
Receptionist and Computer Lab Supervisor, Dean's Office
College of Engineering

Mexican Nacho Hors d'Oeuvres

1 pound lean ground beef
1 large onion, chopped
salt
hot pepper sauce, optional
1 (16-ounce) can refried beans
1 (4-ounce) can mild green chilis, drained
    and chopped
3 cups (12 ounces) shredded Monterey Jack
    cheese
¾ cup taco sauce
¼ cup chopped green onions
1 cup sliced ripe or green olives
guacamole
1 cup sour cream

- Crumble ground beef in frying pan. Add onion. Cook on high heat, stirring until meat is brown; drain. Season meat to taste with salt and hot pepper sauce, if desired.
- Spread refried beans in ovenproof serving dish. Top with meat, green chilis, cheese, and taco sauce.
- Bake, uncovered, at 400° for 20-25 minutes. Remove from oven and garnish with green onions, olives, guacamole, and sour cream.
- Serve with tortilla chips for dipping.

Linda C. Price
System Coordinator
Financial Affairs

Bacon Rolls

¼ cup butter
½ cup water
1½ cups herb-seasoned stuffing mix
¼ pound bulk pork sausage
1 egg, lightly beaten
12 slices bacon, cut in half

- Melt butter in saucepan, add water and bring to a boil. Remove from heat and stir in stuffing mix. Add uncooked sausage and egg. Mix well. Cover and chill 30 minutes.
- Shape into 24 logs, wrap with bacon, and secure with wooden picks.
- Place on a rack in a broiler pan. Bake at 375° for 20 minutes. Turn and bake 15 minutes longer or until lightly browned. Drain on paper towel.
- After draining, cool and place in airtight containers or freeze for up to 30 days.
- To reheat, if frozen, thaw, then place on baking sheet and cover with aluminum foil. Bake at 375° for 10 minutes or until heated.

Debbie Wilson
Medical Receptionist,
Department of Obstetrics and Gynecology
College of Community Health Sciences

Party Beef Balls

2 slices white bread
¼ cup milk
1 pound lean ground beef
1 teaspoon salt
1 tablespoon Worcestershire sauce
1 egg, beaten
1 small onion, chopped
½ teaspoon black pepper
¼ teaspoon cayenne pepper
oil
1 tablespoon soy sauce
8 ounces fresh mushrooms, sliced
lemon juice
margarine
barbecue sauce

- Crumble bread in a medium bowl and moisten with milk. Add beef, salt, Worcestershire sauce, egg, onion, pepper, and soy sauce. Mix lightly and form into small balls.
- Sauté in a small amount of oil until done. Drain well. Meatballs may be made weeks in advance and frozen after cooking.
- Sauté fresh mushrooms in lemon juice and margarine. Combine mushrooms, meat balls, and your favorite barbecue sauce.
- Serve warm in a chafing dish.

Margaret E. (Beth) Rumley Russell '70
York, Alabama

Nothing but the Best!

Brain Food Snacks

4 cups honey graham cereal

1 cup salted nuts

2 cups broken pretzel sticks

¼ cup butter

¼ cup smooth peanut butter

1 cup raisins

- Toss cereal, nuts, and pretzels together in a large bowl.
- Melt butter and peanut butter. Pour over cereal mixture.
- Place in large baking pan and bake at 275° for 25 minutes.
- Remove from oven, add raisins, and pour onto waxed paper to cool.
- Store in an airtight container.

Really good to munch on when studying for exams.

Caroline Powell
Director of Corporate and Foundation Relations
Development Office
Glenn Powell '64 '66
General Counsel
The University of Alabama System

Cocktail Fantastics

1 (16-ounce) box oysterette crackers

1 cup corn oil

1 (7-ounce) package dry ranch-style dressing mix

½ teaspoon garlic powder

1 tablespoon dill

1 tablespoon lemon pepper

paprika

- Combine all ingredients except paprika in a large bowl and mix until well coated.
- Sprinkle with paprika. Store in airtight container.

These are great to serve while watching football and basketball games.

Penny Calhoun Gibson '83 '89
Reference Librarian, Law School Library
School of Law

Curried Chicken Pâté

2 envelopes plain gelatin

1 cup milk

2 chicken bouillon cubes

2 eggs, separated

½ teaspoon Accent seasoning

2 teaspoons curry powder

3 cups cottage cheese

2 tablespoons lemon juice

2 cups finely chopped cooked chicken

¼ cup chutney

¼ cup diced pimento

2 tablespoons minced onion

1 cup whipping cream

- Sprinkle gelatin over milk in a medium saucepan. Add bouillon cubes and egg yolks. Mix well. Place over low heat. Stir constantly until gelatin and cubes are dissolved and mixture thickens slightly, about 5 minutes. Remove from heat. Stir in Accent seasoning and curry powder.
- Beat cottage cheese with mixer on high speed until smooth. Stir into gelatin mixture. Add lemon juice, chicken, chutney, pimento, and onion.
- Chill, if necessary, until mixture mounds slightly when dropped from spoon.
- Beat egg whites until stiff, but not dry, and fold into mixture. Fold in whipped cream, and spoon into an 8 to 9-inch springform pan. Chill until firm. Remove from refrigerator 15 to 20 minutes before serving.
- **Yield: 50 buffet servings.**

Martha Juanita Crump
Gurley, Alabama

Easy Crab Appetizers

1 (10-ounce) can refrigerated crescent rolls

1 (7-ounce) can crabmeat, drained and flaked

1 (8-ounce) can water chestnuts, drained and diced

1 cup (4 ounces) finely shredded Swiss cheese

½ cup mayonnaise

2 tablespoons minced green onions, including tops

1½ teaspoons dill

1 teaspoon lemon juice

salt and pepper to taste

- Separate rolls along perforations into eight pieces. With a sharp knife, cut each piece into fifths.
- Combine remaining ingredients; spread on rolls. Fold ends over mixture to make small "packages." Place on ungreased cookie sheet.
- Bake at 350° for 15 to 20 minutes, checking to make sure they do not burn.

Connie Cotazino Sulentic
Administrative Coordinator,
Culverhouse School of Accountancy
College of Commerce and Business Administration

Marinated Crab Claws

2 pounds fresh crab claws

1 large bottle Kraft House Italian Dressing

½ (.7-ounce) package Good Seasons Italian
   Dressing

1 generous tablespoon Tony Chachere's
   Seasoning

2 (4-ounce) cans black olives, sliced or
   whole

1 bunch green onions, chopped

juice of large lemon

oil and vinegar to taste

lettuce

red and yellow bell pepper rings

- Spread crab claws in a large dish.
- Mix Italian dressing, dry Italian dressing mixture, Tony Chachere's seasoning, olives, green onions, and lemon juice. Pour over crab claws. Add 2 parts of vinegar for every 1 part of oil in an amount sufficient to cover claws.
- Cover, shake well, and marinate, refrigerated, 6 to 8 hours. Do not marinate any longer, or flavors will be too strong.
- Drain and serve in a bowl lined with lettuce. Garnish with bell pepper.

Don't waste your money on crab claws that have been frozen. This recipe is a hit everywhere it is served. Alumni attending the reception in Doster before the bonfire at homecoming look forward to it each year.

Janée and Jo Bonner '82
Alexandria, Virginia

Elaine's Shrimp Mold

1 (10¾-ounce) can cream of shrimp soup

1 (8-ounce) package cream cheese

1½ envelopes unflavored gelatin

1 pound shrimp, cooked, shelled and diced

½ cup chopped celery

1 cup mayonnaise

- Heat soup over medium heat. Add cream cheese and stir until melted.
- Add gelatin and stir until thickened. Add remaining ingredients. Pour into greased 1-quart mold and chill.
- Unmold and serve with assorted crackers.

H.T. Boschung '49 '50 '57
Professor Emeritus, Department of Biological Sciences
College of Arts and Sciences

Fruit Shish Kebobs

bananas, cut into ¾-inch slices

3 tablespoons orange juice concentrate

1 cup toasted coconut

1 (15¼-ounce) can pineapple chunks

1 cup seedless grapes

2 (6-ounce) jars maraschino cherries

- Dip banana slices in orange juice concentrate, then roll in coconut.
- Alternate with pineapple chunks, grapes, and cherries on wooden skewers.

Debbie Wilson
Medical Receptionist,
Department of Obstetrics and Gynecology
College of Community Health Sciences

Game Day Brunch Pizza

1 (8-ounce) can refrigerated crescent rolls
6 eggs, beaten
½ pound bacon, cooked and crumbled
1 cup (4 ounces) shredded cheddar cheese
1 (4-ounce) can sliced mushrooms, drained

- Unroll crescent dough on a lightly greased 12-inch pizza pan; firmly press perforations to seal.
- Combine remaining ingredients. Pour over dough.
- Bake at 375° for 12 to15 minutes.

Megan Morris
Athens, Alabama

Golden Cheesies

1 cup butter, room temperature
2½ cups all-purpose flour
1 teaspoon salt
1 cup sour cream
3 cups (12 ounces) shredded cheddar cheese
paprika

- Cut butter into flour and salt with pastry blender. Add sour cream and form into a ball. Divide dough into four balls and chill until firm.
- Roll one ball on floured surface. Sprinkle with ¾ cup cheese. Roll up jellyroll-style. Place on ungreased cookie sheet, seam side down. Cut halfway through at 1-inch intervals. Sprinkle with paprika. Repeat with remaining dough.
- Bake at 350° for 30 minutes.

Nedria Smelser
Tuscaloosa, Alabama

Spinach Bread

2 (10-ounce) packages frozen spinach, defrosted
½ cup butter, melted
garlic salt
freshly ground black pepper
hot sauce
¼ pound Monterey Jack cheese, grated
2 loaves French bread

- Defrost spinach in microwave, drain, and press dry. Add to melted butter. Stir and let cool.
- Add garlic salt and pepper to taste, dash of hot sauce, and grated cheese. Combine well.
- Slice top off French bread and scoop out ½ inch of bread. Fill cavity with spinach mixture.
- Bake for 10-12 minutes at 350°, until cheese is melted, and bread slightly toasted.
- Slice and serve.
- **Yield: 8 servings.**

Serve as appetizer or in place of garlic bread.

Tom Davis '70
Senior Associate Director
Undergraduate Admissions

Nothing but the Best!

Sausage Biscuits

1 pound grated cheese
1 pound hot sausage
3 cups biscuit mix

- Combine all ingredients and roll in walnut-size balls.
- Bake at 350° for 10 minutes.

These freeze well.

Camille W. Cook '45 '48
Professor Emerita of Law
School of Law

Poppy Seed Sandwiches

3 teaspoons butter, melted
4 tablespoons spicy mustard
2 tablespoons brown sugar
3 tablespoons poppy seeds
2 packages small dinner rolls
2 cups (8 ounces) shredded Mozzarella
    cheese
2 (8-ounce) packages thinly sliced deli ham

- Combine butter, mustard, sugar, and poppy seeds.
- Slice unseparated rolls in half horizontally. Spread butter mixture over both sides.
- Place ham on bottom half of rolls. Sprinkle with cheese. Put top part of rolls over cheese and press lightly. Cover with foil.
- Bake on 250° for 20 minutes. Cut apart and serve.

Kay Branyon
Secretary, Department of American Studies
College of Arts and Sciences

Sweet and Sour Sausage Appetizers

1 (10-ounce) package brown and serve
    sausage links
½ cup light brown sugar
1 tablespoon cornstarch
½ teaspoon salt
1 (15½-ounce) can pineapple chunks,
    drained, juice reserved
¼ cup white vinegar
½ cup water
1 green pepper, cut into ¾-inch squares
½ cup maraschino cherries

- Cut links into thirds and brown lightly.
- Mix sugar, cornstarch, and salt in saucepan. Add ½ cup reserved pineapple juice, vinegar, and water. Boil until thickened.
- Add pineapple, green pepper, cherries, and sausage.
- Serve hot from chafing dish, with toothpicks.

Kay Culton
Director, Freshman Writing Lab
Center for Athletic Student Services

Tomato and Olive Crostini

1 (3-ounce) package sundried tomatoes (not packed in oil)
¾ cup olive salad
15 slices canapé-size sourdough or French bread
1 large garlic clove
extra virgin olive oil
3 to 4 ounces feta cheese

- Rehydrate sundried tomatoes by covering with water and heating in microwave approximately 1 to 2 minutes. Soak for 5 minutes.
- Drain and place in food processor with olive salad. Blend until coarsely ground together.
- Heat over very low heat in a skillet and keep warm.
- Toast the bread until lightly browned on both sides. Rub on one side with garlic clove and brush lightly with the olive oil.
- Place one heaping teaspoon of the tomato mixture on each toast. Crumble cheese lightly over top.
- Broil until the cheese begins to melt. Serve immediately.

Dianne C. Teague '85 '89
Information Specialist/Assistant Registrar
Graduate School

Green Chili Pie

2 (4-ounce) cans chopped green chiles
8 ounces shredded sharp cheddar cheese
2 eggs, beaten
2 tablespoons milk
salt
cumin powder
corn chips

- Mix green chiles with cheese. Place in a pie plate or quiche dish.
- Combine eggs and milk. Pour over cheese mixture.
- Bake in a 400° oven for 10 minutes or until just set.
- Sprinkle with salt and a dash of cumin.
- Serve with corn chips.

This is my own original recipe and everyone who has tried it really likes it!

Betty Hardy Judice '57 '78
Tuscaloosa, Alabama

Nothing but the Best!

Sausage, Cheese, and Olive Crescents

Bread:

1 package instant rapid-rise yeast

1 teaspoon sugar

½ cup warm water

4 cups bread flour

1 teaspoon oregano

2 teaspoons basil

1 tablespoon olive oil

1 cup water

Filling:

7 ounces low-fat smoked sausage

1 cup shredded non-fat mozzarella cheese

2 tablespoons Parmesan cheese

¼ cup sliced green olives

1 (4-ounce) can chopped ripe olives with jalapeño flavor

2 tablespoons Dijon mustard

- For the bread, add yeast and sugar to the warm water. Place flour, oregano, basil, and olive oil in the bowl of a food processor with a plastic dough blade. Add yeast mixture and begin to process. Slowly pour remaining one cup water through feed tube until dough forms a cohesive ball. Allow machine to run for 45 seconds to knead the dough.
- Add more flour, if necessary, to assure dough is not sticky. Remove from machine and place in a lightly oiled bowl. Turn once to cover the top with oil.
- Cover and place in a warm spot to rise until doubled, 45 minutes to an hour.
- For the filling, process sausage until finely chopped.
- Add remaining ingredients and pulse until just blended. Do not overprocess.
- Punch dough down and divide into four pieces. Roll each piece out on a lightly floured surface into a ¼-inch thick strip approximately 3 inches wide by 18 inches long.
- Cut into triangles. Place a tablespoon of filling at the wide end of each triangle and roll up into a crescent roll shape.
- Place on a lightly greased baking sheet and allow to rise until doubled, about 15 minutes.
- Bake in a preheated oven until browned and firm, 15 to 20 minutes.
- Serve warm or cool.

These freeze well. Thaw at room temperature before re-heating.

Rae K. Eighmey
Wife of John Eighmey, Professor,
Department of Advertising and Public Relations
College of Communication

Black Bean and Cheese Roll-Ups

1 can black beans, rinsed and drained
6 large flour tortillas
1 (8-ounce) package cream cheese, softened
1 cup (4 ounces) grated sharp cheddar cheese
1 bunch green onions, chopped
1 red bell pepper, chopped
garlic salt
salt and pepper
tomato salsa or guacamole

- Mash beans and spread on tortillas.
- Combine cheeses, onions, bell pepper, garlic salt, and salt and pepper to taste. Spread over beans.
- Roll up tortillas jellyroll-style. Wrap each roll with plastic wrap and refrigerate for 3 to 4 hours.
- When ready to serve, slice into ½-inch slices.
- Serve with tomato salsa or guacamole.

Lee Horn '87 '90
Florence, Alabama

Pineapple Cheese Ball

2 (8-ounce) packages cream cheese, softened
½ cup finely chopped green pepper
1 medium can crushed pineapple, well
    drained
2 tablespoons finely chopped onion
chopped pecans

- Mix all ingredients except pecans.
- Form into a ball and roll in pecans.
- Chill and serve with crackers.

Ann S. Fulmer
Secretary, Department of Human Nutrition
and Hospitality Management
College of Human Environmental Sciences

Best Cheese Ball

1 (8-ounce) package cream cheese, softened
1 cup (4 ounces) grated sharp cheddar cheese
1 (7-ounce) package Hidden Valley
    Original Dressing Mix
1 teaspoon chopped onion
pecans

- Mix all ingredients except pecans well with hands.
- Shape into a ball and roll in pecans.
- Chill and serve with crackers.

Judy M. Andrzejewski '89
Birmingham, Alabama

Nothing but the Best!

Holiday Cheese Ball

1 (8-ounce) package cream cheese, softened
2 cups (8 ounces) grated sharp cheddar
    cheese
4 ounces Roquefort or Bleu cheese
1 garlic clove, pressed
3 tablespoons Worcestershire sauce
¼ teaspoon cayenne pepper
1 cup chopped parsley, divided
1 cup chopped pecans, divided

- Using mixer, combine all ingredients except half of parsley and half of pecans.
- Shape into ball and roll in remaining parsley and pecans.

Betty Joyce Cain Mills '50
Birmingham, Alabama

Beef and Cheese Ball

6 ounces smoked or chipped beef, finely
    chopped
2 pounds cream cheese, softened
2 cups (8 ounces) grated sharp cheddar
    cheese
2 tablespoons Worcestershire sauce
¼ cup pickle relish
⅛ teaspoon hot pepper sauce
¼ teaspoon onion salt
dash of white pepper
chopped parsley or grated pecans

- Combine all of the ingredients except parsley and pecans. Mix well.
- Form into a ball and roll in parsley or pecans.
- Serve with assorted crackers.
- **Yield: One very large, or two small balls.**

Sally Edwards '75 '77
Director, Child Development Resources and Services
College of Human Environmental Sciences

Cheese Spread

1 (5-ounce) jar bacon cheese spread
1 (5-ounce) jar Old English cheese spread
4 ounces cream cheese, softened
¼ teaspoon garlic powder
¼ teaspoon onion powder
paprika

- Warm cheeses in microwave until soft.
- Add garlic and onion powder, mixing well. Sprinkle with paprika.
- Serve with crackers.

Nedria Smelser
Tuscaloosa, Alabama

 *Appetizers*

Quick and Easy Holiday Cheese Log

1 (8-ounce) package cream cheese, room
  temperature
red or green pepper jelly

- Place cream cheese on serving plate and cover completely with jelly.
- Serve surrounded by crackers.

Makes a pretty dish for the holidays.

Bill Fendley
Director, Institutional Research

Strawberry Cheese Ring

1 pound shredded sharp cheddar cheese
2 tablespoons grated onion
¼ teaspoon black pepper
2 tablespoons milk
1½ cups grated pecans
¼ cup mayonnaise, or enough to blend
  mixture
dash of cayenne pepper
curly leaf lettuce
strawberry preserves

- Place cheese in a large mixing bowl. Add remaining ingredients except lettuce and preserves. Cream with a spoon until smooth.
- Transfer to a platter lined with lettuce and pat out flat with hands, leaving a higher rim around edge.
- Refrigerate until well-chilled. When ready to serve, fill center with preserves.
- Serve with crackers.

This cheese ring is especially nice at Christmas time. The green lettuce and red strawberry preserves make a very attractive presentation.

Leigh Ann Danner Summerford '80
Tuscaloosa, Alabama

Stuffed Edam Cheese

1 (2-pound) Edam cheese
½ teaspoon chervil
1 tablespoon brandy or sherry
2 teaspoons Worcestershire sauce
dash hot pepper sauce
salt and pepper to taste
paprika

- Hollow out the cheese, leaving rind intact.
- Process removed cheese in food processor. Add remaining ingredients, except paprika, and blend well.
- Refill shell and refrigerate.
- Remove from refrigerator 30 minutes before serving and sprinkle lightly with paprika.
- Serve with assorted crackers.

Mary Bolt Lloyd '42
Birmingham, Alabama

Nothing but the Best!

Olive Spread

6 ounces cream cheese, softened
½ cup mayonnaise
½ cup chopped pecans
1 cup chopped stuffed green chilies

- Combine all ingredients and blend well.
- Refrigerate overnight.
- Serve with assorted crackers.

Betty Hardy Judice '57 '78
Tuscaloosa, Alabama

Pecan Spread

8 ounces cream cheese, softened
2 tablespoons milk
1 (2½-ounce) jar sliced dried beef, chopped
¼ cup chopped green bell pepper
2 tablespoons minced onion,
¼ teaspoon pepper
1 cup sour cream
½ cup chopped pecans
2 tablespoons butter

- Blend cream cheese and milk together. Add beef, bell pepper, onion, pepper, and sour cream. Mix well.
- Spoon into a buttered 8-inch pie plate.
- Bake at 350° for 10 minutes.
- Toast pecans at 250° for 10 to 15 minutes. Coat with melted butter.
- Sprinkle pecans on top of baked spread. Bake an additional 8 to 10 minutes.
- Serve hot or cold with assorted crackers.

Beth Gibbs '84 '86
Computer Coordinator
College of Human Environmental Sciences

Shrimp Dip

1 (8-ounce) package cream cheese, softened
4 tablespoons mayonnaise
6 drops hot pepper sauce
juice of ½ lemon
1 small onion, finely chopped
1 package frozen shrimp, thawed and minced
1 teaspoon Worcestershire sauce
paprika

- Combine all ingredients except paprika and mix well.
- Sprinkle with paprika. Chill.
- Serve with favorite crackers or corn chips.

Ann S. Fulmer
Secretary, Department of Human Nutrition
and Hospitality Management
College of Human Environmental Sciences

Layered Nacho Dip

1 (16-ounce) can refried beans
1 package taco seasoning
1 (6-ounce) carton avocado dip
1 (4½-ounce) can chopped ripe olives
1 small onion, chopped
1½ cups shredded Monterey Jack cheese
1 (8-ounce) carton sour cream
2 tomatoes, diced
1 (4-ounce) can chopped green chilies

- Combine beans and taco seasoning. Spread in 12 x 8 x 2-inch dish.
- Layer with remaining ingredients in order given.
- Serve with large corn chips or tortilla chips.

Ann S. Fulmer
Secretary, Department of Human Nutrition
and Hospitality Management
College of Human Environmental Sciences

Artichoke Dip

1 (14-ounce) can artichoke hearts packed in
    water, drained and mashed
1 cup mayonnaise
1 cup Parmesan or Romano cheese

- Mix all ingredients and spread in a baking dish.
- Bake at 350° for 30 minutes.
- Serve with corn chips.

Betty Jo Novak Walker '58
River Forest, Illinois

Ball Game French Onion Dip

24 ounces curd cottage cheese
¼ cup milk
2 tablespoons dry onion soup mix
¼ teaspoon onion salt

- Blend cottage cheese and milk in blender until smooth.
- Add soup mix and onion salt. Blend well.
- Refrigerate overnight.

Nedria Smelser
Tuscaloosa, Alabama

Dill Dip

⅔ cup mayonnaise
⅔ cup sour cream
1 tablespoon minced dried onion
1 tablespoon dried parsley flakes
1 teaspoon dill
1 teaspoon seasoned salt

- Mix all ingredients and chill.
- Serve with your favorite assortment of raw vegetables.

Linda C. Price
System Coordinator, Financial Affairs

Nothing but the Best!

Hot Broccoli and Cheese Dip

2 (10-ounce) packages frozen chopped
    broccoli

1 cup chopped onion

4 tablespoons butter

1 (6-ounce) roll garlic cheese

1 (4-ounce) can mushroom stems and pieces,
    drained

1 (10¾-ounce) can cream of mushroom soup

- Cook broccoli and drain. Set aside.
- In another pan, sauté onion in butter. Add cheese and heat until melted.
- Stir in mushrooms, mushroom soup, and broccoli. Thin the mixture with a small amount of water if too thick.
- Serve hot with corn chips.

Teresa Gilstrap Pruett
Office Assistant, Division of Environmental
and Industrial Programs
College of Continuing Studies

Hot Spinach Dip

2 (10-ounce) packages frozen chopped
    spinach

½ cup chopped onion

½ cup margarine

2 tablespoons all-purpose flour

1 (10¾-ounce) can cream of mushroom soup

1 (12-ounce) package jalapeño cheese

1 (4-ounce) can sliced mushrooms, drained

1 teaspoon Worcestershire sauce

salt to taste

½ teaspoon pepper

cayenne pepper to taste

garlic powder to taste, optional

- Cook spinach and drain very well.
- Sauté onions in melted margarine until tender.
- Add flour and soup and stir until smooth. Add cheese and rest of ingredients, including spinach. Stir well and heat until cheese is melted and dip is hot.
- Serve hot with corn chips or toast points.

Margaret E. (Beth) Rumley Russell '70
York, Alabama

Spinach and Water Chestnut Dip

1 (10-ounce) package frozen chopped
    spinach, thawed and drained
1 (8-ounce) can water chestnuts, drained
    and chopped
½ cup sour cream or plain yogurt
1 cup mayonnaise
1 (1-ounce) package Ranch House Dressing
    Mix
chopped pimento

- Squeeze excess moisture from spinach. Blend
  with remaining ingredients.
- Chill for several hours or overnight.
- Serve with corn chips or crackers.
- **Yield: 3 cups.**

*This is a quick and simple dip to make. It makes a very
attractive presentation when served in a hollowed-out
cabbage, garnished with chopped pimento.*

Leigh Ann Danner Summerford '80
Tuscaloosa, Alabama

Mama's Salsa

2 large tomatoes, chopped
1 (4-ounce) can black olives, drained and
    chopped
1 (4-ounce) can green chilies, drained and
    chopped
4 green onions, chopped
3 tablespoons olive oil
1½ tablespoons white vinegar
1 teaspoon garlic salt
salt and pepper to taste

- Mix all ingredients gently.
- Serve with corn chips.

Easy and delicious.

Erin Henry McWaters '83
Mobile, Alabama

Bloody Mary Dip

1 (8 ounce) package cream cheese, softened
½ cup ketchup
1 (8 ounce) carton sour cream
3 green onions, finely chopped
¾ teaspoon ground celery seed
½ teaspoon gound black pepper
¼ teaspoon Hot N' Spicy seasoned salt
¾ teaspoon hot sauce

- Beat cheese and ketchup until smooth and fluffy.
- Stir in remaining ingredients.
- Cover and refrigerate until chilled.
- Serve with corn chips or raw vegetables.
- **Yield: 2½ cups.**

Mitzie Burleson '88
Selma, Alabama

Nothing but the Best!

Hot Shrimp Dip

1 pound cream cheese, softened
1 medium onion, chopped
1 medium tomato, chopped
4 chopped banana peppers or 1 small can
    chili peppers
¾ to 1 pound chopped cooked shrimp (fresh
    or canned)
1 tablespoon garlic juice
½ teaspoon salt
3 chopped torrido peppers

- Combine all ingredients in a saucepan. Heat until cheese is melted.
- Serve warm in a chafing dish, with corn chips.

Wilma Greene '59 '60
Assistant Professor, Department of Clothing,
Textiles, and Interior Design
College of Human Environmental Sciences

Mary's Vegetable Dip

2 eggs, well beaten
3 tablespoons sugar
3 tablespoons vinegar
1 tablespoon butter
1 (8-ounce) package cream cheese, softened
½ green bell pepper, finely chopped
½ medium onion, chopped
1 ounce chopped pimentos

- Combine eggs, sugar, vinegar, and butter in a saucepan. Cook over low heat until thickened.
- Add remaining ingredients and beat until smooth.
- Cover and chill overnight.
- Serve with fresh vegetables.

Virgene M. Ficken
Administrative Secretary, Dean's Office
Capstone College of Nursing

Championship Cheese and Chicken Dip

¾ cup chopped onion
butter
milk
2 pounds pasteurized process cheese, cubed
1 can white chunk chicken, drained
black pepper to taste

- Sauté onion in small amount of butter until cooked but not brown. Set aside.
- Fill bottom of saucepan with milk. Over low heat, add cheese cubes a few at a time, stirring continuously until all are melted.
- Add remaining ingredients, including onions, and continue heating until warm. Do not microwave. To reheat, add a little more milk to prevent sticking.
- Serve with tortilla chips.

Britt Barley
Athens, Alabama

Dried Beef and Cheese Dip

2 small jars dried beef, minced
2 (8-ounce) packages cream cheese, softened
   (may use fat-free)
1 small carton sour cream (may use fat-free)
4 tablespoons chopped bell pepper
4 tablespoons chopped green onions
1 cup chopped pecans

- Combine all ingredients except pecans. Place in a baking dish.
- Top with pecans.
- Bake at 300° for 30 minutes.
- Serve with corn chips or crackers.

Judy Aldridge
Tuscaloosa, Alabama

Chili Con Queso Dip

1 pound ground beef or 1 pound sausage
¼ cup chopped green onion
1 (15 ounce) can tomato sauce with tomato
   bits
1 (4-ounce) can chopped green chilies
2 pounds pasteurized process cheese, cubed
1 teaspoon Worcestershire sauce
garlic powder
salt and pepper

- Brown meat and onions. Drain well.
- Add tomato sauce, chilies, and cheese. Cook slowly, stirring, until cheese is melted and dip is smooth. Add seasonings to taste.
- Serve in a heated dish with tortilla chips.

Gene Stallings
Head Football Coach
Intercollegiate Athletics

- **Variation**: Increase meat to 1½ pounds ground chuck and 1 pound bulk pork sausage, regular or hot. Subsitute 1 (10-ounce) can tomatoes and diced green chilies for tomato sauce and green chilies. Add 1 (10¾-ounce) can cream of mushroom soup.

Beverly C. Smith
Executive Secretary, Dean's Office
New College

Bean and Salsa Dip

1 (31-ounce) can refried beans
1 (16-ounce) jar salsa
Monterey Jack and Colby cheese, shredded

- Spray a 13 x 9-inch baking dish with cooking spray. Spread beans in baking dish.
- Top with salsa and enough cheese to cover dish.
- Bake at 350° for 20 minutes.
- Serve with tortilla chips.

Skeet Hobbs
Wife of Head Basketball Coach, David Hobbs

Jean Lumpkin's Hot Mexican Dip

2 cans refried beans with sausage

1 package taco seasoning mix

2 cups sour cream

2 cups (8 ounces) grated cheddar cheese

- Combine refried beans and taco seasoning mix. Spread in a 9 x 12-inch casserole dish.
- Spread sour cream over bean mixture. Sprinkle with cheese.
- Bake at 250° for 20 minutes or until cheese is melted.
- Use as a dip with corn or tortilla chips.

Frances Hansford '78
Wife of Nathaniel Hansford, Professor and
Former Dean, School of Law
Tuscaloosa, Alabama

Olive and Green Chili Salsa

2 (4¼-ounce) cans chopped ripe olives, drained

2 (4-ounce) cans chopped green chilies

2 tomatoes, peeled and chopped

3 chopped green onions

2 garlic cloves, pressed

1 tablespoon red wine vinegar

1 teaspoon pepper

seasoning salt to taste

- Combine all ingredients. Cover dish and chill overnight.
- Serve with chips.

Debbie St. John
Secretary, Dean's Office
College of Arts and Science

Sombrero Dip

2 pounds ground beef

1 cup chopped onion

1 cup hot ketchup

4 to 5 tablespoons chili powder

2 teaspoons cumin

salt to taste

1 large can refried beans

2 cups (8 ounces) shredded cheese

1 cup chopped onion

1 cup chopped green olives

- Brown meat and onions. Drain well.
- Add ketchup, chili powder, cumin, salt, and beans. Stir well to combine.
- Dip may be refrigerated or frozen at this point.
- Before serving, reheat. Garnish with cheese, onions, and green olives.
- Serve in chafing dish with corn chips.

Sally Edwards '75 '77
Director, Child Development Resources and Services
College of Human Environmental Sciences

Bama Punch

2 packages strawberry Kool-Aid
1 gallon water
1 (46-ounce) can pineapple juice
1 (12-ounce) can frozen lemonade
    concentrate
1 package frozen strawberries
3 to 4 cups sugar
ginger ale, optional

- Dissolve Kool-Aid in water and freeze.
- When ready to serve, thaw Kool-Aid a little bit.
- Combine remaining ingredients, and add Kool-Aid to make slushy.

Ricky Thompson
Athens, Alabama

Homecoming Fruit Slush Punch

1½ cups pineapple juice
½ cup orange juice
½ cup grapefruit juice
1 cup ginger ale

- Combine juices. Pour one-quarter into a container and refrigerate.
- Pour remaining mixture into a shallow container; cover tightly, and freeze until ice crystals form.
- Transfer semi-frozen juice to blender, and add chilled juice. Process until slush is formed.
- Transfer to punch bowl and add ginger ale.

J.J. Doster Cafe
College of Human Environmental Sciences

OAA Christmas Punch

2 cans Hawaiian Punch
2 (12-ounce) cans frozen orange juice
1 (46-ounce) can pineapple juice
1 jar red cherries
1 (32-ounce) bottle ginger ale

- Chill ingredients.
- Combine all ingredients except ginger ale in a punch bowl.
- Add ginger ale immediately before serving.

OAA Punch has become a tradition at the Christmas Open House in the Office for Academic Affairs.

Dot Martin '63 '86
Assistant Academic Vice President for Administration
Office for Academic Affairs

Presbyterian Punch

8½ cups water, divided

3 cups sugar

1 (16-ounce) can frozen orange juice concentrate

1 (6-ounce) can frozen lemonade concentrate

1 (46-ounce) can pineapple juice

juice of 2 lemons

3 mashed bananas

2 quarts ginger ale

- Make a simple syrup by boiling 6 cups of water and 3 cups of sugar for 3 minutes.
- Add orange juice and lemonade concentrates, remaining water, pineapple juice, lemon juice, and mashed bananas.
- Stir to combine well and freeze.
- About one-half hour before serving, place frozen base in punch bowl and let thaw until slushy. Add ginger ale and serve.

A fifth of rum may be added with the ginger ale, but in that case, change the name!

Judy M. Andrzejewski '89
Birmingham, Alabama

Watermelon Strawberry Froth

2 cups strawberries, hulled

1 cup seeded and diced watermelon

juice of 2 oranges

juice of 1 lime

1 to 2 tablespoons sugar

- Combine strawberries, watermelon, and juice in a blender. Process until smooth and well blended.
- Add sugar to taste.
- Serve over ice with a straw.

Sherry Smart Harvey
Administrative Specialist
Seebeck Computer Center

Butler Old Fashioned

2 ounces bourbon

½ jigger cherry juice or simple syrup

2 dashes bitters

1 jigger orange juice

orange slice

cherry

- Pour bourbon into double old fashioned glass.
- Add cherry juice or simple syrup and bitters.
- Top with orange juice and stir well.
- Fill glass with ice and garnish with orange slice and cherry.

Cecil Butler Williams
Wife of Ernest Williams, UA Trustee Emeritus

Bloody Mary Mix

2 large cans tomato juice
1 onion, cut crisscross but kept whole
2 lemons, cut in half
2 tablespoons prepared horseradish
2 tablespoons cracked pepper
hot pepper sauce
Worcestershire sauce
celery salt
salt

- Combine tomato juice, onion, lemons, horseradish, and pepper. Add remaining ingredients to taste.
- Let sit for 24 hours.
- When ready to serve, remove lemon and onion and squeeze juice from them.

Serve to Bama fans at a pregame brunch.

Leanne and Alan Spencer '77
Alexandria, Virginia

Dynamite

1 gallon vanilla ice cream
1 fifth brandy or a good bourbon
nutmeg

- Soften ice cream in a large bowl.
- Add brandy, stirring or beating until mixture has a smooth consistency.
- Freeze for at least 24 hours to mellow.
- Serve, sprinkled with nutmeg, in punch cups or small glasses.
- **Yield: 30 (5-ounce) servings.**

Makes a delightful Christmas drink. Keeps well in freezer.

Marwood H. Goetz
Husband of Helen M. Goetz, Professor Emerita,
Department of Consumer Sciences
School of Home Economics
Tucson, Arizona

Orange Slush

1 (12-ounce) can orange juice concentrate
2 (6-ounce) cans frozen limeade concentrate
2 (6-ounce) cans frozen lemonade
    concentrate
3 cups water
1 cup sugar
2 cups vodka
lemon-lime carbonated drink

- Combine all ingredients except lemon-lime carbonated drink.
- Freeze overnight.
- When ready to serve, fill tall glasses two-thirds full of slush and top with carbonated drink.

Margaret E. (Beth) Rumley Russell '70
York, Alabama

Peach Fuzz

2 unpeeled peaches, sliced
1 (6-ounce) can frozen pink lemonade
6 ounces vodka
1 tray ice cubes
mint sprigs

- Place all ingredients except mint in a blender.
- Blend until frothy.
- Serve in Jefferson cups garnished with mint.
- **Yield: 4 servings.**

May be used as a dessert.

If the vodka is omitted, the Peach Fuzz makes a wonderful snack for children on a summer afternoon.

Leatha A. Darden '62 '64
Associate Professor, Department of Clothing, Textiles,
and Interior Design
College of Human Environmental Sciences

Sangria

1 cup vodka
1 cup sugar
1 liter hearty burgundy, chilled
1 (46-ounce) can pineapple juice, chilled
1 (32-ounce) bottle lemon-lime carbonated
   drink, chilled
lemon slices
lime slices

- Mix all ingredients except lemon and lime slices.
- Garnish with lemon and lime.

Teresa Gilstrap Pruett
Office Assistant, Division of Environmental
and Industrial Programs
College of Continuing Studies

Russian Tea

2 teaspoons whole cloves
2 sticks cinnamon
1 gallon water
7 tea bags
2 cups sugar
juice of 4 oranges
juice of 3 lemons
grated rind of 2 lemons

- Put cinnamon and cloves in a bag.
- Bring water to a boil. Add tea bags and cinnamon bag. Boil for 3 minutes and steep for 2 minutes.
- Add remaining ingredients, stirring well. Remove tea bags and spices.
- Serve hot.

Lee Horn, '87 '90
Florence, Alabama

Lime Tea

5 cups water
5 regular-sized tea bags
1 (6-ounce) can frozen limeade concentrate
⅓ cup sugar

- Bring water to boil. Pour over tea bags, cover, and steep for 5 minutes. Do not use a metal pot for steeping.
- Remove tea bags. Pour hot tea over one small can of frozen limeade.
- Stir in sugar until dissolved.
- Serve over ice.

The "Sunny South" gets very hot during the summer months and tea is one of our favorite beverages. This makes a really refreshing althernative to the usual glass of tea. More sugar can be added to taste but these measurements make it thirst-quenching.

Marian Loftin '58
Regional Director, Dothan Office
Economic and Community Affairs

Olivia's Almond Tea

2 cups strong tea, decaffeinated may be used
2 quarts water
1½ cups granulated sugar
1 cup orange juice
6 tablespoons lemon juice
1 teaspoon vanilla extract
1 teaspoon almond extract
lemon slices, optional

- Mix and heat all ingredients except lemon slices thoroughly.
- Garnish with lemon slices, if desired.
- **Yield: 16 servings.**

Mila Key Johnston '68
Greensboro, Alabama

Nothing but the Best!

Breads
&
Breakfast

Breads & Breakfast

Nothing but the Best!

Apple Bread

½ cup shortening

1 cup sugar

1 teaspoon vanilla

2 eggs

1 tablespoon buttermilk

2 cups self-rising flour

1 teaspoon grated lemon rind

1½ cups peeled and chopped apples

½ teaspoon cinnamon

1 tablespoon sugar

- Cream shortening, sugar, and vanilla together until fluffy.
- Blend in remaining ingredients, except cinnamon and 1 tablespoon sugar.
- Pour into greased loaf pan and sprinkle with cinnamon and sugar.
- Bake at 350° for 1 hour.

Beth Gibbs '84, '86
Computer Coordinator
College of Human Environmental Sciences

Banana Bread

½ cup margarine

1 cup sugar

3 ripe bananas, mashed

2 eggs, beaten

2 cups flour

1 teaspoon baking soda

pinch of salt

½ cup chopped nuts

- Cream margarine and sugar.
- Add bananas, eggs, flour, soda, and salt.
- Fold in nuts.
- Bake in loaf pan at 325° for about 65 minutes. Insert knife to test doneness.
- Remove from pan while hot and cool on a wire rack.

Teddy Gambril
Wife of Don Gambril, Associate Athletic Director
Intercollegiate Athletics

Famous Kona Inn Banana Bread

6 large bananas, ripened
2½ cups plain flour
1 teaspoon salt
2 teaspoons baking soda
1 cup butter or margarine, softened
2 cups sugar
3 large eggs
1 cup black walnuts (optional)

- In large bowl, mash bananas and set aside.
- In medium bowl, sift together flour, salt, and soda. Set aside.
- In another bowl, cream together butter, sugar, and eggs. Add dry ingredients and bananas alternately to creamed mixture. Mix well. Stir in nuts.
- Pour into 2 well-greased loaf pans.
- Bake at 350° for 60 minutes or until toothpick comes out clean.
- **Yield: 16 servings.**

Shirley Florence
Coordinator of Administrative Affairs and Registrar
College of Community Health Sciences

Cranberry Bread

2 cups flour
½ teaspoon salt
1½ teaspoons baking powder
½ teaspoon baking soda
1 cup sugar
1 egg, beaten
2 tablespoons butter, melted
½ cup orange juice
2 tablespoons hot water
½ cup pecans, chopped
1 cup cranberries, cut in half
grated rind of 1 orange

- Stir dry ingredients together.
- Add egg, butter, orange juice, and hot water. Combine only until dry ingredients are moistened.
- Fold in nuts, cranberries, and orange rind.
- Pour into greased loaf pan and bake at 350° for 35 to 40 minutes, or until cake tester comes out clean. When cool, wrap in plastic wrap and store in refrigerator for at least 24 hours before serving.

Helen M. Goetz
Professor Emerita of Consumer Sciences
School of Home Economics

Nothing but the Best!

Cranberry Nut Bread

2 cups cranberries
⅔ cup pecans, coarsely chopped
2 cups all-purpose flour, sifted
1 cup plus 2 tablespoons sugar
1¾ teaspoons baking powder
½ teaspoon baking soda
¾ teaspoon salt
2 tablespoons margarine, melted
¼ cup water
⅓ cup orange juice
1 egg, well beaten
1 teaspoon grated orange rind

- Line two small loaf pans with wax paper; grease.
- Rinse, sort, and cut cranberries into halves. Add nuts.
- Sift dry ingredients together into a bowl.
- Melt margarine, cool slightly. Add water, orange juice, and egg.
- Make a well in dry ingredients. Add liquid ingredients and stir just enough to combine ingredients.
- Fold in cranberries, nuts, and orange rind.
- Pour into pans and bake at 350° for about 35 to 45 minutes until lightly browned and cake tester or wooden toothpick comes out clean.
- Cool 10 minutes in pan on cooling rack.
- Freezes well.

Virginia C. Brazeal '50
Tuscaloosa, Alabama

Lemon Bread

½ cup margarine
1 cup sugar
2 eggs
grated rind of 1 lemon
½ cup milk
1½ cups flour
1 teaspoon baking powder
¼ teaspoon salt
½ cup nuts, chopped

Topping:
¼ cup sugar
juice of 1 lemon

- Cream margarine and sugar. Beat in the eggs. Add lemon rind and milk.
- Sift flour, baking powder, and salt together and beat into mixture. Stir in nuts.
- Bake at 325° in a greased loaf pan for 45 to 60 minutes.
- Remove from oven and immediately prick top with fork.
- To make topping, stir together sugar and lemon juice.
- Pour topping evenly over hot bread. Let bread sit for 5 minutes.
- Take from pan and cool on rack. Freezes well!
- **Yield: 12 or more servings.**

Linda Olivet '64 '67
Associate Professor & Assistant Dean
for Graduate Studies & Clinical Affairs
Capstone College of Nursing

Zucchini Bread

3 eggs, beaten

1 cup oil

2 cups sugar

2 cups grated zucchini

2 teaspoons vanilla

3 cups flour

1 teaspoon soda

½ teaspoon baking powder

1 teaspoon salt

1 teaspoon cinnamon

1 teaspoon nutmeg

1 teaspoon allspice

1 cup walnuts or pecans, chopped

1 cup raisins (optional)

- Combine oil, eggs, sugar, and zucchini in a large mixing bowl and mix well.
- Add dry ingredients; mix well. Stir in nuts and raisins. Batter will be thin.
- Bake at 350°. If using a bundt pan, bake 1 hour and 15 minutes. For 2 loaf pans, bake 50 minutes or until done.

Beth Gibbs '84, '86
Computer Coordinator
College of Human Environmental Sciences

Mable Adams' Cheese Bread

1 (12-ounce) can beer

¼ cup sugar

1 tablespoon salt

2 tablespoons oil

½ pound processed American or Swiss cheese

1 ounce sharp cheese

2 (¼-ounce) packages dry yeast

½ cup warm water (105-115°)

6 cups bread flour

- Heat beer, sugar, salt, oil, and cheeses until cheeses are melted. Allow to cool.
- Soften yeast in warm water. Add to cooled mixture.
- Add 2 cups flour and beat until smooth. Add remaining flour to make a stiff dough. Knead.
- Let rise until dough doubles in size.
- Shape into loaves (2 large loaves or 6-8 small ones).
- Let rise until dough doubles in size.
- Bake at 350° for 30-35 minutes for small loaves or 45 minutes for large ones.

This recipe was Mable Adams' "trademark" for the annual Fall Festival Bake Sale at the First United Methodist Church in Tuscaloosa.

Ernestine Jackson '64
Director Emerita, Dietetics Program
School of Home Economics

Nothing but the Best!

Mini Swiss Cheese Loaves

1 (¼-ounce) envelope active dry yeast

¼ cup warm water (105-115°)

2⅓ tablespoons all-purpose flour

2 tablespoons sugar

1 teaspoon salt

¼ teaspoon baking soda

1 (8-ounce) carton plain nonfat yogurt

1 large egg

1 cup (4-ounces) shredded reduced-fat Swiss
   cheese

vegetable cooking spray

2 teaspoons sesame seeds, toasted

- Combine yeast and warm water in 1 cup liquid glass or plastic measuring cup; let stand 5 minutes.
- Combine yeast mixture, 1 cup flour, and add next 5 ingredients in a large mixing bowl. Beat at low speed with an electric mixer 30 seconds. Beat at high speed 2 minutes, scraping bowl occasionally. Stir in remaining flour and cheese, mixing well.
- Divide batter evenly among 8 (5x3x2 inch) loaf pans coated with cooking spray; sprinkle evenly with sesame seeds.
- Cover and let rise in a warm place, free from drafts, for 1 hour. Batter may not double in bulk.
- Bake at 350° for 25 minutes or until golden brown. Remove from pans; serve warm, or cool on a wire rack.

Cheryl Parker
Secretary, Department of Advertising and Public Relations
College of Communication

Nut and Seed Bread

½ cup quick-cooking oatmeal

1 cup plus 6 tablespoons water

1 teaspoon salt

¼ cup sorghum or molasses

2 tablespoons butter

1 (¼-ounce) package dry yeast

¼ cup warm water (105-115°)

½ cup rye flour

½ cup whole wheat flour

¼ cup wheat germ

2 tablespoons bran flakes

¼ cup plus 1 tablespoon nuts

¼ cup plus 1 tablespoon sunflower seeds

2 to 2½ cups white flour

- Combine oatmeal and 1 cup cold water in saucepan. Bring to a boil. Add salt, sorghum, and butter. Stir until butter is melted. Transfer to bowl and let cool.
- Dissolve yeast with ¼ cup warm water. Let stand until foamy.
- Add to cooled oatmeal mixture. Add 6 tablespoons water and beat until smooth. Add the rye and wheat flours and beat. Add bran, nuts, and seeds. Gradually add enough white flour to make a workable soft dough.
- Turn onto floured board and knead until smooth and elastic.
- Place in greased bowl, turning once. Cover and let rise in warm place until doubled in size, about 1 hour and 15 minutes.
- Punch down and divide dough in two equal parts. Knead each part to make a smooth ball. Fold and shape into loaves.
- Put into 2 greased 7½ x 3¾ x 2¼-inch loaf pans. Cover and let rise until almost doubled in bulk, about 55 minutes.
- Bake 35 to 40 minutes at 350°.
- **Yield: Two 14-ounce loaves.**

Frieda Meyer
Professor Emerita of Home Economics
School of Home Economics

Oatmeal Bread

2 (¼-ounce) packages rapid rise yeast
⅓ cup lukewarm water (105-115°)
½ cup honey
6 cups flour
1 cup rolled oats
2 tablespoons butter or margarine
2 teaspoons salt
2 cups lukewarm water (105-115°)
additional flour as needed

- Combine yeast with ⅓ cup lukewarm water in a 2 cup measuring cup and let foam. Add honey to yeast mixture and stir.
- In food processor, process flour, oats, butter, and salt for 1 minute. Add 1 cup of lukewarm water to yeast mixture and stir to combine. With processor running, slowly add the yeast mixture through the feed tube. Add second cup of lukewarm water through feed tube. Process until dough is uniformly moist and elastic and forms ball, adding additional flour as needed.
- Knead on floured board as necessary until dough is easy to handle.
- Place in oiled bowl, cover and let rise until doubled in bulk.
- Remove from bowl; divide in half. Knead each half into a loaf shape.
- Place each loaf in greased 9 x 5 x 3-inch glass loaf pan.
- Let rise until doubled in bulk.
- Bake at 325° for approximately 50 minutes or until done.
- Turn out of pans immediately and cool on wire rack.

In my graduate student days when money was very tight, I gave a loaf of this bread and a small jar of jam to nearly everyone as a holiday gift. My family continues to love the bread, especially when it's hot from the oven.

Lucinda Roff
Dean and Professor
School of Social Work

Bohemian Rye Bread

2 (¼-ounce) packages dry yeast
½ cup warm water (105 - 115°)
¼ cup dark brown sugar
¼ cup molasses
1½ cups hot water
1 tablespoon salt
2 tablespoons butter
2½ cups rye flour
3 tablespoons caraway seeds
3 cups all-purpose white flour
1 egg, beaten
2 tablespoons water
whole caraway seeds for garnish

- In a small bowl, dissolve yeast in warm water.
- In a separate bowl, combine the sugar, molasses, hot water, salt, and butter; cool to lukewarm.
- In a large bowl, combine the two liquids, then stir in the rye flour and caraway seeds. Mix in two cups of white flour.
- Turn dough onto a floured board and knead in the remaining one cup of white flour for about 10 minutes, until dough is smooth and elastic.
- Rinse and thoroughly dry the bowl. Lightly grease the mixing bowl with vegetable oil. Shape dough into a ball, and place in a bowl. Cover with a clean, damp cloth and set bowl in a draft-free place for 1 to 2 hours or until dough has risen to almost doubled in bulk.
- Punch down dough and let rest for about 20 minutes, covered. Divide dough into two balls.
- Place on greased baking sheet, cover with damp cloth and set aside for 30 to 40 minutes or until loaves have risen and almost doubled in bulk.
- Bake at 375° for 25 to 30 minutes. Remove from oven and brush tops of loaves with one beaten egg mixed with 2 tablespoons water. Sprinkle tops of loaves with caraway seeds.
- Return to the oven and continue to bake until well-browned, about 20 minutes more.
- Remove from baking sheet and cool on wire rack.
- HINT: Bread is done baking when it sounds hollow when thumped.

Benita Strnad
Curriculum Materials/Education Reference Librarian
University Libraries

Crusty White Braids

4 to 4 ½ cups all-purpose flour
2 (¼-ounce) packages active dry yeast
2 cups warm water (105-115°)
½ cup cooking oil
2 tablespoons sugar
1 tablespoon salt

- In large mixer bowl, combine 2 cups of flour and the yeast. Add warm water, oil, sugar, and salt to dry mixture.
- Beat with electric mixer on low speed for 30 seconds. Beat 3 minutes at high speed. Stir in enough of the remaining flour to make a moderately stiff dough.
- Turn out onto lightly floured surface; knead until smooth and elastic, 5 to 8 minutes.
- Shape into a ball and place dough in greased bowl, turning once to grease surface.
- Cover; let rise until doubled, about 1 1/2 hours.
- Punch dough down. Divide in half. Divide each half in thirds; shape into 6 balls.
- Cover; let rest for 10 minutes.
- Roll each ball into a 16 inch rope. Line up 3 ropes, 1 inch apart, on a greased baking sheet. Braid very loosely, beginning in the middle. Pinch ends together and tuck under. Repeat with remaining ropes.
- Cover; let rise in warm place until almost doubled, about 40 minutes.
- Bake at 375° for 30 minutes or until bread is golden brown.
- **Yield: 2 loaves.**

Kathy H. Rice
Secretary, Culverhouse School of Accountancy
College of Commerce and Business Administration

Brother Pinion's Scratch Biscuits

2 cups self-rising flour
¾ cup milk (plain or buttermilk)
¼ cup oil or shortening

- Mix together ingredients and knead as little as possible.
- Roll out on a floured counter or bread board and cut with a biscuit cutter or a glass.
- Bake at 375° until brown, about 10 minutes.

Ann Smith Brasher
Accounting Specialist
School of Mines and Energy Development

Butter Biscuits

1 cup butter or margarine
2 cups self-rising flour
1 (8-ounce) carton sour cream

- Mix butter and flour with pastry blender or mixing fork; add sour cream.
- When thoroughly mixed, drop by rounded 1/2 teaspoon-sized amounts onto tiny greased 1 3/4-inch muffin pans.
- Bake at 450° for 8-10 minutes or until slightly browned.
- Serve hot.
- **Yield: 50 biscuits.**

Biscuits are so rich they do not need to be buttered.

Jade Abernathy
Staff Assistant, Department of Advertising and Public Relations
College of Communication

Cheese Biscuits

¼ cup shortening
⅓ cup shredded cheese
2 cups biscuit mix
⅔ cup milk

- Cut shortening and cheese into biscuit mix.
- Add milk and stir with fork to make soft dough. Beat 15 strokes.
- Drop teaspoon-size amounts of dough onto greased baking sheet.
- Bake at 425° for 12-15 minutes.
- **Yield: 12 biscuits.**

Jade Abernathy
Staff Assistant,
Department of Advertising and Public Relations
College of Communication

Nothing but the Best!

Garlic Cheese Biscuits

2 cups biscuit mix
½ cup cheddar cheese, shredded
⅔ cup milk
¼ cup margarine, melted
¼ teaspoon garlic powder

- Mix biscuit mix and cheese. Add milk. Beat vigorously for 30 seconds.
- Drop by spoonfuls on ungreased cookie sheet.
- Bake at 425° for 8 to 10 minutes.
- Mix margarine and garlic powder. Brush on hot biscuits.
- **Yield: 15 biscuits.**

Gail Kimball
Word Processor, Student Services
College of Engineering

Mile High Biscuits

2 cups all-purpose flour
1 cup whole wheat flour
4½ teaspoons baking powder
2 tablespoons sugar
¼ teaspoon salt
¾ teaspoon cream of tartar
¾ cup butter-flavored solid shortening
1 egg, lightly beaten
1 cup milk

- In large bowl, combine flours, baking powder, sugar, salt, and cream of tartar.
- Cut shortening into dry ingredients until mixture resembles coarse meal.
- Add egg and milk, stirring with fork until smooth.
- Knead dough on lightly floured board. Roll dough out to ¾-inch thickness and cut into 2½-inch biscuits.
- Place on greased pan and bake at 450° for 12 to 15 minutes or until done.
- **Yield: 16 to 18 biscuits.**

Patricia A. M. Hodges
Director, Coordinated Programs in Dietetics
College of Human Environmental Sciences

Blueberry Bran Muffins

2 tablespoons oil
2 tablespoons honey
⅔ cup sugar
2 egg whites, beaten
1 to 1½ cups buttermilk
½ teaspoon salt
2 cups self-rising flour
2 cups bran
1 teaspoon baking soda
1 cup blueberries

- Preheat oven to 375°.
- Mix oil with honey and sugar. Add remaining ingredients. Mix just until combined.
- Bake in well-greased muffin tins for 10 to 15 minutes.
- **Yield: 24 muffins.**

Margaret E. (Beth) Rumley Russell '70
York, Alabama

Carrot Muffins

2 cups all-purpose flour
1 teaspoon baking powder
½ teaspoon baking soda
¼ teaspoon salt
⅔ cup brown sugar, firmly packed
1 teaspoon ground cinnamon
½ teaspoon ground nutmeg
½ teaspoon ground ginger
1 egg, slightly beaten
⅔ cup buttermilk
½ cup vegetable oil
1 teaspoon vanilla extract
2 cups grated carrots
½ cup chopped pecans

- Combine flour, baking powder, baking soda, salt, brown sugar, and spices in a medium-size bowl. Make a well in the center of the mixture.
- Combine egg, buttermilk, oil, and vanilla. Add to dry ingredients, stirring until almost moistened. Stir in carrots and pecans.
- Spoon mixture into greased muffin cups, filling about three-quarters full.
- Bake at 375° for about 25 minutes.
- **Yield: 1 dozen muffins.**

Carol L. Hoffman '82
Coordinator of Engineering Graphics, Department of
Mechanical Engineering
College of Engineering

Low Cholesterol Muffins

½ cup corn oil

1 cup honey

¾ cup peanut butter

4 ounces egg substitute

⅓ cup skim milk

2 teaspoons baking powder

½ teaspoon cloves

1 teaspoon cinnamon

½ cup oatmeal

½ cup raisins

¾ cup whole wheat flour

- Blend oil and honey in a bowl. Add remaining ingredients in order listed, mixing well after each addition.
- Spoon into greased muffin cups.
- Bake at 350° for 15-20 minutes or until light golden brown. May bake in tube or loaf pan if preferred. Adjust cooking time accordingly.
- **Yield: 10 to 12 muffins.**

Broxie C. Stuckey '55
Gordo, Alabama

Morning Glory Muffins

2 cups all-purpose flour

1¼ cups sugar

2 teaspoons baking soda

2 teaspoons cinnamon

½ teaspoon salt

2 cups grated carrots

½ cup raisins

½ cup chopped nuts

½ cup grated coconut

1 apple, peeled, cored, and grated

3 eggs

1 cup salad oil

2 teaspoons vanilla

- In a large bowl, combine flour, sugar, soda, cinnamon, and salt. Stir in carrots, raisins, nuts, coconut, and apple.
- In a separate bowl, beat eggs, salad oil, and vanilla. Stir into dry mixture until just combined.
- Spoon into well greased muffin cups, filling to the top.
- Bake at 350° for 20 minutes.
- **Yield: 14 large muffins.**

Milla Dailey Boschung '70 '73 '95
Assistant Dean and Head, Department of Consumer Sciences
College of Human Environmental Sciences

Orange-Date Muffins

1 whole orange, sectioned and seeded
½ cup chopped dates or raisins
1 egg
½ cup butter or margarine
1½ cups all-purpose flour
1 teaspoon baking soda
1 teaspoon baking powder
½ teaspoon salt
¾ cup sugar

- Blend orange pieces in food processor until peel is finely chopped. Add dates, egg, and butter and mix.
- In separate container, stir together dry ingredients.
- Pour orange mixture over dry ingredients and stir only until moistened.
- Bake at 375° for 15-20 minutes.

Milla Dailey Boschung '70 '73 '95
Assistant Dean and Head, Department of Consumer Sciences
College of Human Environmental Sciences

Raisin-Oatmeal Muffins

2 cups oatmeal
¼ cup sugar
1 tablespoon baking powder
½ cup raisins
1 cup milk
3 tablespoons vegetable oil
1 egg, beaten

- Preheat oven to 425°.
- In a medium-size bowl, combine oatmeal, sugar, baking powder, and raisins. Add milk, oil and egg; stir only until dry ingredients are moistened.
- Fill greased muffin cups about two-thirds full.
- Bake for 15 to 20 minutes or until toothpick comes out clean.
- **Yield: 12 muffins.**

Carole R. Burke
Head, Interlibrary Loans/Assistant Professor
University Libraries

Six Week Muffins

5 teaspoons baking soda
2 cups boiling water
1 cup shortening
2 cups sugar
4 eggs
1 quart buttermilk
5 cups flour
1 tablespoon salt
4 cups All-Bran
2 cups 40% Bran Flakes
2 cups chopped dates
1½ cups chopped pecans

- Add soda to boiling water. Let cool.
- Cream shortening and sugar in a mixing bowl. Add unbeaten eggs, one at a time.
- Stir in the buttermilk, flour, and salt. Add water and soda mixture.
- In a very large bowl, combine All-Bran, Bran Flakes, dates, and pecans. Add flour mixture.
- Store covered in a refrigerator.
- When ready to bake, don't stir batter; just spoon it into well-greased muffin tins. Fill tins about two-thirds full.
- Bake at 375° for 20 minutes.
- **Yield: 7 dozen.**

Dough lasts six weeks in the refrigerator.

Erin Henry McWaters '83
Mobile, Alabama

Whole Wheat Banana Muffins

2-3 medium bananas, mashed
⅔ cup brown sugar
⅓ cup oil
2 eggs
¾ cup all-purpose flour
¾ cup whole wheat flour
1 teaspoon baking soda
1 teaspoon baking powder
½ teaspoon salt
½ cup chopped nuts, optional
¼ cup sugar
½ teaspoon cinnamon

- Mash bananas. Combine bananas, brown sugar, oil, and eggs. Beat until well mixed.
- In another bowl, mix flours, soda, baking powder, and salt. Add to banana mixture and combine. If desired, add nuts to batter.
- Pour into well-greased muffin tins.
- Mix sugar and cinnamon together. Sprinkle on muffins before baking.
- Bake at 350° for 20 minutes.

Using whole wheat flour adds extra texture, flavor, and fiber.
Milla Dailey Boschung '70 '73 '95
Assistant Dean and Head, Department of Consumer Sciences
College of Human Environmental Sciences

Whole Wheat Muffins

1 egg, well beaten
1 cup brown sugar
½ teaspoon salt
1 teaspoon vanilla
1 cup sour cream
1 cup whole wheat flour
1 teaspoon baking powder
1 scant teaspoon baking soda

- Beat together egg, sugar, salt, and vanilla. Stir in remaining ingredients.
- Fill greased muffin cups and bake at 375° for 10-15 minutes.

Milla Dailey Boschung '70 '73 '95
Assistant Dean and Head, Department of Consumer Sciences
College of Human Environmental Sciences

Spoon Bread

1¼ cups cornmeal, sifted
2 cups water
2 cups milk
2 eggs, separated
2 tablespoons butter, melted
1½ teaspoons salt
2 teaspoons baking powder

- Mix cornmeal and water. Cook over low heat until thick, stirring constantly.
- Add milk, beaten egg yolks, butter, and salt. When smooth, fold in beaten egg whites and baking powder.
- Pour immediately into a greased 2-quart baking pan.
- Bake at 350° for 45 minutes or until brown.

*From the **University Club Cookbook**, published in the early 1960s.*

Jane and John Curry '63
Tuscaloosa, Alabama

Easy Cornbread

2 (8½-ounce) packages corn muffin mix
1 (8-ounce) can cream style corn
2 large eggs
½ cup plain nonfat yogurt
½ cup (2 ounces) shredded reduced-fat
   cheddar cheese
¼ to ½ cup milk

- Combine all ingredients in a bowl. Stir just until moistened.
- Pour into a lightly greased 13 x 9-inch pan.
- Bake at 400° for 17-20 minutes or until golden brown.

Dr. Rodney W. Roth
Professor, Educational Research and Former Dean
College of Education

Nothing but the Best!

Broccoli Cornbread

½ cup melted butter
½ cup chopped onion
1 teaspoon salt
¾ cup cottage cheese
10 ounce package frozen, chopped broccoli
    (thawed and drained)
4 eggs, lightly beaten
1 (8½-ounce) box corn muffin mix

- In a mixing bowl, blend all ingredients except corn muffin mix. Stir in muffin mix.
- Pour into greased 13 x 9-inch pan.
- Bake at 400° for 20-25 minutes.
- Serve warm.

Carol Sue Martin
Wife of James A. Martin, Associate Professor,
Department of Aerospace Engineering
College of Engineering

Mexican Cornbread

3 eggs, beaten
3 cups cornbread mix
2½ cups milk
½ cup oil
1½ cups grated Longhorn cheese
1 cup cream-style corn
1 (4-ounce) can green chili peppers, diced
1 onion, chopped
3 teaspoons sugar

- Mix all ingredients in order given.
- Place in a greased 13 x 9-inch pan.
- Bake at 400° for approximately 30 minutes or until golden brown.

Teresa Gilstrap Pruett
Office Assistant, Division of Environmental
and Industrial Programs
College of Continuing Studies

Big Al's Yeast Rolls

2 tablespoons instant active yeast
1 pound plus 13 ounces bread flour
⅔ cup nonfat dry milk solids
⅓ cup plus 1 tablespoon granulated sugar
1 tablespoon salt
6 tablespoons vegetable oil
2 cups warm water, 90-110°
nonstick spray

- Place yeast, flour, nonfat dry milk, sugar, and salt in mixing bowl. Using dough hook, if available, blend on low speed for 2 minutes.
- Add oil; blend on low speed an additional 2 minutes. Gradually add water; mix on low speed for 1 minute.
- If using dough hook, knead with mixer on medium speed for 10 minutes; to knead by hand, remove dough from bowl and place on floured board. Knead for about 10 minutes; dough should be smooth and elastic.
- Spray pan with nonstick spray.
- Pinch off dough into 2-ounce balls, about the size of a ping-pong ball, and shape until smooth and round; place on prepared pan placing ½ inch apart.
- Cover loosely with plastic film or foil. Place in warm place to proof about 30-50 minutes; rolls should double in size.
- Remove cover and bake in 400° oven for about 18 to 20 minutes, or until lightly browned.

J.J. Doster Cafe
College of Human Environmental Sciences

Nothing but the Best!

Butterhorn Rolls

1 cup milk
½ cup shortening
1 (¼-ounce) package yeast
½ cup granulated sugar
1 teaspoon salt
3 eggs, slightly beaten
4 cups flour
butter, melted

- Scald milk and remove from heat. Add shortening and stir until melted.
- Combine yeast and sugar. When milk mixture is lukewarm (105-115°), add yeast mixture and stir to dissolve yeast.
- Pour milk and yeast mixture into an electric mixer bowl. Add salt and eggs and mix well. Add the flour, 1 cup at a time, beating dough at high speed to mix.
- Cover bowl with a dampened towel. Let dough rise until doubled in size, about 2 to 3 hours.
- Divide dough into three sections. The dough will be very sticky. Add only enough flour to handle dough, keeping it as soft as possible. Do not knead the dough.
- Roll each dough section into a circle about ⅓-inch thick. Brush each circle with melted butter and cut into 12 pie-shaped wedges. From wide edge, roll each wedge and place on greased baking sheet with the pointed end underneath. Brush tops with melted butter.
- Let rise again until doubled in size.
- Bake at 400° for 12-15 minutes.

Rona Donahoe
Associate Professor, Department of Geology
College of Arts and Sciences

Extra Good Rolls

2 cups warm water (105-115°)
½ cup sugar
1½ teaspoons salt
2 (¼-ounce) packages yeast
1 egg, beaten
½ cup oil
approximately 7 cups bread flour

- In a large mixing bowl combine water, sugar, and salt, stirring until sugar is dissolved. Sprinkle yeast on top of water mixture. Let dissolve for 5 minutes.
- Stir in 1 egg. Beat in, by hand, approximately 3½ cups of flour. Add oil and mix well. Add enough remaining flour to make a dough that is no longer sticky and that can be worked with the hands.
- Turn out onto a floured surface and knead for 6 to 8 minutes.
- Place in a greased bowl and let rise until doubled in bulk, 2 to 4 hours. Punch down.
- Then either make into the type of roll desired or brush with oil. Cover tightly and refrigerate. It will keep in the refrigerator for 4 to 5 days. Punch down occasionally.
- When ready to bake rolls, form rolls as desired. Let rise until doubled
- Bake at 425° for approximately 15 to 18 minutes.
- **Yield: 3 to 4 dozen, depending on the type of roll made.**

Rolls can be made cholesterol free by using 2 egg whites in place of the whole egg.

Margaret E. (Beth) Rumley Russell '70
York, Alabama

Mayonnaise Rolls

1 cup self-rising flour
½ cup milk
2 tablespoons mayonnaise

- Mix all ingredients together and blend well.
- Spoon into greased muffin tins and let rise 1 hour.
- Bake at 400° until brown. Let rolls rest in pan a few minutes before removing.
- **Yield: 8 medium rolls.**

Mary Bolt Lloyd '42
Birmingham, Alabama

Nothing but the Best!

Special Day Waffles

2 cups all-purpose flour
3 teaspoons baking powder
1 teaspoon baking soda
1 teaspoon salt
2 cups buttermilk
4 eggs, well beaten
1 cup oil

- Heat waffle iron according to manufacturer's directions.
- Sift together flour, baking powder, soda, and salt.
- Combine buttermilk and beaten eggs. Add to flour mixture. With hand mixer or electric mixer at high speed, beat until smooth. Stir in oil.
- When waffle iron is ready to use, pour batter into center of lower half until it spreads about 1 inch from edge. Bring cover down gently, and bake until golden brown and crisp.
- **Yield: 6 to 8 waffles.**

To make lower in cholesterol and lower in fat, use 4 egg whites, well beaten, and only ½ cup oil.

Margaret E. (Beth) Rumley Russell '70
York, Alabama

Apple-Walnut Pancakes

1 cup whole wheat flour
1 cup white flour
1 teaspoon salt
2 teaspoons baking powder
1 tablespoon brown sugar
2 cups milk
2 eggs, well beaten
2 tablespoons oil
1 cup diced apples
½ cup chopped walnuts

- Combine dry ingredients.
- Blend together milk, eggs, and oil. Add to dry ingredients and stir until just mixed.
- Add diced apples and walnuts.
- Bake on moderately hot, lightly greased griddle.
- **Yield: 4 to 6 servings.**

Frieda Meyer
Professor Emerita of Home Economics
School of Home Economics

Virginia's Mini Blinis

2 (8-ounce) packages cream cheese, softened
1½ cups sugar, divided
2 egg yolks
2 (1 pound) loaves thin white bread, crust removed
1 cup butter, melted
1½ tablespoons cinnamon

- Combine cream cheese, ½ cup sugar, and egg yolks. Blend.
- Roll bread with rolling pin until very thin.
- Spread with cream cheese mixture.
- Roll into finger rolls and dip in butter.
- Combine remaining 1 cup sugar and cinnamon. Dip rolls in cinnamon mixture.
- Bake at 400° for about 10 minutes.
- **Yield: 65 rolls.**

Mini Blinis are wonderful with morning coffee.

Mrs. Madolyn Clipson '69
Associate Professor Emerita,
Department of Business Education
College of Education

GMC Ham and Egg Soufflé

1 cup sliced mushrooms
butter
12 slices bread, crusts removed
2 cups cubed ham
¼ cup chopped green bell pepper
1 cup shredded cheddar cheese
6 eggs, beaten
3 cups milk
½ teaspoon dry mustard
1 tablespoon flour
1 teaspoon salt

- Sauté mushrooms in small amount butter until tender.
- Cover bottom of greased 9 x 13-inch glass baking dish with bread. Layer with ham. Top with mushrooms and pepper. Sprinkle with cheese.
- Combine eggs, milk, mustard, flour, and salt. Pour over ingredients in dish. Cover and refrigerate overnight.
- Bake uncovered at 325° for 1 hour.

Betty Jo Novak Walker '58
River Forrest, Illinois

Nothing but the Best!

Bacon, Egg, and Cheese Brunch Strata

4 cups cubed dry bread

2 cups grated cheddar cheese

10 eggs, beaten

4 cups milk

1½ teaspoons dry mustard

¼ teaspoon onion powder

freshly ground pepper

8 slices bacon, cooked and crumbled

½ cup sliced fresh mushrooms

½ cup chopped tomato

- Grease 13 x 9 x 2-inch baking pan. Arrange bread cubes in pan and sprinkle with cheese.
- Combine eggs, milk, mustard, onion powder and pepper. Pour egg mixture evenly over bread.
- Sprinkle with bacon, mushrooms, and tomato. Cover with foil and refrigerate overnight.
- Heat oven to 325°. Bake, uncovered, until set, about 1 hour. Cover loosely with foil if top browns too quickly.
- **Yield: 10 to 12 servings.**

Egg casseroles were always a favorite at pre-game brunches. It is especially nice that they can be made ahead of time.

MarLa Sayers, Honorary Cookbook Chair
Wife of Dr. Roger Sayers, University of Alabama President
1988-1996

Mexican Brunch Casserole

1 pound pork sausage

9 eggs, beaten

1 teaspoon salt

½ teaspoon pepper

½ cup milk

⅓ cup chopped bell pepper

1 (4-ounce) jar sliced mushrooms, drained

1 (2-ounce) jar diced pimentos, drained

3 cups grated sharp cheddar cheese

1 cup picante sauce

- Brown sausage in skillet. Drain fat.
- Combine eggs, salt, pepper, and milk.
- Layer sausage, bell pepper, mushrooms, pimentos, and cheese in lightly greased casserole dish.
- Pour egg mixture over casserole and stir. Top with picante sauce
- Bake at 375° for 30 minutes, or until eggs are set.
- **Yield: 8 servings.**

Mary Ann Cole Scott '67
Tucker, Georgia

Fancy Egg Scramble

5 tablespoons butter, divided
1 cup diced Canadian bacon
¼ cup diced green onion
12 eggs, beaten
⅛ teaspoon paprika
2 tablespoons butter
2 tablespoons flour
½ teaspoon salt
⅛ teaspoon pepper
2 cups milk
1 cup grated cheddar cheese
1 (3-ounce) can mushroom pieces, drained
2½ cups fresh bread crumbs
melted butter
paprika

- In a large skillet, melt 3 tablespoons butter. Add bacon and onions and sauté until onions are tender.
- Add eggs and scramble until set. Remove from heat.
- Melt remaining butter in a saucepan. Stir in flour, salt, and pepper. Add milk. Cook, stirring constantly, until thickened. Add cheese and continue cooking until cheese is melted.
- Fold mushrooms and egg mixture into cheese sauce.
- Place in a 12 x 7 x 2-inch casserole.
- Toss crumbs with melted butter and paprika. Sprinkle over eggs. Cover and chill until 30 minutes before serving.
- Bake at 350° for 30 minutes.
- **Variation**: Substitute 1 pound browned and drained sausage for Canadian bacon.

Suzanne Crump '65, '79
Wife of Dr. Don Crump, Associate Academic Vice-President
Office for Academic Affairs

Nothing but the Best!

Mushroom Frittata

1 cup sliced fresh mushrooms
⅔ cup chopped onion
⅔ cup chopped green bell pepper
1 cup coarsely chopped zucchini
1 teaspoon minced garlic
2 teaspoons vegetable oil
2 eggs, beaten
3 egg whites
⅓ cup half and half
½ teaspoon salt
⅛ teaspoon pepper
1½ cups soft bread crumbs
1 (8-ounce) package cream cheese, cut in
    ½-inch cubes
1 cup grated sharp cheddar cheese

- Preheat oven to 350°.
- Sauté mushrooms, onions, bell pepper, zucchini, and garlic in oil until tender.
- Beat eggs, egg whites and cream; add salt and pepper. Combine with vegetables.
- Add bread crumbs, cream cheese and cheddar cheese. Mix well, being careful not to break up cream cheese cubes while stirring.
- Place in a greased 9-inch pie pan and bake for 45 minutes.
- **Yield: 6 servings.**

Great with salad and French bread.

Karen Greenlee Conner '72
Birmingham, Alabama

Summer Squash and Zucchini Frittata

3 tablespoons olive oil, divided
2 small summer squash, sliced
2 small zucchini
1 onion, sliced
¼ pound zucchini blossoms, optional
5 eggs
2 tablespoons grated Parmesan cheese
salt and pepper
1 tablespoon chopped parsley

- Preheat oven to 400°.
- Heat 2 tablespoons of olive oil in a sauté pan. Sauté summer squash, zucchini, and onions until tender.
- If using zucchini blossoms, remove pistils and sauté blossoms until softened.
- Beat eggs; stir in Parmesan cheese, 1 teaspoon olive oil, salt, pepper, and parsley.
- Pour over squash, and scramble gently with wooden spoon. When bottom is set, remove to oven and bake until top is firm.
- To serve, drizzle with remaining oil.
- **Yield: 4 to 6 servings.**

Lydia Roper
Associate Professor, Department of Clothing,
Textiles, and Interior Design
College of Human Environmental Sciences

Garlic Cheese Grits Casserole

1 cup uncooked grits
½ cup butter
1 (6-ounce) roll garlic cheese
2 eggs, beaten
½ cup milk
salt

- Cook grits according to package directions.
- Cut butter and cheese into small pieces and stir into warm grits to melt.
- Combine eggs, milk, and salt; add to grits mixture.
- Pour into buttered 2-quart casserole. Cover and bake 30 minutes at 350°, or until set.
- **Yield: 6 to 8 servings.**

Suzanne Crump '65 '79
Wife of Dr. Don Crump, Associate Academic Vice-President
Office for Academic Affairs

Nassau Grits

8 slices bacon, cooked, drippings reserved
1 medium onion, chopped
1 medium green bell pepper, chopped
1 (16-ounce) can tomatoes, drained
¼ teaspoon sugar
1½ cups uncooked grits
6 cups water

- Sauté onions and peppers in reserved bacon drippings. Stir in tomatoes and sugar. Simmer for 30 minutes.
- Cook grits in water. Stir cooked grits into tomato mixture.
- Pour into casserole and crumble bacon on top. Serve hot.
- **Yield: 10 servings.**

Delicious served with fish.

Carole Sloan '66
Wife of Dr. Bernard Sloan '71 '72, Dean, New College

Nothing but the Best!

Picnic Basket Quiche

pastry shell (see recipe below)
1 (8¼-ounce) can crushed pineapple
¼ cup chopped green onion
¼ cup chopped green bell pepper
1 tablespoon butter
2 eggs, beaten
¾ cup half and half
¾ cup shredded Muenster cheese
¼ teaspoon salt
¼ teaspoon dry mustard
⅛ teaspoon white pepper
dash nutmeg
1 (4-ounce) package thinly sliced cooked
   ham
5 slices tomato, thinly sliced
1 tablespoon grated Romano cheese

- Prepare pastry shell. Set pan on baking sheet, and bake on lowest rack of moderately hot oven (375°) for 15 minutes.
- Place pineapple in wire strainer and drain well.
- Sauté onion and bell pepper in butter for 1 minute. Remove from heat and stir in pineapple.
- Combine eggs, half and half, cheese, salt, mustard, white pepper, and nutmeg.
- Layer ham slices in partially baked pie shell. Spoon pineapple mixture over ham. Carefully pour egg mixture over pineapple.
- Return to oven, and bake 20 minutes longer. Top with tomato slices and sprinkle with Romano cheese. Continue cooking 15 minutes longer, or until filling is set.
- Remove from oven and cool at least 15 minutes before cutting.
- **Yield: 8 servings.**

Crust for Picnic Basket Quiche

1½ cups all-purpose flour, sifted
¾ teaspoon salt
¼ teaspoon tarragon, crumbled
½ cup shortening
3 to 4 tablespoons cold milk

- Combine flour, salt and tarragon. Cut in shortening until particles are the size of peas.
- Sprinkle with 3 to 4 tablespoons of milk, adding just enough to make a stiff dough that can be shaped into a ball.
- Roll out on lightly floured board to an 11-inch circle.
- Fit into a greased 8-inch layer cake pan and trim edge slightly above rim of pan.
- Chill while preparing remaining ingredients.

Ruth Gregg '78
Hamilton, Alabama

Quick Crab Quiche

1 deep dish pie shell, unbaked

3 eggs, beaten

1 (6-ounce) can crabmeat, drained and flaked

1 (2.8-ounce) can fried onion rings, crushed

1 cup sour cream

1 cup shredded cheddar cheese

- Prick bottom and sides of pie shell with a fork. Bake at 400° for 3 minutes. Remove from oven and again gently prick with a fork. Bake 5 minutes longer. Cool.
- Combine remaining ingredients, mixing well. Spoon into pastry shell.
- Bake at 350° for 35 minutes or until set. Let stand 10 minutes before serving.

Margaret Balentine '70 '76
Associate Professor Emerita, Home Economics Education
College of Human Environmental Sciences

Grillades

4 pounds beef or venison rounds, sliced ½-inch thick

8 tablespoons bacon grease, divided

½ cup flour

¾ cup chopped celery

1 cup chopped onion

2 cups chopped green onions

1½ cups chopped green bell pepper

2 cloves garlic, minced

2 cups chopped tomatoes

½ teaspoon tarragon

⅔ teaspoon thyme

1 cup water

1 cup red wine

3 teaspoons salt

½ teaspoon black pepper

2 bay leaves

½ teaspoon hot sauce

2 tablespoons Worcestershire sauce

3 tablespoons chopped parsley

- Remove fat from meat. Cut meat into serving-sized pieces and pound it to ¼-inch thickness.
- In a Dutch oven, brown meat in 4 tablespoons bacon grease. As meat browns, remove to warm plate.
- Add remaining bacon grease and flour to Dutch oven. Stir and cook to make a dark brown roux.
- Add green onions, onions, celery, green pepper, and garlic. Sauté until limp.
- Add tomatoes, tarragon, and thyme. Cook for 3 minutes.
- Return meat to pan. Add water, wine, salt, pepper, bay leaves, hot sauce, and Worcestershire sauce. Lower heat, stir and continue cooking. Simmer, covered, approximately 2 hours, until meat is very tender.
- Remove bay leaves, stir in parsley and cool. Let the grillades sit several hours or overnight in refrigerator. More liquid may be added.
- Serve over grits with green salad and garlic bread for supper; or over grits with eggs for Sunday or Mardi Gras brunch.

Tom Davis '70
Senior Associate Director
Undergraduate Admissions

Nothing but the Best!

Salads

Salads

Cranberry Salad

1 (12-ounce) package cranberries

2 cups sugar

1 (3-ounce) package cherry-flavored gelatin

1 cup hot water

2 (1.3-ounce) packages Dream Whip

1 (12-ounce) package miniature
   marshmallows

1 large bunch of seedless grapes

1 cup chopped nuts

- Chop cranberries and add sugar. Chill overnight in refrigerator.
- Next morning, dissolve gelatin in 1 cup of hot water. Add to cranberries and refrigerate until firm.
- Mix Dream Whip package according to directions, omitting vanilla. Fold into gelatin mixture.
- Add remaining ingredients.
- Chill at least 2 hours before serving.

Debbie Riley
Staff Assistant, Housing and Residential Life

Cranberry-Cherry Salad

1 (6-ounce) package cherry-flavored gelatin

2 cups boiling water

1 (16-ounce) can cranberry jelly sauce

1 cup sour cream

1 (8-ounce) can crushed pineapple, drained

½ cup coarsely chopped walnuts, optional

- Dissolve gelatin in boiling water.
- Cut cranberry sauce into cubes with a spoon and add to gelatin.
- Cool in refrigerator until mixture is consistency of unbeaten egg whites.
- Fold in remaining ingredients. Avoid overstirring.
- Chill in refrigerator until firm.
- **Yield: 12 servings.**

Veronica Purcell
Clerical Assistant, External Degree Program
New College

Holiday Salad

2 (3-ounce) packages lime-flavored gelatin
3 cups hot water
1 (8-ounce) package cream cheese
1 large apple, coarsely chopped
1 cup chopped celery
1 cup chopped pecans
½ cup drained red and green cherries
2 cups drained crushed pineapple

- Dissolve gelatin in hot water.
- Cut cream cheese in small pieces. Add with remaining ingredients to gelatin mixture. Combine well.
- Refrigerate until firm.
- **Yield: 8 servings.**

Joyce Best
Mobile, Alabama

Lemon Lime Salad

1 (3-ounce) package lemon-flavored gelatin
1 (3-ounce) package lime-flavored gelatin
2 cups boiling water
1½ cups creamed cottage cheese
1 (8-ounce) can crushed pineapple
1 (6-ounce) can evaporated milk
¾ cup chopped pecans
½ cup mayonnaise
½ teaspoon lemon juice

- Add gelatins to water and stir until completely dissolved. Chill until thick.
- Combine remaining ingredients and add to gelatin. Stir well and refrigerate until set.
- **Yield: 9 to 12 servings.**

Debbie Riley
Staff Assistant, Housing and Residential Life

Mandarin Orange Salad

2 (15-ounce) cans mandarin oranges
2 (3-ounce) packages orange gelatin
2½ cups apricot juice
1½ cups miniature marshmallows
whipped topping
grated cheese

- Drain oranges and reserve juice. Heat juice and add enough water to make 1½ cups. Bring to a boil; then add gelatin and stir until dissolved.
- Add apricot juice.
- Chill until partially jelled.
- Add fruit and marshmallows. Top with whipped topping. Sprinkle grated cheese on top.
- **Yield: 8 servings.**

Dale A. Phillips
Investigator, Department of Public Safety

Pretzel Salad

Crust:
2 cups crushed pretzels
¾ cup butter, melted
3 tablespoon sugar or Nutrasweet

Filling:
1 (8-ounce) package cream cheese
1 cup sugar
1 (8-ounce) package whipped topping

Topping:
1 (6-ounce) box strawberry-flavored gelatin
2 cups boiling water
2 (10-ounce) packages frozen strawberries

- For crust, combine pretzels, butter, and sugar.
- Press into a 9 x 12-inch pyrex pan.
- Bake 8 minutes at 400°.
- Cool.

- For filling, beat cream cheese and sugar together.
- Fold in whipped topping.
- Spread over crust.

- For topping, dissolve gelatin in water.
- Add strawberries.
- Cool in refrigerator for 10 minutes.
- Pour mixture over filling and chill until congealed.

Lisa Parker
Administrative Specialist, Dean's Office
College of Human Environmental Sciences

Congealed Vegetable Salad

1 (3-ounce) package lemon-flavored gelatin
1 cup boiling water
¾ cup mayonnaise
¼ cup vinegar
1 teaspoon prepared mustard
1 teaspoon salt
1 tablespoon sugar
1½ cups shredded carrots
1½ cups finely chopped celery
1 (15¼-ounce) can tiny peas, drained
1 (10-ounce) can cut asparagus spears,
   drained
1 (2-ounce) jar pimentos, chopped
1 tablespoon chopped green pepper
1 tablespoon chopped onion

- Dissolve gelatin in boiling water.
- Add mayonnaise, vinegar, mustard, salt, and sugar; beat until well blended.
- Add vegetables to gelatin mixture.
- Pour into a mold and chill.
- **Yield: 8 to 12 servings.**

Better if prepared a day before serving.

Mary A. Crenshaw
Dean and Professor Emerita
School of Home Economics

Alan's Favorite Orange Salad

1 (20-ounce) can pineapple chunks
1 (15-ounce) can mandarin oranges
1 (3-ounce) package instant vanilla pudding
   mix
3 teaspoons orange-flavored drink mix
3 small bananas

- Drain pineapple and oranges, reserving liquid.
- In a medium bowl, stir pudding mix and orange drink mix together. Add reserved fruit juice and mix well. Stir in fruit.
- Chill for at least 2 hours before serving.
- **Yield: 6 servings.**

May be used as a salad or a dessert.

Shirley Florence
Coordinator of Administrative Affairs and Registrar
College of Community Health Sciences

Variation: Substitute 1 (29-ounce) can mixed fruit for the mandarin oranges.

Lisa Brister
Assistant Director, Housing and Residential Life

Orange Salad Bowl with Celery Seed Dressing

8 cups torn salad greens

2 (15-ounce) cans mandarin oranges, drained

1 cup pecans or peanuts

Celery Seed Dressing:

⅓ cup sugar

1 teaspoon salt

1 teaspoon dry mustard

⅓ cup vinegar

1 small onion

1 cup salad oil

1 tablespoon celery seed

- Combine ingredients and toss with celery seed dressing.

- Combine dressing ingredients, mix well, and chill thoroughly.
- **Yield: 8 to 12 servings.**

Becky Ladewig
Chair Emerita, Department of Human Development
and Family Studies
College of Human Environmental Sciences

Audrey's Peach-Pecan Salad

1 (3-ounce) package lemon-flavored gelatin

1 cup boiling water

1 (4-ounce) package cream cheese

½ cup evaporated milk

½ cup mayonnaise

¼ cup lemon juice

1 (15-ounce) can sliced peaches in light syrup, drained and cut into chunks

½ cup chopped celery

1 cup chopped pecans

lettuce

- Dissolve gelatin in boiling water. Place in refrigerator to cool, but do not allow to set completely.
- Combine cream cheese, milk, and mayonnaise with mixer. Add gelatin and lemon juice and blend until smooth.
- Stir in peaches, celery, and pecans. Pour this mixture into a lightly greased bundt pan or mold and refrigerate for several hours.
- Serve chilled on a bed of lettuce.
- **Yield: 10 to 12 servings.**

Gail Davis
Northport, Alabama

Tuscaloosa Salad

juice of one lemon
4 large apples, diced
3 stalks celery, chopped
¼ cup raisins
⅓ cup chopped pecans or walnuts
1 cup low-fat plain yogurt
lettuce leaves

- Sprinkle lemon juice over apples to prevent discoloration.
- Combine apples, celery, raisins, pecans, and yogurt in a bowl. Toss to coat well.
- Arrange on a bed of lettuce.
- **Yield:** 6 to 8 servings.

Sissy Thompson
Athens, Alabama

Six Fruit Salad

½ cup orange juice
3 apples, peeled and diced
3 bananas, sliced
1 (29-ounce) can Bartlett pears
1 (5-ounce) can mandarin oranges
1 (20-ounce) can chunk pineapple
1 (10-ounce) jar maraschino cherries
¾ cup confectioners sugar
poppy seeds

- Pour orange juice over apples and bananas to prevent discoloration.
- Drain pears, orange sections, pineapple, and cherries, reserving 1 tablespoon of juice each from pineapple and cherries.
- Combine all fruit, including reserved juice.
- Add sugar and toss to dissolve.
- Sprinkle with poppy seeds.
- **Yield:** 12 servings.

Kay Branyon
Secretary, Department of American Studies
College of Arts and Sciences

Twenty-Four Hour Salad

1 (3-ounce) package vanilla pudding
1 cup whipped topping
1 (29-ounce) can fruit cocktail, drained
1 (15-ounce) can mandarin orange sections, drained
1 (10-ounce) jar maraschino cherries, drained
2 bananas, sliced

- Prepare pudding according to package instructions.
- Stir in whipped topping, fruit cocktail, orange sections and cherries. Refrigerate overnight.
- Add bananas shortly before serving.
- **Yield:** 6 servings.

Hugh W. Kilpatrick III
Staff Architect, Facilities Planning and Design

Alabama Ambrosia

8 oranges, peeled, seeded, and sectioned
1 (20-ounce) can of crushed pineapple
1 (12-ounce) bag frozen grated coconut
½ cup powdered sugar

- In a large bowl, arrange a layer of orange sections. Top with a layer of pineapple, including its juice.
- Sprinkle with coconut and sugar.
- Repeat these layers until everything is used up.
- Chill at least 8 hours.
- **Yield: 8 to 10 servings.**

Sissy Thompson
Athens, Alabama

Black and White Bean Salad

1 (15.8 ounce) can great northern beans, rinsed and drained
1 (15.8 ounce) can black beans, rinsed and drained
1¼ cups chopped, peeled, and seeded tomatoes
¾ cup diced red bell pepper
¾ cup diced yellow bell pepper
¾ cup thinly sliced green onions
½ cup salsa
¼ cup red wine vinegar
2 tablespoons chopped fresh cilantro
¼ teaspoon salt
⅛ teaspoon ground pepper
10 cups finely shredded Romaine lettuce
1 teaspoon lime juice

- Combine beans and tomatoes in a large bowl, stirring gently. Add peppers and green onions. Stir gently to combine. Set bean mixture aside.
- Combine salsa, vinegar, cilantro, salt, and pepper in a small bowl; stir with a wire whisk until well blended. Pour over bean mixture, and toss gently.
- Line a large serving bowl with shredded lettuce; top with bean mixture. Sprinkle with lime juice.
- **Yield: 10 servings.**

Martha Steele
Production Control Technician
Seebeck Computer Center

Marinated Broccoli and Cauliflower Salad

4 stems fresh broccoli

1 head cauliflower, broken into flowerets

10 large fresh mushrooms, sliced

1 medium green or red bell pepper, chopped

4 stalks celery, chopped

1 onion, sliced and separated into rings

½ cup vinegar

1½ cups vegetable oil

1 cup sugar

2 teaspoons dry mustard

1 teaspoon salt

2 tablespoons poppy seeds

- Remove flowerets from broccoli and cut into bite-sized pieces. Reserve stems for another use.
- In an airtight container, combine broccoli and cauliflower flowerets, mushrooms, bell pepper, celery, and onion rings.
- In a saucepan, combine vinegar, vegetable oil, and sugar. Heat over medium heat, stirring constantly until sugar is dissolved. Remove from heat.
- Add dry mustard, salt, and poppy seeds. Cool. Pour over vegetables.
- Cover with air tight lid and keep in refrigerator for 24 hours, stirring occasionally.
- **Yield: 10 to 12 servings.**

You may add cherry tomatoes (quartered) or other fresh vegetables. The secret to this recipe is to let the vegetables marinate 18-24 hours.

Judy Bonner '69 '73
Dean, College of Human Environmental Sciences

Broccoli, Raisin, and Walnut Salad

1 pound, 10 ounces fresh broccoli

¾ cup seedless raisins

¾ cup mayonnaise

3 tablespoons granulated sugar

3 tablespoons distilled vinegar

6 tablespoons chopped walnuts

- Remove flowerets from broccoli and cut into bite-sized pieces; place in a large bowl. Reserve stems for another use. Add raisins to broccoli and toss gently.
- In small mixing bowl, whisk together mayonnaise, sugar, and vinegar. Pour over broccoli mixture and gently mix well.
- Cover tightly. Chill for at least 2 hours or overnight.
- Add half of nuts to salad, combining well. Sprinkle remaining nuts over top.

J.J. Doster Cafe
College of Human Environmental Sciences
(Courtesy of Heather Silas, Spring 1995)

Broccoli and Bacon Salad

Dressing:
1 cup mayonnaise
½ cup sugar
2 tablespoons white vinegar

Salad:
2 large heads broccoli
½ cup finely chopped red onion
½ cup golden raisins
6 slices bacon

- Combine dressing ingredients 24 hours ahead and refrigerate.
- Remove flowerets from broccoli and cut into bite-size pieces. Use broccoli stems in other dishes.
- Cook bacon until crisp. Crumble.
- Just before serving, layer broccoli, onion, raisins, and bacon in a large bowl. Top with dressing and toss gently to combine.
- **Yield: 8 to 10 servings.**

Simple, never-fail recipe which always receives rave reviews. Even teenagers and picky eaters will love this sweet and sour dish. Sounds strange, looks colorful, and tastes terrific.

Hazel Bruchey
Office Manager, School of Music
College of Arts and Sciences

Chinese Cabbage Salad

1 head cabbage, chopped
8 green onions, sliced
2 (3-ounce) packages chicken-flavored
    ramen noodles, crushed
1 cup slivered almonds
¼ cup sesame seeds
¼ cup sunflower seeds

Dressing:
1 cup oil
¼ cup sugar
¼ cup wine vinegar
2 packages seasoning from noodles

- Place all salad ingredients in a large bowl.
- Mix together dressing ingredients and pour over salad.
- Refrigerate overnight.
- **Yield: 8 servings.**

Cindy Bowes
Programmer Analyst, Systems Development

Cashew Cole Slaw

⅔ cup mayonnaise

⅓ cup sour cream

¼ cup Italian dressing

¼ teaspoon celery seeds

salt and pepper to taste

½ cup chopped green onions

1 (10-ounce) package frozen baby sweet
    peas, thawed

¼ pound bacon, cooked and crumbled

1 cup unsalted, roasted cashews

½ medium cabbage, shredded

- Mix mayonnaise, sour cream, Italian dressing, celery seed, and salt and pepper to taste; refrigerate for two hours.
- Just before serving, add onions, peas, bacon, and cashews to dressing mixture.
- Pour over cabbage and toss.
- **Yield: 8 servings.**

For sweet cole slaw add ⅓ cup sugar.

Marion Reed
Expediter II, Purchasing

Shoepeg Corn Salad

2 (12-ounce) cans shoepeg corn, drained

2 tomatoes, seeded, drained and chopped

1 bell pepper, chopped

1 purple onion, chopped

1 cucumber, chopped

½ cup sour cream

¼ cup mayonnaise

2 tablespoons white wine vinegar

½ teaspoon celery seed

½ teaspoon dry mustard

½ teaspoon salt

½ teaspoon pepper

- Place corn, tomatoes, bell pepper, onion, and cucumber in a salad bowl.
- Blend sour cream, mayonnaise, and vinegar together. Add seasonings.
- Pour over vegetables, cover and chill overnight.
- **Yield: 6 servings.**

Note: You can use low-fat or fat-free sour cream and mayonnaise.

Pam Parsons '80, '93
Director of Development
College of Arts and Sciences

Nothing but the Best!

Corn and Pea Salad

¾ cup white vinegar

¼ cup canola oil

1 cup sugar

1 teaspoon salt

1 teaspoon pepper

2 (14½-ounce) cans whole kernel corn, drained

2 (15¼-ounce) cans green peas, drained

5 green onions, chopped

6 celery stalks, chopped

1 green pepper, chopped

- Combine vinegar, canola oil, sugar, salt, and pepper in a saucepan. Heat until sugar melts. Cool completely.
- Place remaining ingredients in a large bowl.
- Toss with vinegar mixture.
- Refrigerate 24 hours before serving.

Keeps up to one week in refrigerator.

Betty Pilegge
Wife of Joe Pilegge, Professor Emeritus, Department of
Political Science
College of Arts and Sciences

Confetti Salad

Salad:

1 (15¼-ounce) can green peas, drained

1 (16-ounce) can French green beans, drained

1 (12-ounce) can white shoepeg corn, drained

1 (2-ounce) large jar pimento, drained and diced

1 cup diced red onion

1 cup chopped celery

1 green pepper, chopped

Marinade:

½ cup sugar

½ cup oil

½ cup white vinegar

1 teaspoon salt

1 teaspoon pepper

- Place all salad ingredients in a large salad bowl.
- Blend marinade ingredients together. Pour over salad ingredients and mix.
- **Yield: 10 servings.**

Peggy Jessee
Associate Professor, Department of Human Development and
Family Studies
College of Human Environmental Sciences

Caesar Salad

4 garlic cloves
4 flat anchovies
3 ounces extra virgin olive oil
½ teaspoon dry mustard
2 teaspoons lemon juice
dash of hot sauce
4 ounces dry grated Romano cheese
1 medium bunch Romaine lettuce

- Combine garlic, anchovies, olive oil, mustard, lemon juice, and hot sauce in a small food processor. Process until dressing is smooth and without large pieces.
- Wash the Romaine, spin dry, and tear into pieces. Place in a large glass salad bowl.
- Toss lettuce with dressing. When the salad is tossed, add the cheese and toss again.
- Serve on large salad plates.
- **Yield: 4 to 6 servings.**

James G. Taaffe
Provost and Vice President for Academic Affairs, 1990-1996

Calhoun Layered Salad

½ head lettuce, torn into bite-size pieces
1 celery stalk, chopped
1 large bell pepper, chopped
1 small onion, chopped
1 (15¼-ounce) can green peas, drained
1 (8-ounce) can sliced water chestnuts, drained
½ cup sour cream
½ cup mayonnaise
dash of garlic salt
1 cup grated cheese
4 hard boiled eggs, chopped
1 cup bacon bits

- Place lettuce in a large glass salad bowl. Cover with celery, then bell pepper, followed by onions. Top with peas and finish with water chestnuts.
- Combine sour cream, mayonnaise and garlic salt. Spread over salad.
- Sprinkle with cheese, eggs, and bacon bits.
- Cover and refrigerate overnight. Do not toss until ready to serve.
- **Yield: 6 to 8 servings.**

Penny Calhoun Gibson
Reference Librarian, Law School Library
School of Law

- **Variation**: Omit onion and water chestnuts. Add a layer of shredded carrots. Use 2 cups salad dressing plus 2 tablespoons sugar for dressing.

Ann Smith Brasher
Accounting Specialist, School of Mines and Energy Development

Tailgaters Potato Salad

6 to 8 medium size potatoes, cooked, peeled,
    and diced
4 hard boiled eggs, chopped
3 to 4 dill pickles, chopped
½ cup salad dressing (more if needed)
1 small onion, chopped
1 teaspoon sugar
1 teaspoon vinegar
½ teaspoon salt
1 to 2 tablespoons prepared mustard or spicy
    brown mustard
paprika for garnish

- Combine all ingredients except paprika in a large bowl.
- Sprinkle with paprika.
- **Yield: 8 servings.**

Donna Laughmiller
Decatur, Alabama

Sour Cream Potato Salad

7 medium potatoes, peeled and diced
⅓ cup Italian salad dressing
4 hard boiled eggs
¾ cup celery, diced
⅓ cup green onions, chopped
1 cup mayonnaise
½ cup sour cream
½ teaspoon spicy mustard
salt to taste
celery seeds to taste

- Cook potatoes; drain well.
- Marinate potatoes in Italian salad dressing for at least 2 hours, or overnight.
- Separate egg yolks from whites. Dice whites and mix with potatoes. Add celery and green onions.
- Mash egg yolks and mix with mayonnaise, sour cream, and mustard. Add small amount of salt and celery seeds.
- Add to potatoes and toss.
- **Yield: 8 servings.**

Angie Webb '61
Birmingham, Alabama

Curried Rice Salad

1 (4⅓-ounce) box Original Long Grain
   Rice-A-Roni
¾ cup chopped green bell pepper
1 small onion or 8 green onions, chopped
1 (2¼-ounce) can chopped black olives,
   drained
1 (6-ounce) jar marinated artichokes
⅔ cup mayonnaise
1 teaspoon curry powder

- Cook rice as directed on package.
- Add bell pepper, onion, and black olives. Drain artichokes and reserve marinade. Add artichokes to rice.
- Combine mayonnaise and curry powder. Add to rice mixture. If salad seems dry, add small amounts of the reserved marinade.
- Chill at least 5 hours before serving.

Mary Catherine Beasley
Professor Emerita, Consumer Sciences
School of Home Economics

Sauerkraut Salad

Marinade:
2 cups sugar
1 cup vinegar
½ teaspoon ground black pepper
4 to 6 drops hot sauce

Salad:
1 (32-ounce) jar sauerkraut
3 cups chopped celery
1 (2-ounce) jar pimentos, drained
1 large onion, thinly sliced
1 large green bell pepper, chopped

- For marinade, place sugar, vinegar, black pepper, and hot sauce in a saucepan. Heat until sugar melts. Set aside to cool to room temperature.
- For salad, mix together sauerkraut, with juice, celery, pimentos, onion, and green pepper in a 4-quart glass container.
- Pour marinade over vegetables.
- Cover and store in refrigerator for 24 hours before serving.
- **Yield: 10 servings.**

Lee W. Rabe
Assistant Professor, Department of Clothing,
Textiles, and Interior Design
College of Human Environmental Sciences

Nothing but the Best!

Spinach, Bacon, and Water Chestnut Salad

10 cups fresh spinach, torn into bite-size
    pieces
½ pound bacon, cooked, drained, and
    crumbled
2 (8-ounce) cans sliced water chestnuts,
    drained
4 hard cooked eggs, sliced
1 cup salad oil
¼ cup balsamic vinegar
¾ cup sugar
1 tablespoon Worcestershire sauce
2 teaspoons salt
⅓ cup ketchup
1 small onion, diced

- Layer spinach, bacon, water chestnuts, and eggs in a salad bowl.
- In a saucepan, combine remaining ingredients. Cook over medium heat, stirring occasionally, until sugar is dissolved. Cool.
- A few minutes before serving, toss salad with dressing.
- **Yield: 8 to 10 servings.**

Judy Bonner '69 '73
Dean, College of Human Environmental Sciences

Spinach Salad with Soy Ginger Dressing

10 ounces fresh spinach
1 (8-ounce) can water chestnuts, drained
    and sliced thin

Soy Ginger Dressing:
3 tablespoons water
2 tablespoons cider vinegar
2 tablespoons soy sauce
4 teaspoons vegetable oil
½ teaspoon sugar
⅛ teaspoon ground ginger
1 small clove garlic, crushed (optional)

- Rinse spinach well. Tear leaves from stem and discard stems. Drain leaves and dry on paper towels.
- Place spinach and water chestnuts in salad bowl.
- Combine all dressing ingredients in a jar with a tight lid. Shake vigorously.
- Pour dressing over spinach and toss lightly.
- **Yield: 6 servings.**

Carole R. Burke
Head, Interlibrary Loan
University Libraries

Onion Salad

3 medium white onions, chopped
⅓ cup sweet pickle cubes
1 tablespoon mayonnaise
1 tablespoon mustard
pinch of salt and pepper

- Mix onions with sweet pickles.
- Add mayonnaise, mustard, salt, and pepper. Chill.

Delicious served with fried fish.

Gloria F. Ellis
Secretary, Development Services
Office of Development

Hot Chicken Salad

3 cups cooked chicken, diced
1 cup finely chopped celery
½ cup sliced almonds, toasted
½ cup round buttery cracker crumbs
2 tablespoons chopped onion
1 (10¾-ounce) can cream of chicken soup
1 (2-ounce) can mushroom stems and pieces, drained
½ cup mayonnaise
½ cup crushed potato chips

- Combine all ingredients except potato chips and toss gently.
- Spoon into a greased 1½-quart casserole dish.
- Bake at 375° for 15 minutes. Sprinkle potato chips on top; bake 15 minutes more.
- **Yield: 6 servings.**

Cheryl Parker
Secretary, Department of Advertising and Public Relations
College of Communication

Chicken Salad

4 cups cooked and cubed chicken
2 cups chopped celery
4 tablespoons chopped ripe olives
6 hard cooked eggs, diced
1 teaspoon seasoned salt (or more, to taste)
¾ cup mayonnaise
¾ cup sour cream
2 tablespoons grated onion
2 tablespoons lemon juice

- Combine all ingredients.
- Chill and serve.
- **Yield: 6 to 8 servings.**

Teddy and Don Gambril
Associate Athletic Director

Carousel Mandarin Chicken

2 to 3 cups diced cooked chicken
1 cup diced celery
2 tablespoons lemon juice
1 tablespoon minced onion
1 teaspoon salt
⅓ cup light mayonnaise
1 cup seedless green grapes
1 (11-ounce) can mandarin oranges, drained
½ cup slivered almonds, toasted
lettuce leaves
additional mandarin orange slices, optional

- Combine chicken, celery, lemon juice, onion and salt. Chill well.
- Add mayonnaise, grapes, oranges, and almonds to chicken mixture; toss until well mixed.
- Serve on lettuce leaves, garnished with additional orange slices, if desired.
- **Yield: 6 servings.**

Broxie Stuckey '55
Gordo, Alabama

Wild Rice and Chicken Salad

1 (6-ounce) package long grain and wild
    rice
1 pound boneless chicken breasts, cooked and
    cut into ½-inch cubes
½ teaspoon salt
¾ cup mayonnaise
1 tablespoon lemon juice
¾ cup seedless red grapes, cut in halves
¾ cup sliced celery
¾ cup coarsely chopped cashews
2 tablespoons finely chopped onion
lettuce leaves
grapes
cashews

- Prepare rice according to package directions. Refrigerate until chilled.
- In small bowl, stir together salt, mayonnaise, and lemon juice.
- In large bowl, combine chicken, grapes, celery, chopped cashews, onion, and chilled rice. Fold in mayonnaise mixture.
- Refrigerate 2-3 hours.
- To serve, mound individual salad portions on lettuce leaves. Garnish with grapes and cashews.
- **Yield: 6 to 8 servings.**

Leigh Ann Danner Summerford '80
Tuscaloosa, Alabama

Tortellini Salad with Chicken and Artichokes

1 (9-ounce) package refrigerated cheese-filled
    tortellini
1 (5-ounce) can chicken breast meat,
    undrained
1 (14-ounce) can artichokes, drained and
    quartered
1 (2¼-ounce) can sliced ripe olives, drained
2 tablespoons olive oil
2 tablespoons white wine vinegar
2 teaspoons Italian seasoning
1 teaspoon Dijon-style mustard
1 teaspoon salt
⅛ teaspoon ground pepper
¼ cup grated Parmesan cheese
lettuce leaves
tomato wedges

- Cook tortellini according to package instructions. Drain and cool.
- Stir in chicken, artichokes, and olives. Set aside.
- Combine olive oil, vinegar, Italian seasoning, mustard, salt, and pepper. Mix well and pour over salad ingredients.
- Add grated Parmesan cheese and gently toss. Cover and refrigerate.
- Serve on lettuce and garnish with tomato wedges.
- **Yield: 4 servings.**

Carol L. Hoffman '82
Coordinator, Engineering Graphics
Department of Mechanical Engineering
College of Engineering

Nothing but the Best!

"War Chicken" Salad

1 whole chicken fryer
2 carrots, shredded
½ cup low calorie buttermilk dressing
¼ cup low calorie creamy cucumber dressing
¼ cup water
2 boiled eggs, chopped
salt to taste

- Boil the chicken until tender. Pull off all of the fat and skin and discard. Remove chicken from bones and chop into small pieces.
- Combine remaining ingredients. Pour over chicken and toss.
- Chill.
- **Yield: 6 servings.**

Jimmy Hill
Courtland, Alabama

Pasta Chicken Salad

2 cups dry pasta shells
1 cup sour cream
1 cup mayonnaise
1 package Hidden Valley Ranch Salad
    Dressing Mix-Original Flavor
½ teaspoon garlic salt
1 to 1½ cups chopped cooked chicken
1 tablespoon fresh chives, chopped*

*green onion tops may be substituted for chives

- Cook pasta according to package directions. Drain.
- Combine remaining ingredients and pour over pasta. Toss.
- Chill.
- **Yield: 6 to 8 servings.**

Paige and Lee Horn '87, '90
Florence, Alabama

Shrimp and Crab Salad with Avocado and Mandarin Oranges

1 pound cooked shrimp

1 pound cooked crab meat

2½ tablespoons lemon juice, divided

1 cup mayonnaise

¼ cup chopped parsley

3 tablespoons chives

1 tablespoon minced onion

1 teaspoon seasoned salt

¼ teaspoon thyme

¼ teaspoon pepper

lettuce leaves

1 large avocado

1 large tomato

1 can mandarin oranges

4 ripe olives

- Combine shrimp and crab. Toss with 1½ tablespoons lemon juice. Chill.
- Mix mayonnaise with parsley, chives, onion, salt, thyme, pepper, and remaining lemon juice. Add to seafood mixture and mix well.
- Arrange lettuce leaves on individual plates and top with a mound of seafood mixture.
- Cut avocado into quarters, remove seed and skin, and cut each quarter into thirds. Place slices in a starburst on top of the seafood.
- Cut tomato into wedges. Arrange tomato wedges and mandarin oranges around salad.
- Top each salad with one ripe olive.
- **Yield: 6 servings.**

Leatha A. Darden '62 '64
Associate Professor, Department of Clothing, Textiles, and
Interior Design
College of Human Environmental Sciences

Shrimp and Crab Salad

1 pound crab meat

1 pound medium cooked shrimp, chopped

1 stalk celery, chopped

½ teaspoon seasoned salt

1 teaspoon lemon juice

dash cayenne pepper

dash Worcestershire sauce

4 tablespoons mayonnaise

2 teaspoons Durkee Sandwich and Salad
   Sauce

- Mix all ingredients well.
- **Yield: 8 servings.**

Anabel and Isabel Vartanian '57
Hopewell, Virginia

Nothing but the Best!

Oriental Tuna Salad

2 (9-ounce) cans chunk light tuna in spring
    water
1 cup mayonnaise
1 tablespoon minced onion
1 tablespoon lemon juice
1 teaspoon soy sauce
1 scant teaspoon curry powder
1 cup finely chopped celery
1 large can Chinese noodles
1 (10-ounce) package frozen green peas
lettuce cup

- Combine tuna, mayonnaise, onion, lemon juice, soy sauce, curry powder, and celery.
- Add peas and noodles just before serving.
- Serve in a lettuce cup.

Variation: Crabmeat, shrimp, or a combination may be substituted for the tuna.

Carolyn T. Stewart '57
Associate Professor Emerita, Department of Clothing,
Textiles, and Interior Design
School of Home Economics

Tuna-Cheese Salad

1 (7-ounce) package macaroni shells
1 (9-ounce) can tuna
1 cup cubed cheese
¾ cup chopped sweet pickle
½ cup finely chopped onion
½ cup chopped celery
1 cup mayonnaise
salt and pepper to taste

- Cook macaroni shells according to package directions. Drain in colander and rinse with cold water. Chill.
- Mix together macaroni, tuna, cheese, pickle, onion, and celery. Add mayonnaise. Toss together lightly but thoroughly. Add salt and pepper to taste.
- Refrigerate at least 3 hours before serving.
- **Yield: 8 to 10 servings.**

Frieda Meyer
Professor Emerita of Home Economics
School of Home Economics

Wurstsalat (Sausage Salad)

4 tablespoons oil

5 teaspoons vinegar

1 teaspoon sugar

½ teaspoon salt

⅛ teaspoon black pepper

8 ounces summer sausage, cut into ½-inch
  cubes

2 dill pickles, chopped

2 stalks celery, chopped

1 medium onion, chopped

1 green pepper, chopped

1 (16-ounce) package frozen green peas,
  cooked without butter

lettuce leaves

- Combine oil, vinegar, sugar, salt, and black pepper in a small jar; shake well to blend.
- Combine sausage, pickles, celery, onion, green pepper, and cooked peas; toss lightly. Add dressing; toss lightly.
- Chill at least 20 minutes.
- Serve on lettuce leaves.
- **Yield: 4 to 6 servings.**

Hint: Cook frozen peas by placing the peas in a colander and pouring 2 quarts of salted boiling water over them.

This recipe multiplies well for parties and makes a good buffet dish.

Lee W. Rahe
Assistant Professor, Department of Clothing, Textiles, and
Interior Design
College of Human Environmental Sciences

Italian Sweet-Sour Salad Dressing

½ cup vegetable oil

⅓ cup red wine vinegar

2 tablespoons sugar

½ teaspoon salt

½ teaspoon celery salt

½ teaspoon coarsely ground pepper

½ teaspoon dry mustard

½ teaspoon Worcestershire sauce

¼ teaspoon hot pepper sauce

1 clove garlic, minced

- Combine all ingredients in a jar and shake well.
- Chill.
- Pour over mixed greens and toss.

Paige and Lee Horn '87, '90
Florence, Alabama

$\mathcal{S}$oups

Soups

Nothing but the Best!

Vegetable Basil Soup

1 pound ground beef
½ cup chopped onion
⅛ teaspoon garlic powder
2 beef bouillon cubes
2 (16-ounce) cans chopped tomatoes
3 cups water
1 potato, chopped, unpeeled
1 (16-ounce) package frozen vegetables
1 (4-ounce) can sliced mushrooms
1 teaspoon sugar
1 teaspoon salt
1 tablespoon basil
½ teaspoon pepper

- Sauté ground beef, onion, and garlic powder. Drain well.
- In a large pot, combine bouillon cubes, tomatoes, water, potato, frozen vegetables, mushrooms, beef mixture, and seasonings.
- Bring to a boil, reduce heat, and simmer approximately 30 minutes.

This makes a lightly seasoned soup — adjust seasonings to taste.

Tracy Eason '87
Tuscaloosa, Alabama

French Vegetable Soup

4 large baking potatoes, peeled and chopped
1 large parsnip, peeled and chopped
2 large onions, chopped
1 large carrot, chopped
6 quarts beef stock
1 teaspoon black pepper
1 teaspoon salt
3 tablespoons Dijon mustard
½ cup ketchup
croutons
thinly sliced lemon zest

- Combine vegetables and stock in a large kettle. Bring to a boil, reduce heat, and simmer until tender.
- Remove vegetables from stock and process in batches in a food processor or blender until smooth .
- Return vegetable puree to stock. Add spices, mustard, and ketchup. Heat thoroughly, being careful not to scorch it.
- Garnish with croutons and thin slices of lemon zest.

This soup freezes very well.

Rae K. Eighmey
Wife of John Eighmey,
Professor, Department of Advertising and Public Relations
College of Communication

Roasted Red Pepper Soup

1½ cups chopped yellow onion

3 tablespoons olive oil

1 cup chicken broth

1 cup white wine

1 cup water

salt to taste

pinch cayenne pepper

6 red bell peppers, roasted, peeled, and
    chopped

1 tablespoon lemon juice

½ cup heavy cream

10 fresh basil leaves, julienned

- Sauté onion in olive oil until limp.
- Add chicken broth, wine, water, salt, and cayenne. Bring to a boil; reduce heat and simmer for 20 minutes.
- Add peppers and simmer 10 minutes more. Remove peppers and onion with a slotted spoon. Purée peppers and onion in food processor or blender.
- Return to liquid in saucepan and reheat. Cook approximately 5 minutes longer.
- Stir in lemon juice and adjust seasonings.
- Serve garnished with cream and basil.
- **Yield: 4 servings.**

Tracy Eason '87
Tuscaloosa, Alabama

California Gazpacho

3 pounds tomatoes, peeled and chopped, juice
    reserved

1 clove garlic, chopped

2 cucumbers, peeled and chopped

½ cup minced green bell pepper

½ cup minced onion

⅓ cup olive oil

3 tablespoons vinegar

salt

freshly ground black pepper

¼ teaspoon hot pepper sauce

2 cups tomato juice, frozen in cubes

small croutons

- In a large bowl, combine tomatoes and garlic.
- Add cucumbers, green pepper, onion, and reserved tomato juice. Add olive oil, vinegar, and seasonings.
- Cover and chill thoroughly.
- Serve in chilled bowls with a cube of frozen tomato juice in each bowl. Serve topped with croutons.
- **Yield: 6 servings.**

Joan Jackson
Wife of John E. Jackson, Professor and Head,
Department of Aerospace Engineering
College of Engineering

Chicken Corn Soup

1 (3½-pound) chicken, cut into pieces
3 quarts water
¼ teaspoon saffron
1 tablespoon salt
4 ounces spiral noodles
2 cups fresh corn, cut from cob
freshly ground black pepper
chopped parsley
2 hard-cooked eggs, chopped

- Cover chicken with water. Add saffron and salt and bring to a boil. Lower heat and simmer, covered, until tender, approximately 2 hours.
- Remove chicken from broth. Pull meat from skin and bones. Chop meat and return to broth.
- Bring broth to a boil; add noodles and corn. Cook until noodles are tender.
- Correct seasonings and serve garnished with parsley and egg.

Sherry Smart Harvey
Administrative Specialist
Seebeck Computer Center

Winter Soup

1 whole chicken
lemon juice
salt
pepper
3 (12-ounce) cans beer
1 large onion, chopped
2 teaspoons salt
1 bay leaf
½ teaspoon thyme
1 cup chopped celery
1 clove garlic, pressed
¼ cup chopped parsley
6 carrots, cut in 2-inch pieces and split
16 small whole new potatoes
16 small fresh mushrooms
1 (10-ounce) package frozen peas

- Rub chicken with lemon juice, salt, and pepper and place in a kettle. Add beer, onion, salt, bay leaf, thyme, celery, garlic, and parsley. Bring to a boil, reduce heat, cover and simmer 1½ to 2 hours until chicken is very tender.
- Remove chicken, debone, and pull into small pieces. Return meat to pot and add carrots and potatoes.
- Cover and simmer until vegetables are tender. Add mushrooms and frozen peas, cover and cook about 5 minutes longer.
- Serve with good, dense bread.
- Remove potatoes to store leftover soup, or they will absorb too much of the liquid.

This soup tastes best when the temperature outdoors is below 40°!

Randall Dahl
Director of Admissions and University Registrar
Office of Admissions, Records and Testing

Curried Carrot and Celery Soup

4 large carrots, peeled and cut into
   3-inch pieces
½ teaspoon salt
freshly-ground black pepper
4 stalks celery, chopped
1 large onion, chopped
2 tablespoons butter
3 tablespoons white rice, cooked
1 (13-ounce) can reduced-salt chicken broth
1 teaspoon curry powder
1 pint half and half
orange rind, cut into ¼-inch julienne slices
1 cup water
¼ cup granulated sugar
whipped cream or sour cream, optional

- Steam carrots until semi-soft. Season with salt and pepper.
- In a large saucepan, sauté celery and onion in butter until wilted. Cool slightly.
- Purée carrots, celery, and onion with rice in blender or food processor.
- Return to saucepan and add chicken broth, curry powder, and half and half. Heat thoroughly.
- Poach orange rind in water and sugar for 3 minutes.
- Garnish each serving with a dollop of whipped cream or sour cream, if desired, and orange rind.
- **Yield: 4 to 6 servings.**

Marly Dukes Thomas
Wife of former UA President Dr. Joab Thomas

French Canadian Pea Soup

2 cups dried peas
2 tablespoons butter
1 large onion, thinly sliced
8 cups cold water
1 teaspoon salt
1 small twist lemon peel
2-3 pinches savory
1 ham bone
grated carrots, optional
rice, optional

- Soak dried peas in cold water for 2 hours or more. Drain.
- In a frying pan, melt butter and sauté onion.
- Combine onion, peas, 8 cups cold water, salt, lemon peel, savory, and ham bone. Bring to a boil, reduce heat, cover, and simmer for 2 hours.
- During the last 15 minutes of cooking, add grated carrots or a little rice, if desired.
- **Yield: 10 servings.**

Lise J. Lesher
Wife of C.M. Lesher, Professor, Department of Geology
College of Arts and Sciences

Nothing but the Best!

Potato Soup

6 large potatoes
¼ cup chopped onion
2 chicken bouillon cubes
1 (8-ounce) carton reduced-fat sour cream
8 strips bacon, cooked until crisp and
   crumbled
½ cup reduced-fat butter
½ pound reduced-fat processed cheese spread

- Cover potatoes, onion, and bouillon with water. Bring to a boil, cover, reduce heat, and cook until tender.
- Add remaining ingredients and cook until cheese is melted.

Lisa Brister
Assistant Director, Housing and Residential Life

Cream of Potato Soup

9 potatoes, peeled and cubed
1 (10¾-ounce) can cream of mushroom soup
2 cups milk
¼ cup chopped celery
1 medium onion, chopped
¼ cup margarine
ham or bacon cubes
2 tablespoons flour
⅓ cup grated carrots
salt and pepper
cornstarch, optional
instant mashed potatoes, optional

- Cover potatoes with water, bring to a boil, cover, and reduce heat. Cook until tender. Drain, reserving water.
- Mash potatoes with mixer.
- Mix soup with milk. Add to potatoes.
- Slowly add enough reserved water to reach desired consistency. Heat thoroughly.
- Sauté celery and onion in margarine. Add cubes of ham or bacon. Cook until tender and lightly browned. Add to soup.
- Add flour, carrots, and salt and pepper to taste. Put in crock pot on low until heated.
- Thicken with cornstarch or instant potatoes, if desired. If soup becomes too thick, stir in more reserved water.
- **Yield: 6 to 8 servings.**

Gail Kimball
Word Processor, Engineering Student Services
College of Engineering

Best Ever Potato Soup

8 large white or red potatoes, peeled and diced

2 celery stalks, chopped

1 large onion, chopped

1 teaspoon salt

1 (13-ounce) can evaporated milk

4 heaping teaspoons chicken bouillon
   granules

8 teaspoons bacon drippings

1 teaspoon dried parsley flakes

6 pats butter

grated cheddar cheese

crumbled bacon

pepper to taste

- In a large 6-quart saucepan, cook potatoes, celery, onion, and water until tender.
- Add salt, milk, bouillon, bacon drippings, and parsley flakes; stir well. Return to boil, reduce heat and simmer 30 minutes, stirring frequently.
- Serve in individual bowls garnished with butter, cheese, bacon, and pepper.
- **Yield: 6 to 8 servings.**

Ruby Morrison
Associate Professor, Nursing
Capstone College of Nursing

Crock Pot Potato Soup

6 medium potatoes, peeled and chopped

2 medium onions, chopped

1 large carrot, chopped

1 stalk celery, chopped

4 chicken bouillon cubes

1 tablespoon parsley flakes

5 cups water

1 tablespoon salt

pepper, to taste

⅓ cup butter

1 (13-ounce) can evaporated milk

chopped chives

- Place all ingredients, except milk and chives, in a 4-quart crockpot. Cover and cook on low 10 to 12 hours.
- Stir in evaporated milk during last hour.
- If desired, mash potatoes with a masher before serving.
- Serve topped with chives.
- **Yield: 8 servings.**

Judy Arnold
Assistant Registrar, Record's Office
Office of Admissions, Records, and Testing

Mexican Soup

1 (10-ounce) can tomatoes with green chilies
1 (15-ounce) can chili with beans
1 (10¾-ounce) can tomato soup
1 (10¾-ounce) can vegetable beef soup
1 (12-ounce) can whole kernel yellow corn,
    drained

- Mash tomatoes and mix with remaining ingredients in large stockpot. Heat to a boil.
- Serve with corn or tortilla chips.

Betty Hardy Judice '56 '78
Tuscaloosa, Alabama

Cioppino

1 tablespoon olive or vegetable oil
1 large onion, sliced
2 cloves garlic, pressed
1 (16-ounce) can stewed tomatoes
¾ cup dry red wine
¼ teaspoon dried oregano
¼ teaspoon dried basil
¼ teaspoon salt
⅛ teaspoon cracked pepper
12 clams
1 small red bell pepper, seeded and chopped
1 small green bell pepper, seeded and chopped
½ pound medium shrimp, shelled
1 (1 to 1½-pound) live lobster, cut into
    pieces and cleaned

- In a 6-quart kettle or Dutch oven, heat oil. Sauté onion and garlic until golden.
- Add tomatoes, wine, oregano, basil, salt, and cracked pepper. Simmer uncovered, 20 minutes.
- Scrub clams and soak in cold water.
- Add bell pepper, shrimp, clams, and lobster pieces to stew. Cook gently until shrimp are pink and clams have opened, about 10 to 12 minutes.
- Serve with garlic bread.

Jan Brakefield '75 '77
Coordinator of College Relations
College of Human Environmental Sciences

Bouillabaisse

1 dozen mussels (see note)

1 small red snapper

1 cup water

1 tablespoon olive oil

1 large onion, chopped

2 cloves garlic, pressed

1 green pepper, sliced

1 (16-ounce) can whole tomatoes

¼ teaspoon salt

¼ teaspoon dried thyme leaves

⅛ teaspoon crumbled saffron

1 (2 x ½-inch) strip orange peel

¼ cup sliced fennel, optional

6 sea scallops

6 large shrimp

1 (1-pound) lobster, steamed and cut into
    pieces

3 cups hot cooked rice or 12 slices toasted
    French bread, optional

- Scrub mussels; set aside in a bowl of cool water.
- Rinse snapper and cut into 2-inch chunks. Simmer head and tail in 1 cup water for 20 minutes. Strain and reserve stock.
- Heat oil in an 8-quart heavy kettle or Dutch oven. Sauté onions, garlic, and green pepper until onion is golden. Add tomatoes, reserved fish stock, salt, thyme, saffron, orange peel, and fennel, if desired. Cook gently, uncovered, for 20 minutes.
- Drain mussels; rinse scallops and shrimp. Add mussels, red snapper pieces, scallops and shrimp. Return to boiling; cook gently 5 minutes.
- Stir lobster into bouillabaisse; cook just until fish is cooked through and mussels have opened.
- To serve, place ½ cup rice or 2 pieces French bread in soup plate. Ladle bouillabaisse on top.
- **Yield: 6 servings.**

Any kind of fresh fish or shellfish may be substituted for mussels, snapper, scallops, shrimp, or lobster.

Jan Brakefield '75 '77
Coordinator of College Relations
College of Human Environmental Sciences

Brunswick Stew

chicken and pork, cut into small pieces
2 onions, finely chopped
1 (12-ounce) can tomatoes
1 (14-ounce) can tomato sauce
1 (32-ounce) bottle ketchup
¾ cup vinegar
½ cup barbecue sauce
¼ cup Worcestershire sauce
salt and pepper to taste
6 cans shoepeg corn or 2 bags frozen shoepeg
  corn

- Cook chicken and pork separately. Remove from broth and cut into small pieces. Save broth and chill overnight. Skim fat before using.
- Combine 6 cups reserved broth with all ingredients except corn in a large stockpot. Bring to a boil, cover, and reduce heat. Simmer 3 to 4 hours, stirring often.
- Add corn at the end of cooking so kernels will be crisp.
- **Yield: 25 servings.**

Carole Sloan
Wife of Bernie Sloan, Dean, New College

Easy Camp Stew

1 (3-pound) Boston butt
2 whole chickens
1 pound stew beef
3 (15-ounce) cans tomatoes
2 (15-ounce) cans green peas
1 pound potatoes, chopped
1 pound onions, chopped
1 (20-ounce) bottle ketchup
2 (15-ounce) cans creamed corn
2 (15-ounce) cans whole corn
cayenne pepper
salt

- In advance, cook meat until tender and save the broth. Shred meat.
- In reserved broth, cook all vegetables except corn. Stir occasionally. When vegetables are nearly done, about 15 minutes, add shredded meat and ketchup. Cook an additional 10 minutes.
- Add corn. Cook an additional 5 minutes, stirring continuously. Add cayenne pepper and salt to taste.
- **Yield: 15 servings.**

Billy Helms
Professor and Head, Department of Economics,
Finance, and Legal Studies
College of Commerce and Business Administration

French Stew

5 pounds chuck roast, round or sirloin steak,
    cut into 1½-inch pieces
½ cup butter
1 tablespoon seasoned salt
1 tablespoon salt
¼ teaspoon pepper
2 medium onions, chopped
1 clove garlic, minced
2 carrots, chopped
2 cups dry red wine
1 cup water
1 bay leaf
¼ cup chopped parsley
1 teaspoon dried thyme leaf
4 potatoes, peeled and chopped
1 pound large mushrooms, cut in half
3 tablespoons flour, optional

- Brown beef in butter in large Dutch oven. Add seasoned salt, salt, and pepper.
- Remove meat and brown onion in beef drippings. Return beef and add garlic, carrots, wine, water, bay leaf, parsley, thyme, and potatoes. Bring to a boil, cover, and reduce heat. Simmer for 3 hours. If mixture becomes too thick, add more water or wine.
- Sauté mushrooms and onions over medium heat in butter, then add to stew in the last 15 minutes of cooking.
- If stew is too thin, mix flour well with water, add to sauce, and stir until thickened.

Mona Plyler
Tuscaloosa, Alabama

Chilly Tomato-Corn Chowder

1 (7½-ounce) jar roasted red bell peppers,
    drained and juice reserved

2 coarsely chopped garlic cloves, optional

1 medium cucumber, peeled, seeded, and finely
    diced

½ red bell pepper, seeded and finely diced

2 very ripe tomatoes, seeded and finely diced

1 cup cooked and cooled corn kernels (about
    1 large ear)

2 cups vegetable juice or tomato juice

½ cup fat-free beef or vegetable stock

2 tablespoons red wine vinegar

1 tablespoon chopped fresh basil

salt

diced avocado, optional

sliced scallions, optional

chopped hard-cooked egg, optional

sliced green and/or ripe olives, optional

thinly sliced chile peppers, optional

sour cream, optional

hot sauce, optional

vodka splash, optional

- Purée roasted peppers, with their juice, and garlic in a blender or food processor. Transfer to a large bowl.
- Stir in cucumber, bell pepper, tomatoes, corn, vegetable juice, stock, vinegar, basil, and salt to taste. Cover and chill until very cold, at least 2 hours and up to 24 hours.
- To serve, ladle into bowls and serve with some or all of the following toppings: diced avocado, sliced scallions, chopped hard-cooked egg, sliced green and/or ripe olives, thinly sliced chilies, sour cream, hot sauce, or a splash of vodka.

Hearty enough to make a meal.

Harry Knopke
Vice President for Student Affairs

 Soups

Taos Inn Chile Verde

1 pound beef, diced
1 pound pork or lamb, diced
3 tablespoons peanut oil
1 large onion, finely chopped
4 garlic cloves, finely chopped
¼ cup all-purpose flour
1 (14-ounce) can chicken broth
1 (14-ounce) can beef broth
¼ cup chopped fresh parsley
¼ cup chopped fresh cilantro
3 teaspoons ground cumin seed
1 teaspoon dried oregano
1 cup Mexican beer
6 to 8 large green chilies, roasted, peeled and
  diced
2 large ripe tomatoes, peeled, seeded and diced
salt
freshly ground black pepper
Salsa Cruda (recipe follows)
corn or flour tortilla

- In a large pot, brown meat in peanut oil over medium heat. Remove to a platter.
- Add onion and garlic to pot; cook over medium heat for 10 minutes. Return meat, add flour and cook, stirring 5 minutes or until flour is browned. Add broth, parsley, cilantro, cumin, and oregano. Lightly season with salt and pepper.
- Bring to a boil, reduce heat, and simmer, partially uncovered, for 1 hour.
- Add beer and chilies. Cook an additional 15 minutes. Add tomatoes and continue cooking 15 minutes more.
- Serve hot with Salsa Cruda and hot corn or flour tortillas.
- **Yield: 4 to 6 servings.**

Salsa Cruda

3 or 4 serranos chilies (or jalapeños), seeded
  and deveined
4 whole serranos chili
3 or 4 green onions, including 3 inches of
  green
1 large ripe tomato, peeled and seeded
handful of fresh cilantro
1 teaspoon ground oregano
1 teaspoon ground cumin
1 teaspoon sweet basil
¼ small lime, including peel
salt, to taste

- In a food processor, roughly chop all ingredients. If you want more liquid, add additional tomato or tomato juice.

Jane Green
Instructor, Department of Mathematics
College of Arts and Sciences
Patrick Green
Associate Professor and Chair,
Department of Religious Studies
College of Arts and Sciences

White Chili

1 medium onion, chopped
1 garlic clove, minced
1 teaspoon ground cumin
1 tablespoon salad oil
2 whole large chicken breasts, skinned, boned
    and cut into 1-inch pieces
1 (16-ounce) can white kidney beans,
    drained
1 (15½-ounce) can garbanzo beans, drained
1 (12-ounce) can white corn, drained
2 (4-ounce) cans chopped, mild green chilies
2 chicken bouillon cubes
1½ cups water
hot pepper sauce
parsley sprigs for garnish
1 cup shredded Monterey Jack cheese

- Preheat oven to 350°.
- In small saucepan, sauté onion, garlic, and cumin in oil over medium heat until onion is tender.
- In 2½-quart casserole dish, combine onion mixture with chicken, beans, corn, green chilies, bouillon, and water.
- Cover casserole and bake 50 to 60 minutes until chicken is tender.
- Add hot pepper sauce to taste.
- Garnish with parsley and serve with shredded cheese.
- **Yield: 8 servings.**

Sandra Arnold
Secretary, Department of Journalism
College of Communication

White Lightning Chili

2 tablespoons vegetable oil
1 medium onion, chopped
⅔ cup chopped green bell pepper
½ cup chopped celery
2 pounds lean ground beef
1 (12-ounce) can beer
1 (15-ounce) can tomato sauce
3 tablespoons chili powder
1 tablespoon ground cumin
2 teaspoons oregano leaves
1½ teaspoons salt
¾ teaspoon instant minced garlic
½ teaspoon Italian seasoning
½ teaspoon dry mustard
½ teaspoon ground red pepper
1 bay leaf
tequila

- In a large saucepan, heat oil until hot. Sauté onion, green pepper, and celery for 3 minutes. Push to side of saucepan.
- Add beef and cook until brown, stirring to crumble. Drain.
- Add beer, tomato sauce, chili powder, cumin, oregano, salt, garlic, Italian seasoning, mustard, red pepper, and bay leaf. Bring to a boil. Reduce heat and simmer, covered, stirring frequently, until thickened and flavors have developed, about 2 hours. Add water if necessary.
- Just before serving, stir in tequila and remove bay leaf.
- **Yield: 6 servings.**

Benita Strnad
Curriculum Materials/Education Reference Librarian,
McClure Education Library
University Libraries

Quick and Easy Black Bean Chili

2 (15-ounce) cans black beans, partially
   drained
⅓ cup chopped onion
1 teaspoon garlic, minced
⅓ cup chopped green bell pepper
½ cup diced smoked turkey ham
4 tablespoons honey
1½ teaspoons ground cumin
1 teaspoon red pepper
salt to taste
1 cup canned julienne carrots, drained
salsa
sour cream

- In a large saucepan, combine all ingredients except carrots, salsa, and sour cream. Cook over medium heat for 10 minutes.
- Add carrots. Simmer over low heat for 10 minutes or until chili is thick and vegetables are tender.
- Serve in soup bowls topped with salsa and sour cream.

Great served over chicken quesadillas or chicken enchiladas.

Beth Gibbs '84 '86
Computer Coordinator
College of Human Environmental Sciences

Vegetables & Side Dishes

Vegetables

Nothing but the Best!

Asparagus and Almonds

1 (14½-ounce) can asparagus spears
½ cup slivered almonds
2 tablespoons butter
juice of ½ lemon

- Drain asparagus and warm slowly in skillet.
- Brown almonds in butter.
- Place asparagus in serving dish. Squeeze lemon juice over asparagus and top with almonds.

Skeet Hobbs
Wife of Head Basketball Coach David Hobbs

Asparagus Marinade

4 (14½-ounce) cans asparagus, drained
1 green bell pepper, finely chopped
1 bunch green onions, finely chopped
1 stalk celery, finely chopped
¾ cup light oil
½ cup red wine vinegar
½ cup sugar
½ teaspoon minced garlic
¼ teaspoon paprika

- Layer asparagus in a 9 x 13-inch pan.
- Mix chopped vegetables together and spread over asparagus.
- Combine remaining ingredients and pour over vegetables.
- Chill 4 hours.

Karen Greenlee Conner '72
Birmingham, Alabama

Chilled Asparagus with Pecans

2 (10-ounce) packages frozen asparagus
    spears or 1½ pounds fresh asparagus
¾ cup finely chopped pecans
2 tablespoons vegetable oil
¼ cup cider vinegar
¼ cup soy sauce
¼ cup sugar
pepper to taste

- Cook frozen asparagus according to package directions. If using fresh asparagus, cook in boiling water 6 to 7 minutes, or until tender and still bright green. Drain and rinse under cold water. Drain again.
- Arrange in 1 or 2 layers in oblong serving dish.
- Mix remaining ingredients and pour over asparagus, lifting asparagus so mixture penetrates to the bottom. Sprinkle with pepper.
- Serve chilled.

May be marinated up to 36 hours ahead.

Leigh Ann Danner Summerford '80
Tuscaloosa, Alabama

Vegetables

119

Beets in Orange Sauce

2 tablespoons cornstarch
2 (16-ounce) cans baby beets, drained and
    juice reserved
1 cup orange juice
4 tablespoons lemon juice
2 tablespoons vinegar
2 tablespoons sugar
½ teaspoon salt
4 tablespoons butter
2 tablespoons grated orange peel

- Mix cornstarch with 2 tablespoons reserved beet juice in a saucepan. Add orange juice, lemon juice, and vinegar. Cook until clear.
- Add sugar, salt, and beets. Heat and add remaining ingredients.
- Serve hot.
- **Yield: 6 servings.**

Broxie C. Stuckey '55
Gordo, Alabama

Broccoli Casserole

2 (10-ounce) packages frozen broccoli
2 eggs, beaten
1 cup grated cheddar cheese
½ cup mayonnaise
1 (10¾-ounce) can cream of mushroom soup
crushed round crackers
grated cheddar cheese

- Cook broccoli according to package directions; drain.
- Combine eggs, cheese, mayonnaise, and mushroom soup.
- Add broccoli and pour into casserole dish.
- Top with crackers and additional cheese.
- Bake at 350° for 30 minutes.

Malinn Rivers '86
Northport, Alabama

Low Fat Broccoli Pie

1 (10-ounce) package frozen broccoli,
    thawed and drained
½ cup finely chopped onion
½ cup chopped red or green bell pepper
1 cup finely grated fat-free or reduced fat
    cheese
4 to 5 sprigs fresh rosemary, chopped
1½ cups skim or low-fat milk
¾ cup biscuit mix
6 ounces egg substitute
salt and pepper to taste

- Spray a deep dish pie plate with non-stick cooking spray.
- Combine broccoli, onion, pepper, cheese, and rosemary. Place in prepared dish.
- Mix together milk, biscuit mix, egg substitute, salt and pepper. Pour over broccoli.
- Bake at 400° for 40 minutes.
- **Yield: 6 to 8 servings.**

Elsie Barton
Hoover, Alabama

Nothing but the Best!

Baked Bean Combo

2 (16-ounce) cans Northern beans, drained
1 (15½-ounce) can lima beans, drained
1 (15½-ounce) can kidney beans, drained
2 (15½-ounce) cans pork and beans, drained
8 slices bacon, crisp-cooked and crumbled,
    drippings reserved
4 large onions, chopped
1 cup packed brown sugar
1 teaspoon mustard
½ teaspoon garlic powder
1 teaspoon salt
½ cup apple cider vinegar

- Add onions, sugar, mustard, garlic powder, salt, and vinegar to reserved bacon drippings. Simmer 20 minutes.
- Stir in beans and bacon. Pour into a crockpot.
- Cook for 2 to 3 hours.

Dr. Rodney W. Roth
Professor, Educational Research, Professional Studies and
Former Dean, College of Education

Cauliflower Gratin

3 ounces cheddar cheese, finely grated
1 cup Italian-style bread crumbs
1 teaspoon salt
½ teaspoon black pepper
3 teaspoons paprika
3 teaspoons dried parsley flakes
1½ teaspoons garlic powder
3 pounds frozen cauliflower flowerets,
    partially thawed

- Preheat oven to 350°.
- In mixing bowl, combine cheese, bread crumbs, salt, pepper, paprika, parsley, and garlic powder.
- Spray a cookie sheet with nonstick spray.
- Toss cauliflower in bread crumb mixture until well coated.
- Spread in a single layer on prepared cookie sheet.
- Bake at 350° for about 8 to 10 minutes, until golden brown .
- Serve immediately while hot and crisp.

J.J. Doster Cafe
College of Human Environmental Sciences

Celery Casserole

1 cup croutons
2 tablespoons margarine
2 cups chopped celery
2 cups medium white sauce
½ cup slivered almonds, toasted
1 cup grated cheddar cheese

- Toast croutons in margarine.
- Layer celery in greased casserole dish. Top with white sauce, almonds, cheese, and croutons.
- Bake at 350° for 20 minutes.
- **Yield: 6 servings.**

Ernestine Jackson '64
Assistant Professor Emerita, Department of Human Nutrition
and Hospitality Management
School of Home Economics

Quick Corn Pudding

1 (16-ounce) can whole kernel corn, drained
1 (16-ounce) can cream style corn
2 eggs, beaten
½ cup sour cream
1 small onion, chopped
1 cup corn muffin mix
¼ cup margarine, melted

- Combine corn, eggs, sour cream, onion, and muffin mix. Mix well.
- Pour into a 2-quart casserole which has been sprayed with non-stick cooking spray.
- Pour margarine over corn mixture.
- Bake at 350° for 1 hour. Serve hot.
- **Yield: 6 servings.**

Mary A. Crenshaw
Dean and Professor Emerita of School of Home Economics

Corn Casserole

1 medium onion, chopped
1 green bell pepper, chopped
½ cup margarine
2 cups cooked rice
1 (17-ounce) can cream style corn
1 (12-ounce) can shoepeg corn, drained
1 (14½-ounce) can stewed tomatoes, drained
1 teaspoon Worcestershire sauce
dash hot sauce
salt and pepper to taste
½ cup grated sharp cheddar cheese

- Sauté onion and green pepper in margarine.
- Combine rice, corn, tomatoes, Worcestershire sauce, hot sauce, salt, and pepper. Add to onion mixture.
- Pour into a casserole dish and top with cheese.
- Bake at 350° for 30 to 40 minutes .
- **Yield: 10 servings.**

Judy Bonner '69 '73
Dean, College of Human Environmental Sciences

Nothing but the Best!

Corn and Green Bean Casserole

1 (12-ounce) can white shoepeg corn, drained
1 (16-ounce) can French-style green beans, drained
½ cup chopped celery
¼ cup chopped green bell pepper
½ cup grated sharp cheese
½ cup sour cream
1 (10¾-ounce) can cream of celery soup
salt and pepper
1 package round crackers, crushed
¼ cup margarine, melted

- Mix corn, beans, celery, green pepper, cheese, sour cream, and soup. Add salt and pepper to taste.
- Pour into casserole dish. Top with cracker crumbs and drizzle with margarine.
- Bake at 350° for 45 minutes.

Skeet Hobbs
Wife of Head Basketball Coach David Hobbs

Green Bean Casserole

2 (16-ounce) cans green beans
3 tablespoons bacon drippings
1¼ tablespoons dill seed
3 tablespoons margarine, melted
3 tablespoons flour
1 cup milk
1 tablespoon minced onion
salt and pepper, to taste
dash of hot sauce
buttered bread crumbs or crushed round crackers
sliced almonds, optional

- Combine green beans (with liquid), bacon drippings, and dill seed in a saucepan. Bring to a boil, cover, reduce heat, and simmer 15 minutes.
- Drain, reserving ½ cup liquid.
- In another saucepan blend margarine and flour. Gradually stir in reserved liquid and milk. Cook until thickened, stirring constantly. Add seasonings and hot sauce.
- Combine beans with sauce.
- Place a layer of bean mixture in a casserole dish; top with crumbs, and repeat layers. Finish with almonds, if desired.
- **Yield: 8 servings.**

Beverly C. Smith
Executive Secretary, Dean's Office
New College

Bill's Cucumber Fritters

1 cup pared and diced cucumbers
½ cup diced green onions
½ cup diced white onion
½ cup diced bell pepper
2 tablespoons Creole seasoning
1 teaspoon black pepper
¼ teaspoon garlic powder
½ cup cold water
¾ cup all-purpose flour
½ cup unsalted butter, divided

- Combine cucumbers, onions, bell pepper, and seasonings in a medium bowl.
- Mix water and flour to a paste. Add to cucumber mixture.
- Melt 1 teaspoon butter in a small skillet. Drop 2 tablespoons cucumber mixture per fritter into butter and fry to a golden brown. Remove with slotted spoon and drain on paper towels.
- Add butter as needed.

Bill Persons
Saraland, Alabama

Joe Namath's Favorite Black Eyed Peas

1 bag dried black eyed peas
1 small piece white meat, 1 slice bacon, or
    2 beef bouillon cubes
1 large white onion, chopped
salt to taste

- Soak peas in water overnight .
- Drain and wash thoroughly two or three times.
- Cover peas in water in a large stockpot. Bring to a boil. Add onion, meat, and salt. Return to a boil, reduce heat, and cook over low heat for 1½ to 2 hours. Add water as needed.
- Serve peas with stuffed celery sticks, carrot sticks, radishes, bell peppers, onions, olives, pickles, and cornbread.

We enjoyed having Joe over for lunch when he was a student at The University of Alabama. Black eyed peas and cornbread were his favorite.

Bessie Asbury, '26
Ruth Burchfield, '32
Tuscaloosa, Alabama

Ragú

1 (17-ounce) can English peas, drained
1 bell pepper, chopped
1 (3-ounce) can sliced mushrooms, drained
1 (10¾-ounce) can tomato soup
1 tablespoon Worcestershire sauce
3 hard-boiled eggs, sliced
½ cup grated sharp cheddar cheese

- Combine peas, bell pepper, mushrooms, soup, and Worcestershire sauce in a casserole dish. Top with egg slices.
- Sprinkle with cheese.
- Bake at 350° for 30 to 45 minutes.
- **Yield: 8 servings.**

Jo Bonner '82
Alexandria, Virginia

French-Fried Onion Rings

1 large onion, cut into ¼-inch slices
1⅓ cups self-rising flour
½ teaspoon salt
1 (5⅓-ounce) can evaporated milk
vegetable oil

- Separate onion slices into rings.
- Combine flour and salt; stir well.
- Dip onion rings into milk, then into flour mixture. Repeat. Set aside on paper towels for 10 minutes.
- Fry in deep oil until golden brown. Drain on paper towels.

Kathy H. Rice
Secretary, Culverhouse School of Accountancy
College of Commerce and Business Administration

Bell Pepper Casserole

4 medium bell peppers, seeded and cut into
    strips
crushed cracker crumbs
salt and pepper to taste
grated pasteurized process cheese
liquid butter
milk

- Boil pepper strips until tender. Drain.
- In a greased baking dish, layer cracker crumbs, peppers, salt and pepper to taste, and cheese. Repeat. Pour butter on top. Pour milk around edges.
- Bake at 375° until brown.

Ingredient amounts depend on the size of the baking dish.

Kathryn Rivers
Research Assistant,
Center for Business and Economic Research
College of Commerce and Business Administration

Granddad's Fried Okra and Potatoes

vegetable oil
8 okra pods, sliced
3 medium potatoes, diced
cornmeal
salt and pepper to taste

- Heat oil in frying pan.
- Add okra and potatoes. Sprinkle with cornmeal and stir to coat. Salt and pepper to taste.
- Fry until brown.

Glenda H. Battles
Accounting Clerk
Office of Development Services

Spinach and Artichoke Casserole

2 (14-ounce) cans artichoke hearts, drained and halved
2 (10-ounce) packages frozen chopped spinach
½ cup chopped onion
⅓ cup butter, melted
½ cup sour cream
¼ cup plus 2 tablespooons grated Parmesan cheese, divided
¾ teaspoon salt
¾ teaspoon ground white pepper
dash of cayenne pepper

- Arrange artichoke hearts in a lightly greased 8-inch square baking dish.
- Cook spinach according to package directions; drain well.
- Sauté onion in butter in a large skillet over medium heat, stirring constantly, until tender. Stir in spinach, sour cream, ¼ cup Parmesan cheese, salt, and peppers.
- Spoon spinach mixture over artichokes; sprinkle with remaining Parmesan cheese.
- Bake, uncovered, at 350° for 25 to 30 minutes or until thoroughly heated.
- **Yield: 8 servings.**

Kathy Morrow
Executive Secretary
College of Human Environmental Sciences

Creamed Spinach

1 (10-ounce) package frozen chopped spinach, thawed
¼ cup margarine, melted
1 (3-ounce) package cream cheese, softened
¼ cup Parmesan cheese
½ teaspoon salt

- Press extra moisture out of spinach. Mix with remaining ingredients.
- Place in buttered casserole dish and bake at 350° for 30 minutes.

Kathy H. Rice
Secretary, Culverhouse School of Accountancy
College of Commerce and Business Administration

Nothing but the Best!

Country Club Squash Casserole

3 tablespoons minced yellow onions
1 tablespoon olive oil
1 pound summer squash, thinly sliced
6 tablespoons sour cream
¼ cup Italian-style bread crumbs
2 tablespoons margarine, melted
2 ounces cheddar cheese, grated

- Sauté onions in olive oil in sauté pan until tender.
- Gently combine onions, squash, and sour cream in a bowl. Place in a 1-quart casserole.
- Combine bread crumbs, margarine, and cheese. Sprinkle over squash.
- Bake at 325° until crust browns and squash is tender.

Zucchini squash may be substituted for all or part of the yellow squash

J.J. Doster Cafe
College of Human Environmental Sciences
(Courtesy of Tim Mercer, Fall 1993)

Squash Croquettes

2 pounds yellow squash, sliced
1 medium onion, grated
2 cups fine bread crumbs
1 cup fine cornbread crumbs
2 eggs, beaten
1 ½ teaspoons salt
½ teaspoon white pepper
2 teaspoons sugar
fine bread crumbs, as needed
vegetable oil

- Cook squash in small amount of water until tender. Drain well in a colander, pressing out excess moisture.
- Mash squash. Add onion, 2 cups bread crumbs, cornbread crumbs, eggs, salt, white pepper, and sugar. Chill thoroughly.
- Form in oblong croquettes, adding more bread crumbs if necessary for easy handling.
- Roll in bread crumbs. Fry in deep oil until light golden brown.

A recipe from Britling Cafeterias. Used by permission.

Mary Bolt Lloyd '42
Birmingham, Alabama

Summer Squash Stuffed with Pepperoni and Parmesan

2 yellow summer squash, halved lengthwise
1 tablespoon vegetable oil
2½ tablespoons margarine, divided
1 small onion, chopped
2 tablespoons finely chopped pepperoni
¼ cup grated Parmesan cheese, divided
3½ tablespoons fine bread crumbs, divided
1 tablespoon minced fresh parsley
salt and pepper to taste

- Remove pulp from squash, leaving ¼-inch shells. Chop pulp and reserve.
- Cook shells in hot oil in a covered skillet over medium heat. Turn shells once, cooking about 2 to 3 minutes on each side, or until just tender. Transfer to a rack, cool, and pat dry with a paper towel.
- Add 1½ teaspoons margarine to oil in skillet. Add squash pulp and onion. Cook until onion is tender.
- Stir in pepperoni, 1 tablespoon Parmesan cheese, 1½ tablespoons bread crumbs, parsley, and salt and pepper to taste.
- Fill shells with squash mixture.
- Mix remaining Parmesan cheese and bread crumbs. Sprinkle over squash. Dot with remaining margarine.
- Broil 4 inches from heat for 2 to 3 minutes, or until golden brown.
- **Yield: 4 servings.**

Leatha A. Darden '62 '64
Associate Professor, Department of Clothing,
Textiles, and Interior Design
College of Human Environmental Sciences

Squash Casserole

2 pounds yellow squash, sliced
½ cup chopped onion
1 cup sour cream
1 (10¾-ounce) can cream of mushroom soup
½ cup slivered almonds
1 (8-ounce) package herb-seasoned stuffing
   mix
½ cup margarine, melted

- Cook squash and onion in boiling water until tender. Drain.
- Combine squash mixture, sour cream, soup, and almonds. Mix well.
- Combine stuffing mix, including seasoning packet, and margarine. Spoon half of stuffing into a 2-quart casserole dish, pressing on bottom and along sides.
- Pour squash mixture over stuffing. Sprinkle remaining stuffing on top.
- Bake at 350° for 30 minutes.

Ruth Gibbs
Brilliant, Alabama

Winter Squash Casserole

3 cups chopped winter squash, cooked,
   drained, and mashed
2 eggs, beaten
½ cup brown sugar
½ cup sour cream
1 teaspoon vanilla or rum flavoring
¼ teaspoon cinnamon
⅛ teaspoon nutmeg
⅛ teaspoon salt

- Combine all ingredients. Mix by hand until blended.
- Pour into greased baking dish.
- Bake, uncovered, at 350° for 1 hour.
- **Yield: 6 servings.**
- **Variation**: pumpkin may be substituted for winter squash.

Patricia A. M. Hodges
Director, Coordinated Program in Dietetics
College of Human Environmental Sciences

Summer Basil Tomatoes

4 ripe summer tomatoes, peeled and sliced
   ¼-inch thick
3 tablespoons fresh basil, julienned
Mrs. Dash's seasoning
white wine vinegar
balsamic vinegar

- Arrange tomatoes slices on platter. Sprinkle with basil and Mrs. Dash's seasoning.
- Add equal portions of the vinegars.
- Cover and refrigerate for 30 minutes. Do not prepare sooner because tomatoes will get soggy.
- **Yield: 8 servings.**

Sandra Perkins '84
Academic Advisor, External Degree Program
New College

Mama's Stuffed Tomatoes

6 tomatoes
1 small package yellow rice
½ pound sharp cheddar cheese, grated
2 tablespoons butter
6 slices bacon

- Scoop pulp out of tomatoes, leaving shells intact. Salt inside of shells, invert, and drain on paper towel.
- Cook rice according to package directions. While rice is still hot, add cheese and butter and stir to melt.
- Stuff tomatoes with rice mixture. Top with bacon.
- Bake at 350° for 45 to 60 minutes, until bacon is crisp.

Cecil Williams
Wife of Ernest Williams, UA Trustee Emeritus

Nothing but the Best!

Vegetable-Stuffed Tomatoes

8 fresh ripe tomatoes
salt
1 cup sliced carrots
1 cup peeled and diced cucumber
⅓ cup minced purple onion
¾ cup diced green bell pepper
1 cup diced celery
1 cup finely shredded cabbage
¾ teaspoon salt
¼ cup minced parsley
No Oil Italian Salad Dressing
mayonnaise, optional
parsley sprigs, optional

- Have ready a medium pan of boiling water and a bowl of ice water.
- Drop one tomato at a time in boiling water for 30 seconds. Transfer with slotted spoon to ice water for a moment, then remove and set aside. Repeat with remaining tomatoes.
- Using a sharp knife, skin tomatoes. Cut ½-inch slices from bottom of tomato and reserve slices.
- Using a grapefruit spoon, remove pulp and seeds from tomatoes, leaving shell intact.
- Chop pulp and slices removed from tomatoes and reserve.
- Sprinkle tomato shells lightly with salt and invert on paper towels. Refrigerate until ready to fill.
- Combine carrots, cucumber, onion, bell pepper, celery, cabbage, and ⅔ cup reserved tomato pulp in a plastic bowl. Sprinkle with salt and parsley.
- Top with Italian dressing, cover, and marinate 1 to 2 hours.
- Drain vegetable mixture in a colander. Fill tomato cups and top, if desired, with mayonnaise and a sprig of parsley.

Leatha A. Darden '62 '64
Associate Professor, Department of Clothing,
Textiles, and Interior Design
College of Human Environmental Sciences

Fried Green Tomatoes

2 tablespoons nonfat dry milk
½ cup water
1 egg, beaten
¼ cup all-purpose flour
½ cup yellow cornmeal
½ teaspoon salt
¼ teaspoon black pepper
3 green tomatoes, sliced ¼-inch thick
vegetable oil

- Combine dry milk and water in mixing bowl, whisking until smooth. Add egg and beat until frothy.
- In flat container, combine flour, cornmeal, salt and pepper.
- Dip each tomato slice into milk mixture, coating well. Dredge in flour mixture.
- Add oil to frying pan to ⅛-inch depth; heat to 400°.
- Drop tomato slices individually into oil and brown on both sides. Remove and drain well on paper towels.
- Serve immediately.

J.J. Doster Cafe
College of Human Environmental Sciences
(Courtesy of Gillian Cramer, Spring 1995)

Zucchini and Onion Sauté

1 pound zucchini, grated
½ teaspoon salt
1 cup sliced or chopped onions
2 tablespoons olive oil
dash of pepper
cream, optional

- Place zucchini in colander and sprinkle with salt. Allow to stand until water drains from zucchini, approximately 30 minutes. Squeeze with paper towels to remove excess moisture.
- Sauté onion in oil until tender, but not brown. Add zucchini and sauté over moderate heat until tender, approximately 5 minutes.
- Add pepper and cream, if desired.
- **Yield: 4 servings.**

Ernestine Jackson '64
Assistant Professor Emerita, Human Nutrition and
Hospitality Management
School of Home Economics

Macaroni and Cheese

8 ounces elbow macaroni
2 tablespoons margarine
2 tablespoons flour
½ teaspoon salt
¼ teaspoon pepper
2 cups milk
3 cups shredded sharp cheddar cheese

- Preheat oven to 375°.
- Cook macaroni according to package directions; drain.
- Melt margarine over low heat. Blend in flour, salt, and pepper. Stir in milk and heat to boiling, stirring constantly. Cook until thick. Add cheese and continue cooking until cheese is melted.
- Combine macaroni and sauce, mixing well. Place in baking dish, cover and bake for 30 minutes.

Kathy H. Rice
Secretary, Culverhouse School of Accountancy
College of Commerce and Business Administration

Britling's Macaroni and Cheese

2 cups uncooked macaroni
3 large eggs, beaten
2½ cups milk
¼ cup margarine, melted
1 teaspoon salt
¼ teaspoon white pepper
½ pound grated New York cheese, divided

- Cook macaroni in boiling salted water 10 to 12 minutes. Do not overcook. Drain and rinse.
- Place in a baking dish.
- Combine eggs, milk, margarine, salt, and pepper. Blend well and pour over macaroni.
- Stir in half of grated cheese. Top with remaining cheese.
- Place baking dish in a pan containing an inch of water. Bake at 350° for 45 minutes.
- Let rest a few minutes before serving.

A recipe from Britling Cafeterias. Used with permission.

Mary Bolt Lloyd, '42
Birmingham, Alabama

No Fuss Noodle Bake

1 (8-ounce) package egg noodles, cooked and
   drained
1 (10¾-ounce) can cream of mushroom soup
1 teaspoon salt
1½ cups grated cheddar cheese
1 (10-ounce) package frozen cauliflower,
   partially thawed and cut up
1 (10-ounce) package frozen broccoli,
   partially thawed and cut up
1 cup sour cream
1 medium onion, chopped
¼ teaspoon pepper

- Mix all ingredients in casserole dish.
- Bake, uncovered, at 350° for 30 minutes.

Randall Dahl
Director of Admissions and University Registrar
Admissions, Records, and Testing

Twice Baked Potatoes with Crabmeat

4 large Idaho baking potatoes, baked
½ cup butter
½ cup light cream
1 teaspoon salt
½ teaspoon white pepper
1 tablespoon grated onion
1 (6⅔-ounce) can crabmeat, drained
grated sharp cheddar cheese

- Cut potatoes in half and scoop out pulp, leaving
  shells intact.
- Mash potatoes with butter, cream, salt, pepper,
  and grated onion. Beat until smooth.
- Fold in crabmeat and refill shells. Top with
  grated cheese.
- Bake at 350° for 30 to 45 minutes, or until
  cheese is melted and potato is hot.
- **Yield: 8 servings.**

Jo Bonner '82
Alexandria, Virginia

Roasted Potatoes

1 tablespoon olive oil
1 garlic clove, crushed
¼ teaspoon salt
¼ teaspoon freshly ground pepper
1½ pounds small red new potatoes, scrubbed
    and quartered
1 tablespoon chopped fresh parsley

- Preheat oven to 425°.
- Mix oil, garlic, salt, and pepper in 9-inch square baking dish.
- Add potatoes and turn to coat with oil.
- Bake until tender and browned, approximately 30 to 35 minutes. Sprinkle with parsley.
- **Yield: 6 servings.**

Voni B. Wyatt '81 '89
Personnel Specialist, University Libraries

Microwave Cheesy Potatoes

1 cup chopped onion
1 (10¾-ounce) can cream of mushroom soup
¼ cup margarine
1 (2-pound) bag frozen hash browns
salt
pepper
paprika
1 (8-ounce) carton sour cream
2 cups grated sharp cheddar cheese, divided

- Combine onion, soup, margarine, and potatoes in a large bowl. Add salt, pepper, and paprika to taste.
- Microwave on high for 10 minutes. Stir and add sour cream.
- Microwave on high for 10 minutes more. Stir in three-fourths of grated cheese and microwave until thoroughly heated, about 10 minutes.
- Melt remaining cheese on top.
- **Yield: 8 to 10 servings.**

Gail Kimball
Secretary, Engineering Student Services
College of Engineering

Parsley New Potatoes

1 pound small new potatoes
¼ cup water
1 tablespoon minced fresh parsley
2 tablespoons butter
salt and pepper

- Cut a ½-inch strip of peel from around the middle of each potato.
- Place potatoes in 2-quart casserole dish. Add water and cover with lid.
- Cook in microwave on high, 10 to 12 minutes, or until tender, stirring once during cooking.
- Drain potatoes. Stir in parsley, butter, and salt and pepper to taste.
- **Yield: 4 servings.**

Veronica Purcell
Secretary, External Degree Program
New College

Hash Brown Casserole

1 (2-pound) bag frozen hash brown
    potatoes, thawed
½ cup chopped onion
1 cup shredded cheddar cheese
1 cup sour cream
¼ cup margarine
1 teaspoon salt
1 pinch of pepper
1 (10¾-ounce) can cream of chicken soup
1 cup plain or Italian-style bread crumbs
¼ cup margarine, melted

- Mix potatoes, onion, cheese, sour cream, margarine, salt, pepper, and soup thoroughly in large mixing bowl.
- Pour into greased 11 x 8-inch glass casserole dish.
- Top with bread crumbs and drizzle with margarine.
- Bake at 350° for one hour.
- **Yield: 12 servings.**

Sallie A. Watkins '73 '81
Director of Social Work, Bryce Hospital
and Adjunct Professor of Social Work
School of Social Work

German Potato Bake

4 cups cubed potatoes, cooked
½ pound pasteurized process cheese, cubed,
    divided
2 tablespoons margarine
5 slices bacon, crisp-cooked and crumbled,
    divided
¼ cup sliced green onions, divided
¾ cup salad dressing
¼ cup sour cream
1 (2-ounce) jar chopped pimento, drained
¼ teaspoon pepper
¼ teaspoon paprika

- In a large saucepan, combine potatoes, half of cheese cubes, and margarine. Stir over low heat until cheese is melted.
- Add 2 tablespoons bacon pieces, 2 tablespoons onions, salad dressing, sour cream, pepper, and pimento. Mix well.
- Spoon into a 1½-quart casserole dish. Top with remaining cheese, bacon, and onions. Sprinkle with paprika.
- Bake at 350° for 20 to 25 minutes or until thoroughly heated.
- **Yield: 6 servings.**

Jeanie and David Sexton '68, '92
Brilliant, Alabama

Nothing but the Best!

Pickled New Potatoes

25 very small new potatoes
3 cups vegetable oil
1 cup tarragon vinegar
1 large onion, coarsely grated
¼ cup chopped parsley
3 garlic cloves, minced or mashed
1 tablespoon salt
whole black peppercorns to taste
4 dashes cayenne pepper

- Boil new potatoes in jackets until just tender. Do not overcook. Drain.
- Combine remaining ingredients in a saucepan. Bring to a full rolling boil.
- Pour over warm potatoes and marinate 3 to 4 hours.
- **Yield: 8 servings.**

Reheat and serve as a vegetable or serve at room temperature as a salad. May also be drained and served as appetizers. Can make up to two days before serving.

Barbara J. Hill
Secretary, Department of Mineral Engineering
College of Engineering

Cheese Potato Puff

1 egg, slightly beaten
1 (5⅓-ounce) can evaporated milk
1¼ cups milk
2 teaspoons salt
¼ teaspoon pepper
1¼ cups grated cheddar cheese, divided
4 potatoes, grated
3 tablespoons butter

- Combine egg, milk, salt, pepper, and 1 cup cheese. Add potatoes. Place in buttered casserole dish.
- Top with butter and sprinkle with remaining cheese.
- Bake at 350° for 1½ hours.

Betty Jo Novak Walker '58
River Forest, Illinois

Golden Parmesan Potatoes

¼ cup flour
¼ cup Parmesan cheese
1 teaspoon salt
⅛ teaspoon pepper
6 large potatoes, cut into large pieces
water
⅓ cup butter
chopped parsley

- Combine flour, cheese, salt, and pepper.
- Moisten potatoes with water and shake a few at a time in the flour mixture.
- Melt butter in baking pan. Roll potatoes in the melted butter as you place in pan. Sprinkle with parsley.
- Bake at 350° until golden and tender.

Cheryl Parker
Secretary, Department of Advertising and Public Relations
College of Communication

Hawaiian Yams

2 cups cooked, mashed, and whipped yams

2 cups sugar, divided

1 cup milk

1 egg, beaten

1 teaspoon salt

1 cup flaked coconut

1 teaspoon vanilla

1 (20-ounce) can crushed pineapple, with juice

1 (4-ounce) jar maraschino cherries, with juice

3 tablespoons cornstarch

- Mix yams, 1 cup sugar, milk, egg, salt, coconut, and vanilla.
- Pour into baking dish and bake at 350° for 25 minutes.
- Combine pineapple, cherries, remaining sugar, and cornstarch in a saucepan. Cook over medium heat, stirring, until thick.
- Pour over yam mixture and serve.

Joann Smith Wissinger '77 '84
Leeds, Alabama

Anne's Sweet Potato Casserole

½ cup margarine, softened

3 cups cooked, mashed sweet potatoes

1 cup sugar

2 eggs, beaten

⅓ cup milk

1 teaspoon vanilla

1 teaspoon cinnamon

Topping:

1 cup brown sugar

½ cup all-purpose flour

⅓ cup margarine, melted

1 cup chopped pecans

miniature marshmallows

- Cream together margarine and potatoes.
- Add eggs, milk, vanilla, and cinnamon. Mix well.
- Pour into a 2-quart casserole dish.
- Combine all topping ingredients except marshmallows. Sprinkle over sweet potato mixture.
- Bake at 325° for 30 minutes.
- Remove from oven and cover entire surface of casserole with marshmallows. Return to oven and bake an addtional 5 minutes, or until marshmallows are melted and slightly brown.
- **Yield: 6 to 8 servings.**

Brian Gray
Associate Professor, Department of Management, Science, and Statistics
College of Commerce and Business Administration

Nothing but the Best!

Wild Rice with Mushrooms, Almonds, and Raisins

1 box Uncle Ben's Long Grain Wild Rice
¼ cup sliced mushrooms
½ cup slivered, blanched almonds
½ cup raisins

- Combine all ingredients and cook according to box directions.

Stella Gray Bryant, '90
Tuscaloosa, Alabama

Wild Rice with Mushrooms and Almonds

1 cup uncooked wild rice
¼ cup butter
½ cup slivered almonds
2 tablespoons snipped chives or chopped
    green onions
1 (8-ounce) can mushroom stems and pieces,
    drained
3 cups chicken broth

- Preheat oven to 325°.
- Wash and drain wild rice.
- Melt butter in large skillet. Add rice, almonds, onion, and mushrooms. Cook and stir until almonds are golden brown, about 20 minutes.
- Pour rice mixture into ungreased 1½-quart casserole dish.
- Heat broth to boiling and add to rice mixture.
- Cover and bake 1½ hours, or until all liquid is absorbed and rice is tender and fluffy.
- **Variation**: Add 2 cups cooked turkey or chicken to use as a main dish.

Helga B. Visscher
Reference Librarian, McClure Education Library
University Libraries

Browned Rice

1 cup rice
½ cup margarine
1 medium onion, chopped
2 (10¾-ounce) cans beef consommé
1 (4-ounce) can mushrooms

- In a frying pan, brown rice, margarine, and onion.
- Add consommé and mushrooms.
- Pour into a casserole dish, cover, and bake at 350° for one hour, or until all liquid is absorbed and rice is cooked.

Sara Bryant
Wife of Jennings Bryant, Reagan Chair of Broadcasting
College of Communication

Lemon Apples

½ cup sugar
1 tablespoon cornstarch
1 cup boiling water
2 tablespoons butter
1 ½ tablespoons lemon juice
¼ teaspoon nutmeg
4 large apples, diced
½ cup raisins
½ cup pecans, optional

- Mix sugar and cornstarch in a saucepan. Stir in boiling water gradually. Boil 5 minutes.
- Remove from heat. Add butter, lemon juice, and nutmeg.
- Toss together apples, raisins, and pecans, if using. Cover with syrup and chill.

Karen Redman
Head Teacher, Child Development Center
College of Human Environmental Sciences

Apple Cranberry Casserole

3 cups unpeeled cooking apples, chopped
2 cups raw cranberries
1 cup sugar
¼ cup margarine
1 cup oats, uncooked
1 cup chopped pecans
½ cup brown sugar

- Alternate layers of apples and cranberries in 13 x 9-inch casserole dish.
- Sprinkle with sugar.
- Melt margarine. Stir in oats, nuts, and brown sugar. Spread over apples.
- Bake, uncovered, at 350° for 45 minutes to 1 hour.

This dish is great in the fall and during the holidays.

Annette Sanderson
Wife of Former Head Basketball Coach Wimp Sanderson

Nothing but the Best!

Pineapple Casserole

2 (20-ounce) cans pineapple tidbits, drained
   and juice reserved
2 tablespoons flour
1 cup sugar
2 cups shredded cheddar cheese
1 cup crushed round crackers
¼ cup margarine, melted

- Combine pineapple, flour, sugar, and cheese. Pour into baking dish.
- Pour ⅓ cup reserved pineapple juice over dish.
- Mix cracker crumbs and margarine. Sprinkle over pineapple mixture.
- Bake, uncovered, at 350° for 25 minutes.

Kathy H. Rice
Secretary, Culverhouse School of Accountancy
College of Commerce and Business Administration

Baked Pineapple

1 (20-ounce) can pineapple chunks, drained
   and juice reserved
1 (8-ounce) package cream cheese, cubed
1 cup miniature marshmallows
¼ cup grated sharp cheddar cheese
2 tablespoons flour
½ cup sugar
1 egg, beaten

- Layer pineapple chunks, cream cheese cubes, marshmallows, and cheese in a 2½-quart casserole dish.
- In a saucepan, combine reserved pineapple juice, flour, sugar, and egg. Cook over low heat, stirring constantly, until thickened.
- Pour over casserole and bake at 400° for 10 to 15 minutes.
- **Yield: 6 servings.**

Judy Bonner '69 '73
Dean, College of Human Environmental Sciences

Pineapple Soufflé

1 (20-ounce) can crushed pineapple, drained
3 eggs, beaten
bread crumbs from 8 slices bread, crusts removed
½ cup milk
½ cup margarine, softened
½ cup sugar
brown sugar

- Mix all ingredients except brown sugar.
- Pour into buttered casserole dish.
- Sprinkle with brown sugar.
- Bake at 350° for 35 minutes.
- **Yield: 6 to 8 servings.**

Kay Culton
Director, Freshman Writing Lab Center for Athletic Student
Services

Entrées

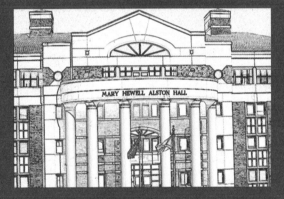

MARY HEWELL ALSTON HALL

Entrées

Nothing but the Best!

Beef Tenderloin

1 (5-7 pound) beef tenderloin
extra virgin olive oil
1 (3-ounce) jar crushed garlic
freshly cracked pepper
salt

- Preheat oven to 500° for 20 minutes.
- Rub tenderloin with olive oil and garlic and sprinkle heavily with pepper. Place in an open pan.
- Reduce oven temperature to 450° and cook for 20 minutes. Turn roast over and cook an additional 20 minutes.
- Turn oven down to 225° and cook for 2 more hours.
- Salt lightly and serve.

Serving beef tenderloin at the cocktail buffet in Doster prior to the bonfire at homecoming is a tradition for alumni and friends of the College of Human Environmental Sciences.

Jo Bonner '82
Alexandria, Virginia

Coach Paul "Bear" Bryant's Favorite Steaks

steaks
salt and pepper to taste
Worcestershire sauce

- Start fire early - let burn down low.
- Before placing steaks on grill cover with salt, pepper, and Worcestershire sauce.
- Turn only once while cooking.

As a student in Letitia Robert's home economics class, I undertook the project of creating a cookbook. I wrote Coach Bryant and asked if he would contribute a recipe for my celebrity section. He graciously responded. Naturally, I cherish the letter from him.

Sharan Huffman Grey
Centreville, Alabama

Eye of Round Roast or Sirloin Tip Roast

eye of round or sirloin tip roast
salt and pepper to taste
bacon, cut into 3-inch strips
large can mushrooms
Worcestershire sauce, optional
parsley flakes

- Preheat oven to 500°. Yes, 500°. Don't be afraid.
- Salt and pepper roast as desired, place in a shallow roasting pan and shove it in.
- Leave the temperature that high for 30 to 45 minutes, until roast is well browned. This procedure seals in the juices of the meat, and when you carve it that wonderful "au jus" will drain out.
- Next, turn the oven down to 250° for about an hour, depending on how rare you want it. The timing above will leave an eye of round roast just pink in the center. An important variable is the diameter of the roast. A sirloin tip roast is thicker, and to get it to the same degree of doneness will take a little longer. A little practice gives you the hang of it.
- About 30 minutes before removing from oven, place bacon all over the top of the roast. This will cook slowly and drip nice juice all over it, and be crisp when the roast is done. Serve the bacon with the roast.
- When ready to serve, place roast on serving platter, and put the roasting pan on stove over medium heat. Add mushrooms, and stir all that good brown stuff in the pan, which will dissolve. Taste it.
- You might want to add just a few drops of Worcestershire, and of course, the ubiquitous parsley flakes.
- Don't add any flour or thickening. There will be lots of this stuff — you may need to add a little water. You'll need a bowl for the gravy and mushrooms.

These are both tender cuts of meat, so don't ruin them by overcooking or doing too much to them. Uncle Ben's Long Grain and Wild Rice mix (just follow the directions on the package), is good with this.

Belle Strong

Nothing but the Best!

Marinade for Steaks

1½ cups salad oil
¾ cup soy sauce
½ cup vinegar
½ cup lemon juice
¼ cup Worcestershire sauce
1 clove garlic, minced
2 tablespoons dry mustard
1 tablespoon pepper
2½ teaspoons salt
1½ teaspoons parsley

- Mix all ingredients and shake well.
- Use as a marinade on any cut of beef. Can be used when cooking in the oven, but is great on the grill.

Stores well in the refrigerator.

Susan and Marshall S. Ginsberg '59
Reston, Virginia

Individual Beef Wellington

8 (5-ounce) beef tenderloin steaks, cut 1-inch thick
1 tablespoon oil
1 (17¼-ounce) package frozen pastry sheets
½ pound creamy liverwurst
¼ cup chopped green onions
2 tablespoons chopped parsley
1 egg, beaten with 1 tablespoon water

- Lightly brown steaks in hot oil over medium high heat. Drain on paper towels; chill.
- Thaw pastry 20 minutes.
- Preheat oven to 400°.
- Stir together liverwurst, green onions, and parsley. Spread evenly on top and sides of each steak.
- On a lightly floured surface, roll each pastry sheet into a 14-inch square. Cut into quarters.
- Brush pastry edges with egg wash and wrap around steaks. Pinch edges to seal. Place on ungreased baking sheet, seam side down.
- Bake 25 minutes.

Olivia Kendrick
Associate Professor, Department of Human Nutrition
and Hospitality Management
College of Human Environmental Sciences

Mother's Eye Round Roast

⅓ cup red wine
⅓ cup soy sauce
¼ cup chopped onion
1 to 2 garlic cloves, minced
1 teaspoon dry mustard
1 teaspoon ginger
1 (3 to 4-pound) eye round roast
garlic slivers, optional

- Combine all ingredients except roast and garlic slivers. Pour into a plastic bag and add roast.
- Marinate in refrigerator for several hours or overnight, turning as needed to evenly marinate. Do not put in a metal container.
- Preheat oven to 400°.
- Remove meat from marinade and wipe dry before placing on a rack in a roasting pan. If desired, cut small slits in meat and insert garlic slivers.
- Roast fat side up for 30 minutes. Reduce heat to 275 to 300° until it is cooked the way you want. Medium rare takes about 40 to 50 minutes. Do not open the oven door.
- Let roast rest for 15 minutes before slicing.
- There will be plenty of juice when it is cut.

Great at room temperature, thinly sliced and served with horseradish sauce.

- **Variation**: Baked Steak. Use steak of your choice and marinate for 1 hour, turning once. Place on a flat rack in a shallow pan. Bake at 400° for 25-35 minutes depending on steak thickness and degree of doneness desired.

Beverly A. Kissinger
Assistant Professor, Department of Clothing,
Textiles, and Interior Design
College of Human Environmental Sciences

Nothing but the Best!

Chinese Green Pepper Beef

½ pound flank steak

2 teaspoons baking soda

6-8 dried Black Forest mushrooms

1 cup boiling water

1 tablespoon vegetable oil

½ teaspoon minced garlic

1 teaspoon minced fresh ginger root

½ cup chopped white or yellow onion

1 large green bell pepper, seeded and cut into
    1-inch squares

1 tablespoon soy sauce

½ cup chicken broth

¼ cup oyster-flavored sauce

1 tablespoon cooking sherry or white wine

1 tablespoon cornstarch

¼ cup cold water

1 tablespoon minced green onion

- Freeze steak for 30 minutes to make slicing easier. Remove and slice into very thin strips. Coat with baking soda and set aside.
- Place mushrooms into small bowl and cover with boiling water. Allow to soften for about 20 minutes. Drain, remove stems, and cut in half.
- Heat wok or high sided frying pan on high. When the pan is hot, pour in the oil and allow the oil to bubble.
- Toss in the garlic, ginger root, onion, and green pepper. Stir for about 2 minutes.
- Push these ingredients to the edge of the pan and in the cleared center, toss in the steak. While stirring the steak, add soy sauce, chicken broth, oyster-flavored sauce, and wine.
- Dissolve cornstarch in cold water. When the steak has turned light brown, add to pan to thicken the sauce. Add more if needed to make sauce thick enough for serving.
- Turn off heat, add green onions, and stir vigorously. Serve immediately.

This dish will serve four people if accompanied with other Chinese dishes for a complete meal.

Ronald R. Robel
Director, Critical Languages Center
Director, Asian Studies Program
College of Arts and Sciences

Bogogi

¾ cup soy sauce
⅔ cup sugar
¼ cup sesame oil
½ teaspoon seasoned salt
¼ teaspoon black pepper
⅛ cup sesame seeds
1 head garlic
3 to 4 pounds beef
2 medium onions, chopped
3 carrots, chopped
2 large green onions, chopped

- Combine soy sauce, sugar, sesame oil, salt, pepper, and sesame seeds. Press garlic and add to soy mixture.
- Thinly slice meat and place in marinade dish. Top with soy mixture. Add onions, carrots, and green onions.
- Cover container, refrigerate, and allow to marinate 2 to 3 hours or overnight.
- Brown in frying pan or wok 10 to 15 minutes, until meat is cooked. Serve over rice.

Chicken or pork may be substituted for beef. This is a Korean dish for garlic lovers.

Patricia A. M. Hodges
Director, Coordinated Program in Dietetics
College of Human Environmental Sciences

Chili

1 pound ground beef
½ cup chopped onions
2 tablespoons shortening
¼ teaspoon garlic powder
2 tablespoons chili powder
1 tablespoon paprika
1 (28-ounce) can tomatoes
1 teaspoon salt
2 (16-ounce) cans kidney beans
cooked rice
grated cheddar cheese, optional

- Brown beef and onions in shortening.
- Add garlic powder, chili powder, paprika, tomatoes, and salt.
- Cover and cook on high until steaming, then reduce heat to simmer. Cook for one hour.
- Add kidney beans and cook for 30 minutes.
- Serve over rice, garnished with cheese, if desired.
- **Yield: 8 servings.**

Linda Campbell Price '63, '65
Systems Coordinator, Office of Financial Affairs

Christmas Chili

1½ pounds ground round steak
2 medium white onions, diced
2 large bell peppers, diced
3 tablespoons chili powder, divided
2 tablespoons garlic powder, divided
1 teaspoon basil
3 (16-ounce) cans stewed tomatoes
3 (16-ounce) cans chili beans
1 (8-ounce) can beer
1 tablespoon black pepper
grated cheddar cheese
chopped onion

- Place beef in an extra large iron skillet. Add onions and bell peppers. Sprinkle with 1½ tablespoons chili powder, 1 tablespoon garlic powder, and basil. Using a wooden spoon, blend together and brown very slowly.
- When the meat is browned, carefully prop the skillet handle on the edge of a Dutch oven and use spoon to move the meat mixture to high side of pan. Allow this to drain for several minutes.
- Carefully spoon out the liquid into a clear glass measuring cup. Put cup in freezer until fat hardens. Carefully remove hardened fat and discard. Reserve liquid.
- Place tomatoes in a food processor and process just long enough to cut up large pieces. Put tomatoes, beans, and beer in a large Dutch oven and bring to a low simmer. Add remaining chili and garlic powder. Add pepper.
- Add reserved liquid and drained meat to Dutch oven. Cook slowly for at least 2 hours.
- Serve with cheese and onion.

First served one Christmas season years ago, the red beans and green peppers caught the eye of guests who immediately named it Christmas Chili.

Carl E. Ferguson, Jr.
Professor of Marketing, Department of Management and Marketing
College of Commerce and Business Administration

Chili Con Carne

2 tablespoons butter
½ cup chopped onion
1 pound ground beef
1¼ cups canned tomatoes
2 cups canned kidney beans
¾ teaspoon salt
½ bay leaf
1 teaspoon sugar, optional
1 tablespoon chili powder
tortillas, crackers, or cornbread

- Melt butter in large skillet and sauté onions.
- Add ground beef. Stir and sauté beef until well done. Drain and discard fat.
- Add remaining ingredients. Cover and cook slowly for about one hour.
- Serve with tortillas or crackers or cornbread.
- **Yield:** 8 servings.

Veronica Purcell
Secretary, External Degree Program
New College

Jennifer's Chili

1½ pounds ground beef
1 (10¾-ounce) can tomato soup
1 (8-ounce) can tomato sauce
1 (15-ounce) can chili beans with jalapeño peppers
1 (1¼-ounce) package chili seasoning mix
chili powder to taste
grated cheese
crackers or tortilla chips

- Brown and drain ground beef; add remaining ingredients except cheese and crackers. Simmer on low for 10-15 minutes.
- Garnish with cheese. Serve with crackers or tortilla chips.
- **Yield:** 5 to 6 servings.

Paige Pierce Cooper '88, '90
Scholarship Coordinator, Student Financial Services

Nothing but the Best!

Judy's Beef Stew

2 pounds boneless stew meat, cut into bite-
    size pieces
flour
¼ cup cooking oil
6 carrots, thickly sliced
5 potatoes, cut into large cubes
1 onion, quartered
2 (10¾-ounce) cans beefy mushroom soup,
    golden mushroom soup, or a combination
4 soup cans of water
2 teaspoons salt
½ teaspoon black pepper
2 to 3 dashes of hot sauce, to taste
1 large bay leaf
1 teaspoon Worcestershire sauce

- Dredge beef with flour and brown well on all sides in hot oil.
- Remove from skillet and drain well on a paper towel.
- In crock pot, layer carrots, potatoes, onions, and stew meat.
- Combine soups, water, and remaining ingredients. Pour over vegetables and meat.
- Cook on high for 2 or 3 hours, then reduce heat to low and cook for another 3 hours.
- **Yield: 8 servings.**

Judith Reeves
Executive Secretary, The Interim Program

Oklahoma Beef Stew

3 tablespoons flour
1 teaspoon salt
½ teaspoon celery salt
¼ teaspoon garlic salt
¼ teaspoon black pepper
½ teaspoon ground ginger
3 pounds lean chuck or round steak, cut into
    2-inch cubes
2 tablespoons shortening or bacon drippings
3 medium onions, sliced
⅓ cup red wine vinegar
½ cup molasses
6 carrots, sliced 1-inch thick
½ cup water
1 (14½-ounce) can tomatoes
½ cup raisins
cooked rice

- Combine flour, salt, celery salt, garlic salt, pepper, and ginger.
- Coat beef with flour mixture and brown in shortening.
- Add onion, red wine vinegar, molasses, carrots, and water. Simmer for 2 hours, uncovered.
- Add tomatoes and raisins. Simmer for 30 minutes more, uncovered.
- Serve over rice.

Roland P. Ficken
Dean Emeritus, College of Community Health Sciences

 Beef

Hobos

4 large potatoes, peeled and chopped
1 small bag carrots, pared and chopped
1 pound ground beef
1 onion, sliced
1 green bell pepper, sliced
salt and pepper to taste
steak sauce

- Boil potatoes and carrots for 15 minutes. Drain.
- Shape beef into patties and place on large square of foil. Add potatoes and carrots. Top with onion and bell pepper. Season with salt, pepper, and steak sauce.
- Seal each foil square and place under broiler for 45-55 minutes. When done, pierce foil with a fork to drain liquids.
- Remove from foil and serve with salad and French bread.

Teresa Burns
Staff Assistant, Housing and Residential Life

Coach Stallings' Favorite Pinto Beans with Ground Beef

2 pounds pinto beans
1 large onion, chopped
1 (14½-ounce) can stewed tomatoes or
    4 fresh tomatoes
1 (16-ounce) can tomato sauce
1 jalapeño pepper, chopped
1 tablespoon chili powder
salt and pepper to taste
1 pound lean ground beef

- Cover beans with water and soak overnight.
- Drain and place in large pot. Cover with water and bring to a boil. Drain again. Add enough water to cover by a few inches.
- Add onion, tomatoes, tomato sauce, jalapeño, chili powder, salt, and pepper.
- Bring to a boil and cover.
- Cook over low heat for approximately two hours. Check often and add water as necessary to keep beans covered.
- Brown ground beef in a separate skillet and drain well.
- Continue cooking until beans are done. Add beef and serve.

Gene Stallings
Head Football Coach

Nothing but the Best!

Cheeseburger Casserole

1 pound ground beef
¼ cup chopped onions
¼ cup chopped green bell pepper
¼ cup ketchup
1 (8-ounce) can tomato sauce
½ pound sliced American cheese
1 large can refrigerated biscuits

- Brown ground beef with onions and peppers. Drain excess fat. Add ketchup and tomato sauce.
- Layer meat mixture with cheese slices in ungreased 1½-quart casserole dish.
- Top with biscuits.
- Bake for 20 to 25 minutes in a preheated 375° oven.
- **Yield: 6 servings.**

Deborah Hamilton '75 '77
Assistant Director, Center for Business and
Economic Research

Shepherd's Pie

3 medium potatoes
1 medium onion, chopped
1 medium green bell pepper, chopped
4 tablespoons butter, divided
2 pounds ground beef
salt and pepper to taste
⅓ cup milk
⅔ teaspoon salt
paprika

- Cover potatoes with water and boil 30 minutes or until easily pierced with a fork.
- Sauté onion and green peppers in 2 tablespoons butter until soft but not brown.
- Add meat and cook until the meat loses its red color; add salt and pepper to taste. Stir often.
- Drain well and place in a 1½-quart baking dish.
- Mash potatoes. Heat milk until hot, but not boiling. Add to potatoes with remaining butter and ⅔ teaspoon salt. Beat until light and fluffy.
- Spread over the meat and sprinkle lightly with paprika.
- Bake at 350° until potato peaks have browned.

A favorite from Tutwiler Dining Hall in the 1940s.

Mary Bolt Lloyd '42
Birmingham, Alabama

Stuffed Italian Shells

1 pound ground beef
1 box jumbo macaroni shells
15 ounces ricotta or cottage cheese
3 eggs
1 pound mozzarella cheese, grated
½ cup bread crumbs
1 (48-ounce) jar spaghetti sauce

- Brown ground beef, drain, and set aside to cool.
- Cook shells according to package directions and drain.
- Mix ricotta cheese and one egg in a bowl.
- In another bowl, mix remaining eggs, mozzarella cheese, and bread crumbs. Add cooled ground beef. Stir in ricotta mixture.
- Spread a small amount of sauce in bottom of baking pan. Fill each shell with meat mixture. Place in pan and top with remaining sauce.
- Bake, covered, at 350° for 30 minutes.
- Uncover and bake an additional 10 minutes.
- **Yield: 8-10 servings.**

Delicious served with a garden salad and bread.

Shirley D. Johnson
Executive Secretary, Capstone College of Nursing

Taco Casserole

1 pound ground beef
1 (1¼-ounce) package taco seasoning mix
1 (10-ounce) can tomatoes
1 package yellow seasoned rice
shredded cheddar cheese
plain taco chips
shredded lettuce
chopped tomatoes
taco sauce, optional

- Brown ground beef; drain. Add taco seasoning mix. Add tomatoes and simmer.
- In another saucepan, cook rice as directed on package.
- Place rice in large casserole dish. Top with meat mixture. Sprinkle with cheese. Bake at 350° until hot and cheese is melted.
- Top with taco chips and return to oven again for a few minutes.
- Remove from oven and top with lettuce and tomatoes. Pour taco sauce over each serving, if desired.

Judy M. Andrzejewski '89
Birmingham, Alabama

Nothing but the Best!

Quick Taco Skillet Casserole

1 pound ground beef
1 (17-ounce) can whole kernel corn, drained
1 (8-ounce) can tomato sauce
1 cup water
1 (1¼-ounce) package taco seasoning mix
1 cup Monterey Jack cheese, cubed
corn chips
taco sauce, optional

- Brown ground beef in a deep skillet; drain off pan drippings.
- Stir in corn, tomato sauce, water, seasoning mix, and cheese; simmer 20 to 25 minutes.
- Serve over corn chips. Top with taco sauce, if desired.

Sandra Arnold
Secretary, Department of Journalism
College of Communication

Round Steak and Potato Casserole

1½ pounds round steak
5 medium potatoes, thinly sliced
6 slices American cheese
2 (10¾-ounce) cans cream of mushroom soup
salt and pepper
⅓ cup water

- Brown beef and cut into bite-size pieces.
- Layer one-third of steak and potatoes, two slices cheese, and one-third of cream of mushroom soup in 2-quart casserole dish. Repeat to make three layers. Salt and pepper each layer. Pour water over top.
- Bake at 375° for 1 hour or until done.

Voni B. Wyatt '81 '89
Personnel Specialist
University Libraries

Beef and Tater Tot Casserole

1 pound ground beef
1 (10¾-ounce) can cream of mushroom soup
1 (32-ounce) bag tater tots

- Place meat in an 8½ x 10-inch casserole dish.
- Top with soup and tater tots.
- Bake at 350° for 30 minutes or until meat is browned.

Teresa Gilstrap Pruett
Office Assistant, Division of Environmental and Industrial Programs
College of Continuing Studies

Twenty-Minute Meat Loaf

Meat Loaf:

1½ pounds ground beef

½ teaspoon salt

¼ teaspoon pepper

2 tablespoons instant onion

1 egg

1 cup soft bread crumbs

1 (8-ounce) can tomato sauce

Sauce:

1 (8-ounce) can tomato sauce

2 tablespoons brown sugar

2 tablespoons parsley flakes

1 teaspoon Worcestershire sauce

- Combine meat loaf ingredients and shape into eight oval loaves.
- Place in shallow baking pan and bake at 450° for 15 minutes. Pour off excess grease.
- Combine sauce ingredients and pour over meat loaves. Bake for 5 minutes longer.
- **Yield: 4 servings.**

Doris K. Townsend '55
Retired Secretary, Department of Mathematics
College of Arts and Sciences

Italian Spaghetti

2 tablespoons olive oil

1 large onion, finely chopped

1¼ pounds ground chuck or round

1 (4-ounce) can chopped mushrooms

2 (15-ounce) cans tomato sauce

¼ cup Worcestershire sauce

½ teaspoon thyme

½ teaspoon rosemary leaves

½ teaspoon oregano

1 teaspoon salt

1 teaspoon pepper

1 (12-ounce) package vermicelli, cooked
    according to package directions

Parmesan cheese

- Brown onion in olive oil. Add beef, cook until browned, and drain off excess fat.
- Add mushrooms, including liquid, tomato sauce, and remaining herbs and spices.
- Heat until bubbly, then cover and simmer over low heat 1½ hours or more. Stir occasionally and add water if necessary.
- Serve over vermicelli and top with Parmesean cheese.

Mary Ann Thigpen '65
Wife of Richard Thigpen '65 '68
Sparkman Professor of Law (Retired), School of Law

Nothing but the Best!

Stromboli

½ pound ground beef

½ cup chopped onion

1 (32-ounce) package frozen bread dough, thawed

2 tablespoons prepared mustard, divided

12 slices American cheese, divided

2 cups shredded mozzarella cheese, divided

2 (3½-ounce) packages sliced pepperoni, divided

2 teaspoons dried Italian seasoning, divided

vegetable oil

- Brown ground beef and onion in a large skillet, stirring until meat crumbles. Drain well, and set aside.
- For each stomboli, place 1 loaf bread dough on a lightly floured surface. Roll dough into a 12-inch square.
- Spread 1 tablespoon mustard over dough to within ½ inch of edges.
- Layer 3 slices American cheese, ½ cup mozzarella cheese, half of pepperoni, and half of beef mixture lengthwise down center third of dough, leaving a ½-inch border at top and bottom of dough; sprinkle with 1 teaspoon Italian seasoning.
- Top with ½ cup mozzarella cheese and 3 slices American cheese. Fold each side of dough over filling. Pinch seam and ends to seal.
- Transfer loaves to greased baking sheets; brush with oil.
- Bake at 350° for 25 minutes or until lightly browned. Cut each loaf into 8 slices.
- **Yield: 8 servings.**

Tracy Burleson '93 '95
Washington, D.C.

Lasagna

1½ pounds ground meat
1 medium onion, chopped
½ green bell pepper, chopped
10 medium fresh mushrooms, chopped
olive oil
oregano
salt
pepper
parsley flakes
garlic
Italian seasoning
1 (16-ounce) jar marinara sauce
1 (8-ounce) can tomato sauce
1 cup red wine
1 (8-ounce) package lasagna noodles
1 pint cottage cheese
10-12 ounces Monterey Jack or mozzarella
    cheese, grated

- Brown meat, drain, and set aside.
- Sauté onion, pepper, and mushrooms in olive oil. Add to meat. Season with oregano, salt, pepper, parsley flakes, garlic, and Italian seasoning. Add marinara sauce, tomato sauce, and red wine.
- Cook lasagna noodles according to package directions and drain.
- Place one-third of noodles in baking dish. Top with one-third of meat sauce and one-half of cottage cheese. Repeat, topping with one-half of Monterey Jack cheese. For final layer, repeat, omitting cottage cheese.
- Bake at 350° for 30 minutes.

Dorothy Beaufait '65
Salem, Oregon

Beef Pot Pie

5 tablespoons canola oil

2 pounds stew beef, cut into ½-inch cubes

2 tablespoons all-purpose flour

1 medium onion, chopped

½ garlic clove, minced

4 cubes beef bouillon

6 cups water

½ cup red wine

¾ teaspoon salt

½ teaspoon Worcestershire sauce

¼ teaspoon black pepper

1½ cups peeled, chopped potatoes, cut into
 ¼-inch cubes

1 cup peeled, chopped carrots, cut into
 ½-inch cubes

1 cup frozen peas

Crust:

2 cups sifted all-purpose flour

1 teaspoon salt

⅔ cup vegetable shortening

6 tablespoons water

- Heat oil in 6-quart pot. Dredge beef cubes with flour and brown, a few cubes at a time, in hot oil. Remove and set aside as they brown.
- Add onion and garlic to pan drippings and cook, stirring occasionally, until onion is transparent. Stir in bouillon and water. Add wine, salt, Worcestershire sauce, and pepper. Cover and bring to a boil. Reduce heat to simmer and cook 1½ hours, stirring occasionally.
- Add potatoes and carrots; cover and simmer 20 minutes. Stir in frozen peas; cover and simmer 7 minutes. Continue simmering until meat is tender.
- Fill 8 (5 x 1½-inch) alumnium foil tart pans with ¾ cup of filling. Cover with pie crust; dust with flour, and prick with fork.
- Pies may now be frozen in individual freezer bags or covered with aluminum foil.
- Before baking, preheat oven to 450°. Center frozen pie on cookie sheet and bake 40 minutes, or until crust is brown.
- Sift flour and salt into 4-quart bowl.
- Cut shortening in with two knives until particles are about the size of corn kernels.
- Sprinkle water over flour, 1 tablespoon at a time, and stir with fork until dough is moist but not sticky.
- Gather dough together, lift out, and press into a ball. Divide dough ball into 8 pieces. Roll each piece between 2 sheets of wax paper until about ½-inch larger in diameter than top of foil pans.

When Sheila and I were in graduate school in the early 1970s, we found this recipe in **Consumer Reports***. It's become a family favorite. I have also experimented with different vegetables and seasonings, but the base recipe is a good place to begin and won't disappoint. A bottle of very dry burgundy wine is a delightful accompaniment to the cooking procees and also enhances the meal.*

Harry Knopke
Vice President for Student Affairs

Beef

Nancy's Chicken

8 to 10 pieces of chicken
1 envelope French onion soup
½ cup Russian dressing
½ cup apricot preserves

- Arrange chicken pieces in a 9 x 13-inch pan.
- Combine remaining ingredients and pour over chicken.
- Bake at 300°, uncovered, for 2 hours. Check after 1½ hours, and if getting too brown, cover lightly with aluminum foil.
- **Yield: 6 servings.**

Frieda Meyer
Professor Emerita, Department of Food Nutrition, and
Institution Management
School of Home Economics

Ruth's Chicken Breasts

8 whole, boned chicken breasts
8 slices uncooked bacon
1 (2½-ounce) jar dried beef
1½ (10 ¾-ounce) cans cream of mushroom
    soup
1½ cups sour cream
paprika or pepper

- Wrap breasts with bacon.
- Line a casserole dish with dried beef and top with chicken.
- Combine soup and sour cream. Pour over chicken. Sprinkle with paprika or pepper. May be covered and refrigerated at this point, and cooked next day.
- Bake, covered, for 2½ hours at 300°. Uncover, and bake 30 minutes more.
- **Yield: 8 servings.**

Ruth Garner '57
Wife of Paul Garner
Dean Emeritus, College of Commerce and Business
Administration

Oven Fried Chicken

1 cup biscuit mix
1 teaspoon paprika
1½ teaspoons poultry seasoning
1½ teaspoons salt
4 pieces skinless chicken
butter-flavored cooking spray
margarine, melted

- Combine biscuit mix, paprika, poultry seasoning, and salt in a plastic bag.
- Add chicken, one piece at a time, and shake to coat.
- Place in a casserole dish coated with cooking spray. Drizzle with a small amount of margarine.
- Bake uncovered at 375° for 1 hour.
- **Yield: 4 servings.**

Kathy H. Rice
Secretary, Culverhouse School of Accountancy
College of Commerce and Business Administration

Nothing but the Best!

Potato Chip Oven Fried Chicken

4 skinless chicken breasts
½ cup margarine, melted
1 (7-ounce) can Pringles plain chips, crushed
garlic salt

- Dip chicken into margarine to coat and roll in crushed chips.
- Place in a glass baking dish. Cover with any remaining chips. Sprinkle with garlic salt to taste.
- Bake uncovered at 375° for 45 minutes.

Tastes like fried chicken without all of the mess.

Leslie Almond
Wife of Kevin Almond, Director of Academic Program
for Intercollegiate Athletics

Poulet Celestine

4 chicken breast halves
½ cup butter
½ pound mushrooms, chopped
2 large ripe tomatoes, peeled, seeded, and chopped
1 cup white wine
½ cup beef broth
¼ cup brandy
salt and pepper
cayenne pepper
3 tablespoons finely chopped parsley
2 medium finely chopped garlic cloves

- In a large skillet, brown chicken in butter over medium heat.
- Add mushrooms and tomatoes and sauté 5 minutes over medium to high heat.
- Add white wine, broth, brandy, salt and pepper, and a good pinch of cayenne pepper. Cook 15 minutes.
- Remove chicken to a platter and keep warm. Skim fat off the sauce, and reduce over high heat for 5 minutes. Add parsley and garlic; cook for 30 seconds. Pour sauce over chicken and serve immediately.

Patrick Green
Chairman and Associate Professor of Religious Studies
Jane Green
Instructor of Mathematics
College of Arts and Sciences

Lemon Chicken

1 pound skinless, boneless chicken breasts or
    tenders, cut into bite-sized pieces
1 medium onion, finely chopped
2 cloves garlic, crushed
2 tablespoons butter
1 tablespoon cornstarch
1 (13¾-ounce) can chicken broth
1 large carrot, thinly sliced
2 tablespoons lemon juice
½ teaspoon salt
1 cup snow pea pods
3 tablespoons chopped parsley
1½ cups uncooked minute rice

- Sauté chicken, onion, and garlic in butter until chicken is lightly browned, about 5 minutes.
- Stir in cornstarch and cook for one minute. Add chicken broth, carrot, lemon juice, and salt. Bring to a full boil.
- Stir in pea pods, parsley and rice. Cover; remove from heat. Let stand for 5 minutes. Fluff with a fork.

Shirley Culp
Administrative Specialist, University Honors Program

President's Choice Chicken

1 broiler chicken
1 tablespoon salad oil
1 tablespoon butter
1 medium onion, chopped
¼ cup brown sugar
1 cup water
1 cup ketchup
¼ cup lemon juice
3 tablespoons Worcestershire sauce
2 tablespoons vinegar
1½ teaspoons prepared mustard
½ cup chopped celery
dash of red pepper
salt

- Heat oil and butter in skillet. Add chicken and brown on both sides.
- Remove chicken and place in a deep casserole dish.
- Add onion to skillet and cook until tender. Add remaining ingredients and simmer for about 30 minutes.
- Pour over chicken, cover and bake in 350° oven for 1 hour.

Shirley Culp
Administrative Specialist, University Honors Program

Quick Chicken and Dumplings

4 chicken breasts
flour
2 cans refrigerated crescent rolls

- Cover chicken with water, bring to a boil, and simmer for one hour. Remove from pot, skin and debone, and return to broth. Bring broth to a boil.
- Flour rolls and cut into strips. Drop into boiling broth. Reduce heat and simmer 20 minutes.
- **Yield: 4 to 6 servings.**

Ann Smith Brasher
Accounting Specialist,
School of Mines and Energy Development

Supersonic Quick Chicken and Dumplings

1⅔ cups biscuit mix
⅔ cup milk
2 (16-ounce) cans fat free, low sodium chicken broth
2 (5-ounce) cans chicken breast in water, undrained
¾ teaspoon poultry seasoning
Salt and pepper to taste

- Combine biscuit mix and milk.
- Bring broth to medium boil in Dutch oven. Drop biscuit mix by tablespoons into broth. Cook, uncovered, 5-8 minutes. Do not stir too much. Reduce heat, cover, and cook for 5-8 minutes more.
- Add chicken, poultry seasoning, and salt and pepper to taste. Cook one more minute. Serve immediately.
- **Yield: 4 servings.**

Sandra Perkins
Advisor/Contract Coordinator
New College

Chicken Rotel

1 whole chicken
2 large onions, chopped
1 large green bell pepper, chopped
¼ cup margarine
12 ounces vermicelli
3 (10-ounce) cans Rotel tomatoes
2 tablespoons Worcestershire sauce
1 (16-ounce) can green peas, drained
1 (4-ounce) can mushrooms, drained
salt and pepper to taste
1 pound Velveeta cheese, shredded

- Cook chicken, cool, debone, and chop. Reserve broth.
- Sauté onion and green pepper in margarine until tender.
- Cook vermicelli in chicken broth, but don't overcook.
- Add Rotel and Worcestershire sauce to vermicelli. Add peas, mushrooms, salt and pepper to taste. Add chicken and mix well.
- Pour into 3 large casserole dishes sprayed with cooking spray. Top with cheese.
- Bake at 350° until bubbling, about an hour.

Freezes well uncooked.

Bill Alford
College of Engineering

Mexican Chicken

4 skinless, boneless chicken breasts
2 (10¾-ounce) cans cream of chicken soup
2 (10-ounce) cans Rotel tomatoes
3 cups shredded cheese
1 package (10) frozen flour tortillas

- Cook chicken on high 20 to 30 minutes in pressure cooker with water. Start timing after pressure cooker starts whistling.
- Shred cooked chicken.
- Combine soup and tomatoes.
- Spray baking dish with cooking spray. Layer bottom of dish with one-third of tortillas. Pour one-third of soup mixture over tortillas. Top with one-third of chicken. Sprinkle with 1 cup cheese. Repeat with two more layers.
- Bake at 350° for one hour. Let cool for 15 minutes.

Ann Smith Brasher
Accounting Specialist,
School of Mines and Energy Development

Quick Fajitas

4 boneless chicken breasts
¼ cup water
2 tablespoons steak sauce
1 tablespoon brown sugar
1 bunch green onions, cut into 1-inch
    segments
1 red bell pepper, sliced
1 green bell pepper, sliced
dried red pepper flakes to taste
flour tortillas

- Cut chicken into bite-size strips.
- Heat brown sugar, water, and steak sauce in a skillet. Add chicken and cook until done. Remove chicken and set aside.
- Add green onions, peppers, and pepper flakes to skillet. Steam to desired crispness. Return chicken to pan and stir.
- Serve in warm flour tortilla shells.
- **Yield: 6 servings.**

Kim H. Jones
Sales Clerk, University Supply Store

Coach Stallings' Texas Chicken Enchiladas

3 large chicken breasts
1 cup chopped onion
1 clove garlic, minced
2 tablespoons margarine
1 (16-ounce) can tomatoes, chopped
1 (8-ounce) can tomato sauce
¼ cup chopped green chilies
1 teaspoon sugar
1 teaspoon ground cumin
½ teaspoon salt
12 corn tortillas
2½ cups shredded Monterey Jack cheese
¾ cup sour cream

- In a saucepan, simmer chicken breasts covered in water until tender. Drain and remove skin and bones. Sprinkle with salt. Cut into 12 strips and set aside.
- In saucepan, cook onion and garlic in margarine until tender. Add tomatoes, tomato sauce, chilies, sugar, cumin, and salt. Bring to a boil and reduce heat. Simmer covered for 20 minutes. Remove from heat.
- Dip each tortilla in tomato mixture to soften. Place one piece of chicken and 2 tablespoons cheese on each tortilla, roll up and place seam down in a long baking dish.
- Blend sour cream into remaining sauce mixture and pour over tortillas. Sprinkle with remaining cheese.
- Cover and bake at 350° until thoroughly heated.

Gene Stallings
Head Football Coach

Chicken

167

Cheesy Chicken

4 chicken breasts, cooked and cubed
1 cup shredded cheddar cheese, divided
1 (10¾-ounce) can cream of chicken soup
1 cup milk
1 (8-ounce) package refrigerated crescent
    dinner rolls

- Mix chicken, ½ cup cheese, and 2 tablespoons soup. Form into eight balls.
- Wrap crescent roll around each ball, leaving part of ball uncovered. Place in casserole dish, uncovered side down.
- Combine milk, remaining soup, and remaining cheese in saucepan. Heat, stirring, until sauce is smooth and cheese is melted. Pour over chicken.
- Bake at 350° for 25-30 minutes.
- **Yield: 8 servings.**

Doris K. Townsend '55
Retired Secretary, Department of Mathematics
College of Arts and Sciences

Chicken Cheese Enchiladas

12 corn tortillas
½ cup oil
2 cups grated Monterey Jack cheese
2 cups cooked and deboned chicken
¾ cup chopped onion
½ cup margarine
¼ cup flour
2 cups chicken broth
salt and pepper to taste
1 (4-ounce) can jalapeño peppers
1 cup low-fat sour cream
salsa

- Heat oil in small skillet and cook tortillas one at a time until pliable.
- Place 2 tablespoons cheese, 2 tablespoons chicken, and 1 tablespoon onion in each tortilla. Roll up and place seam down in a greased 9 x 13-inch pan.
- In a saucepan, melt margarine, add flour and cook over low heat until smooth. Add broth slowly and continue stirring until mixture begins to thicken. Add salt and pepper to taste. Remove from heat and stir in peppers and sour cream. Pour over tortillas.
- Bake, uncovered, at 350° for 20 minutes. Top with remaining cheese. Bake an additional 5 minutes.
- Serve with salsa.

Billy Helms
Head, Department of Economics, Finance, and Legal Studies
College of Commerce and Business Administration

Chicken in Foil

1 chicken breast
1 medium potato, sliced
2 carrots, sliced
6 button mushrooms
1 thin slice of onion
salt and pepper to taste
1 tablespoon butter
⅓ cup white wine

- Shape a large piece of foil to hold ingredients.
- Place chicken breast, potato slices, carrot slices, and mushrooms on foil. Top with onion slice. Sprinkle with salt and pepper to taste. Dot with butter. Add wine.
- Seal foil and bake at 375° for 1 hour.

Shirley Florence
Administrative Specialist
College of Community Health Sciences

Chinese Chicken and Asparagus

1 chicken breast, cut into 1-inch thick slices
2 tablespoons cornstarch, divided
8 spears asparagus
1 tablespoon vegetable oil
½ teaspoon minced garlic
½ cup straw mushrooms
½ teaspoon sugar
1 teaspoon soy sauce
½ teaspoon salt
dash pepper
¼ cup chicken broth
1 tablespoon white wine
¼ cup cold water
1 tablespoon minced green onion

- Dust chicken with 1 tablespoon cornstarch.
- Peel asparagus spears and cut into 1-inch pieces at an angle.
- Heat a wok or high-sided frying pan on high. When hot, add oil and heat until bubbling. Toss in asparagus and garlic and stir-fry for 2 minutes. Push the asparagus to the edges of the pan and add chicken. Stir-fry until chicken turns white.
- Add mushrooms, sugar, soy sauce, salt, pepper, chicken broth, and wine. Stir vigorously for 1 to 2 minutes.
- Combine remaining cornstarch and cold water. Add to wok to thicken sauce. Remove from heat, toss in green onions, and serve.

Ronald R. Robel
Director, Critical Languages Center
Director, Asian Studies Program
College of Arts and Sciences

Chicken and Green Bean Casserole

4 chicken breasts, cooked and diced
2 (15-ounce) cans green beans
2 (10¾-ounce) cans cream of chicken soup
2 (8-ounce) cans water chestnuts, sliced
1 cup mayonnaise
1 (2-ounce) jar pimentos, optional
1 teaspoon pepper
½ teaspoon salt
1 teaspoon curry powder
2 tablespoons lemon juice
1 can French fried onion rings

- Combine all ingredients except onion rings and place in casserole dish.
- Bake at 350° for 25 minutes. Top with onion rings and continue cooking until brown.
- **Yield: 6 to 8 servings.**

Helen M. Goetz
Professor and Chair Emerita,
Department of Consumer Sciences
School of Home Economics

Chicken and Broccoli Bake

6 chicken breasts
salt and pepper
¼ cup oil
1 (10¾-ounce) can cream of chicken soup
½ cup sherry
¼ teaspoon garlic powder
2 (10-ounce) packages frozen broccoli, thawed and drained
1 cup shredded cheddar cheese
¼ cup grated Parmesan cheese

- Season chicken with salt and pepper. Heat oil in skillet and brown chicken.
- In a medium bowl, combine soup, sherry, and garlic powder.
- Layer broccoli, cheddar cheese, and chicken in a 7 x 12-inch baking dish; top with soup mixture.
- Bake at 350° for 20 to 25 minutes. Sprinkle with Parmesan cheese and continue baking 10 minutes longer.
- **Yield: 6 servings.**

Patricia LaRue West Thrasher '68
Garland, TX

Nothing but the Best!

Chicken and Broccoli Casserole

1 broccoli stem
4 boneless chicken breasts, cooked
2 (10¾-ounce) cans of cream of chicken,
    mushroom or celery soup
1 tablespoon lemon juice
½ tablespoon Worcestershire sauce
½ cup mayonnaise
½ cup grated cheese
1 cup plain bread crumbs
liquid margarine

- Cook broccoli and drain well. Cut broccoli and chicken into bite-sized pieces and place in a buttered casserole dish.
- Combine soup, lemon juice, Worcestershire sauce, and mayonnaise in a bowl. Spread over chicken.
- Sprinkle with cheese.
- In a small bowl, moisten bread crumbs with margarine. Spread over cheese.
- Bake, uncovered, at 350° for 30-45 minutes.

Shirley Culp
Administrative Specialist, University Honors Program

Chicken Divan

2 (10-ounce) packages frozen broccoli spears
4 chicken breasts, boned and skinned
2 (10¾-ounce) cans cream of mushroom
    soup
1 cup mayonnaise
1 tablespoon lemon juice
1 cup grated cheddar cheese
½ cup bread crumbs
1 teaspoon curry powder

- Cook broccoli according to package directions, reducing cooking time to 2 minutes. Drain and place in a greased 2½-quart casserole.
- Steam chicken breasts for 20 minutes. Arrange over broccoli.
- Combine soups, mayonnaise, and lemon juice. Pour over chicken. Sprinkle with cheese
- Toss crumbs with curry powder. Spread over cheese.
- Bake at 350° for 30 minutes.
- **Yield: 4 servings.**

Cheryl Parker
Secretary, Department of Advertising and Public Relations
College of Communication

Chicken Pot Pie

4 chicken breasts, cooked, skinned, and boned
4 hard boiled eggs, finely chopped
1 (15-ounce) can English peas, drained
1 (15-ounce) can cut carrots, drained
2 (10¾-ounce) cans cream of chicken soup
milk
1 cup skim milk
1 cup self-rising flour
¾ cup mayonnaise

- Layer chicken, eggs, peas, and carrots in a greased 10 x 13-inch casserole dish.
- Stir soup with enough milk to make it pour evenly. Pour over casserole.
- Combine milk, flour, and mayonnaise. Spoon over casserole.
- Bake for one hour in preheated 300° oven.

Ann Smith Brasher
Accounting Specialist, School of Mines
and Energy Development

Easy Chicken Pie

3 pounds chicken
1 (10¾-ounce) can cream of chicken soup
2 cups chicken broth
½ cup margarine, melted
1 cup self-rising flour
1 cup buttermilk
½ teaspoon black pepper

- Boil chicken until tender. Debone and cut into bite-sized pieces. Place in greased 13 x 9-inch casserole dish.
- Heat soup and broth together. Pour over chicken.
- Combine margarine, flour, and buttermilk. Spoon over chicken. Sprinkle with pepper.
- Bake in 300° oven for one hour.

Donjette Yarbrough
Wife of James D. Yarbrough, Dean,
College of Arts and Sciences

Chicken Jerusalem

2 tablespoons oil
1 (2½ to 3-pound) chicken, quartered
flour
½ pound fresh mushrooms, chopped
1 (6-ounce) jar marinated artichoke hearts, drained
2 cloves garlic, minced
½ teaspoon oregano
freshly ground black pepper
2 cups canned or fresh tomatoes
½ cup sherry

- Heat oil in a large pan. Dredge chicken in flour and brown in oil. When golden brown, remove from pan and place in a casserole dish.
- Cover with mushrooms and artichoke hearts.
- Combine garlic, oregano, pepper, and tomatoes in a bowl. Pour over chicken.
- Bake at 350° for 1 hour or until tender. Add sherry during last few minutes of cooking time.
- **Yield: 4 servings.**

Erin Bradley
Designer, University Press

Chicken Tetrazzini

6 ribs celery, chopped
1 large onion, chopped
½ red bell pepper, chopped
½ green bell pepper, chopped
3 tablespoons butter
1 (4-ounce) jar sliced mushrooms
2 cups chicken stock
1 tablespoon Worcestershire sauce
black or red pepper to taste
1 (10¼-ounce) can cream of mushroom or cream of celery soup
½ pound cheddar cheese, grated
1 (6-ounce) bottle of stuffed olives, drained and sliced, optional
3 whole chicken breasts, cooked and chopped
½ pound spaghetti, cooked until tender in chicken stock
1 cup broken pecans, optional
1 stack round crackers, crushed
½ cup butter, melted

- Sauté celery, onion, and bell pepper in butter until tender. Add mushrooms and cook briefly.
- Stir in stock, Worcestershire sauce, pepper, soup, and cheese. Add olives, if desired.
- Add chicken and correct seasoning. Add spaghetti. If mixture seems dry, stir in additional stock.
- Place in 13 x 9-inch baking dish and top with pecans and crackers. Pour butter over crumbs.
- Bake at 350° for 1 hour.
- **Yield: 16 generous servings.**

Annette Sanderson
Wife of Former Head Basketball Coach, Wimp Sanderson

Thigpen Tetrazzini

1 large bell pepper, finely chopped
1 large onion, chopped
3 tablespoons butter
1 (10-ounce) package vermicelli
1½ cups chicken broth
1 pound sharp cheddar cheese, grated and
    divided
1 (5-pound) hen, cooked and diced
¼ cup chopped pimento
3 (10¾-ounce) cans cream of mushroom
    soup
¾ teaspoon celery salt
¼ teaspoon pepper
1½ tablespoons Worcestershire sauce
slivered almonds

- Sauté onion and bell pepper in butter until soft.
- Cook vermicelli in broth and drain. Add onion mixture. Add half of cheese and all remaining ingredients, except almonds. Stir.
- Place in casserole dish and top with remaining cheese.
- Bake 15 minutes at 300°. Top with almonds and continue baking until almonds are toasted.

Mary Ann Thigpen '65
Wife of Richard Thigpen '65 '68
Sparkman Professor of Law (Retired), School of Law

Chicken Spaghetti

1 onion, chopped
½ bell pepper, chopped
2 stalks celery, sliced
1 teaspoon oregano
1 teaspoon basil
1 teaspoon garlic powder
1 teaspoon Italian seasoning
1 teaspoon parsley flakes
1 tablespoon olive oil
6 boneless chicken breasts, cut in 1-inch
    cubes
1 (12-ounce) can stewed tomatoes
1 (15-ounce) can tomato sauce
1 (4-ounce) jar mushrooms
cooked spaghetti

- In a non-stick skillet, sauté onion, bell pepper, celery and spices in olive oil until tender. Add chicken and sauté until chicken is no longer pink.
- In a saucepan, combine tomatoes, tomato sauce, and mushrooms. Add chicken mixture. Simmer for 1 hour.
- Serve over spaghetti.

Linda Southern
Program Assistant, Alumni Affairs

Nothing but the Best!

Pollo Alla Dante (Manicotti with Chicken)

Wine Sauce:

½ cup butter

½ cup flour

1½ teaspoons salt

dash of white pepper

1 cup milk

3½ cups chicken broth, divided

½ cup white wine

Filling:

1½ cups finely chopped cooked chicken or
  turkey

5 ounces Gruyère or Swiss cheese, grated

⅓ cup wine sauce (reserved from above)

¼ cup white wine

1 egg, beaten

1 tablespoon minced parsley

1 clove garlic, crushed

1 package eggroll wrappers

3 tablespoons Parmesan cheese

- Preheat oven to 350°. Combine chicken, cheese, reserved wine sauce, wine, egg, parsley, and garlic in large bowl. Spoon two tablespoons of mixture down the center of each eggroll skin and fold one flap over the other.

- Cover the bottom of a 2-quart oblong baking dish with a little of the wine sauce. Lay filled egg roll skins (manicotti) in the baking dish, seam side down, about one inch apart. Top with remaining sauce.

- Cover and bake for 20-25 minutes. Uncover and spoon any unabsorbed sauce over the top. Sprinkle with Parmesan cheese. Bake about 10 to 15 minutes longer to brown lightly.

- **Yield: 4 to 6 servings.**

This is a classic Italian dish. You may substitute fancy white crabmeat, lean ham, or tender cooked beef for the chicken.

*Connie Sulentic
Administrative Coordinator,
Culverhouse School of Accounting
College of Commerce and Business Administration*

Chicken in Tomato Sauce

6 chicken breast halves, skinned
2 tablespoons butter
3 tablespoons olive oil
1 small onion, chopped
3 tablespoons flour
1½ cups of chicken broth
1 (8-ounce) can tomato sauce
¼ cup sherry
2 tablespoons parsley
salt and pepper, to taste
cooked pasta

- In a large skillet, sauté chicken in butter and olive oil until browned. Remove from skillet.
- Add onion and sauté until tender. Add flour and stir for 1 minute. Add broth, tomato sauce, and sherry. Stir. Add parsley, salt, and pepper. Return chicken to sauce.
- Cover and cook over low heat for 45 minutes or until chicken is tender.
- Serve with your favorite pasta.
- **Yield: 6 servings.**

Lynne S. April '76
Director, Accounting and Reporting, Financial Affairs

Country Club Chicken Casserole

2½ cups cooked chicken, cut into large pieces
2 cups cooked rice
1 cup finely chopped onions
1 cup finely chopped green peppers
⅓ cup sliced pimentos
1 teaspoon garlic salt
¼ teaspoon pepper
1 (10¾-ounce) can cream of mushroom soup
½ cup mayonnaise
1 tablespoon chopped parsley
1 cup grated cheddar cheese
ripe olives, optional

- Combine all ingredients except cheese and olives. Toss lightly. Turn into a greased shallow 2-quart casserole.
- Sprinkle with cheese.
- Bake at 350° for 25 minutes or until thoroughly heated.
- Garnish with ripe olives, if desired.
- **Yield: 6 servings.**

Jackie McPherson
Secretary, Dean's Office
College of Human Environmental Sciences

Nothing but the Best!

Poppy Seed Chicken Casserole

2 cups chopped cooked, deboned chicken
2 (10¾-ounce) cans cream of chicken soup
1 cup sour cream
1 package round crackers, crushed
½ cup margarine, melted
2 tablespoons poppy seeds

- Place chicken in casserole dish.
- Combine soup with sour cream and pour over chicken. Sprinkle with cracker crumbs. Pour margarine over the cracker crumbs and top with poppy seeds.
- Bake at 350° for 30 to 40 minutes.
- **Yield: 4 servings.**

Kay Branyon
Department of American Studies
College of Arts and Sciences

Chicken Casserole

1 cup chopped celery
1 tablespoon grated onion
2 tablespoons chopped green pepper
2 cups minced cooked chicken
3 tablespoons butter
4 tablespoons flour
1 cup milk
1 cup chicken stock
½ cup grated cheddar cheese
1 (10¾-ounce) can cream of mushroom soup
2 cups crushed potato chips

- Cook celery, onion, and green pepper until tender in a small amount of water or stock. Add chicken.
- Melt butter and stir in flour. Gradually add milk and chicken stock, stirring until thick. Add cheese and soup.
- Layer potato chips, chicken mixture, and sauce, ending with chips, in a buttered 3-quart casserole.
- Bake at 350° until brown and bubbly.
- **Yield: 6 servings.**

Jill R. Hicks '70
Academic Advisor,
College of Commerce and Business Administration
Bobby Ray Hicks, Associate Director, Undergraduate
Admissions

Chicken Almondzini

¾ cup mayonnaise

⅓ cup flour

2 tablespoons instant minced onion

1 teaspoon garlic salt

2¼ cups milk

1 cup shredded Swiss cheese

⅓ cup dry white wine

1 (7-ounce) package vermicelli, cooked and drained

2 cups chopped cooked chicken

1 (10-ounce) package frozen broccoli, thawed and drained

1¼ cup sliced or slivered almonds, divided

1 (4-ounce) can mushrooms, drained and sliced

¼ cup chopped pimento

- Combine mayonnaise, flour, onion, and garlic salt. Gradually add milk; cook over low heat, stirring constantly, until thickened. Add cheese and wine; stir until cheese melts.
- In large bowl combine mayonnaise mixture, vermicelli, chicken, broccoli, ¾ cup almonds, mushrooms, and pimento. Toss lightly. Pour into an 11¾ x 7½-inch pan. Top with remaining almonds.
- Bake at 350° for 40 to 45 minutes.

Mary Crenshaw
Dean and Professor Emerita
School of Home Economics

Chicken and Wild Rice

1 box long grain and wild rice

8 cooked chicken breasts, cut into bite-size pieces

1 (10¾-ounce) can cream of mushroom soup

½ green bell pepper, chopped

1 cup sliced celery

1 cup sliced mushrooms

1 (3-ounce) package almond slivers

- Cook rice according to package directions.
- Combine chicken, rice, soup, bell pepper, celery, and mushrooms. Place half in a heavily buttered casserole and top with almonds. Repeat.
- Cook, covered, at 350° for 30 minutes. Uncover and cook an additional 10 to 15 minutes.
- **Yield: 10 servings.**

Tom Davis '70
Senior Associate Director, Undergraduate Admissions

Nothing but the Best!

Country Captain Chicken

8 chicken breast halves

4 tablespoons margarine, divided

1 onion, sliced very thin

1 green pepper, chopped

2 cloves garlic, minced

2 (15-ounce) cans tomatoes

1½ teaspoons salt

1 teaspoon white pepper

1½ teaspoons curry powder

1½ teaspoons powdered thyme

cooked rice

sliced almonds

chopped parsley

white raisins, plumped in hot water and
    drained

- Brown chicken breasts in 2 tablespoons margarine; set aside.
- Brown onions, green pepper, and garlic in remaining margarine. Add tomatoes and seasonings. Cook until bubbling.
- Place chicken in a roasting pan. Top with sauce.
- Cover and bake at 350° until done.
- Serve over rice, garnished with almonds, parsley, and raisins.

This recipe was served by Mrs. Freeman, housemother of the Pi Beta Phi house in the 1960s. It was a favorite.

Mary Kidd Jackson '65
Hartwell, Georgia

Jan's Famous Barbecued Chicken

¼ cup butter
1 lemon
1 tablespoon vinegar
1 (10-ounce) jar Durkee sauce
6 skinless chicken breasts

- Melt butter in saucepan. Add juice from lemon plus entire lemon. Add vinegar and Durkee sauce. Bring to a boil, reduce heat, and simmer for 10 minutes.
- Grill chicken until done, basting frequently with sauce.
- **Yield: 6 servings.**

Makes a delicious alternative to tomato based barbecued chicken.

Donna Davenport Petty '68 '84
Wife of Mickey Petty, Professor of Management
College of Commerce and Business Administration

Chicken Salad Pie

½ cup mayonnaise
2 cups chopped cooked chicken breast
¾ cup grated sharp New York cheese
½ cup chopped celery
½ cup drained crushed pineapple
½ cup chopped pecans
½ teaspoon paprika
½ teaspoon salt
1 (9-inch) pie shell, baked
½ cup whipped cream
¼ cup mayonnaise

- Combine mayonnaise, chicken, cheese, celery, pineapple, pecans, paprika, and salt. Pile into pie shell.
- Fold together whipped cream and mayonnaise. Spread over chicken mixture.

Olivia Kendrick
Associate Professor, Department of Human Nutrition
and Hospitality Management
College of Human Environmental Sciences

Nothing but the Best!

Glazed Roast Pork

1 (5 to 6-pound) pork roast
1 teaspoon salt
¼ teaspoon pepper
1 cup cider
1 (10-ounce) jar red currant jelly
1 cup consommé

- Wipe roast with damp cloth and trim off excess fat. Season with salt and pepper. Place in open roasting pan.
- Roast in 325° oven 35 to 40 minutes per pound, or until meat thermometer registers 185°.
- An hour and a half before meat is done, remove from oven and pour all fat from pan. Heat cider with jelly until blended and pour over meat. Return to oven and continue roasting, basting frequently.
- To serve, remove meat from pan and skim excess fat from sauce. Stir in consommé and bring to a boil. Serve this delicious gravy with roast.

Angie Webb '61
Birmingham, Alabama

Dijon Pork Tenderloin

1 to 3 pounds pork tenderloin
salt and pepper to taste
Dijon mustard

- Pat meat with paper towel to remove moisture.
- Salt and pepper to taste on all sides. Coat with Dijon mustard.
- Bake, uncovered, at 350° for 30 minutes per pound, turning tenderloin over halfway during cooking process.

Linda Campbell Price
Student Services, Financial Affairs

Orange Glazed Pork Loin

1 (6-ounce) orange marmalade
1½ teaspoons soy sauce
1 teaspoon garlic powder
pinch of pepper
1 tablespoon water
1½ teaspoons thyme
1 (3-pound) boneless pork loin

- Combine all ingredients except pork.
- Brush meat with half of the sauce. Bake at 350°, covered, for 45 minutes.
- Uncover and spread with remaining sauce. Continue baking for 45 minutes or until done.

Kathy Morrow
Executive Secretary, Dean's Office
College of Human Environmental Sciences

Marinated Pork Tenders

¼ cup soy sauce
1 tablespoon grated onion
1 clove garlic, mashed
1 tablespoon vinegar
¼ teaspoon cayenne pepper
½ teaspoon sugar
2 pork tenderloins
bacon strips

- Combine soy sauce, onion, garlic, vinegar, cayenne, and sugar in a plastic bag. Add pork and marinate, refrigerated, overnight.
- Remove tenders from marinade and wrap together with strips of bacon. Reserve marinade.
- Bake, uncovered, at 350° for 1½ hours, basting several times with reserved marinade.
- Serve with flavored rice dish.
- **Yield: 4 to 5 servings.**

Lynne S. April '76
Director, Accounting and Reporting
Financial Affairs

Nothing but the Best!

Mexican Rice and Pork Chops

2 lean pork chops
salt
pepper
flour
oil
½ cup uncooked rice
¼ cup chopped onion
¼ cup chopped green pepper
½ cup bottled taco sauce
½ cup water
½ teaspoon chili powder
¼ teaspoon salt
1 tablespoon sliced ripe olives

- Dredge pork chops in salt, pepper, and flour. Brown in a small amount of oil.
- Remove from pan and add rice, onion, and green pepper. Sauté until rice is brown and onions are transparent. Add taco sauce, water, chili powder, and salt. Mix well.
- Place rice mixture in casserole dish. Top with pork chops. Cover.
- Bake at 350° for 30 minutes or until done. Check after 15 minutes and add water if too dry.
- Garnish with olives.

Beth Russell '70
York, Alabama

Bohemian Pork Chops

4 pork chop cutlets
1 egg, beaten
2 tablespoons milk
2 teaspoons curry or more, to taste
¼ cup bread crumbs or crushed saltines
butter
1 (10-ounce) package frozen broccoli, thawed
4 tomatoes, sliced
½ pound mushrooms, sliced
½ cup heavy cream
cooked rice

- Pound cutlets with tenderizing hammer.
- Combine egg and milk. Blend together curry and bread crumbs. Dip cutlets in milk mixture, then dredge in crumbs to coat well.
- Melt a small amount of butter in frying pan and brown pork. Remove to a greased casserole dish. Surround cutlets with broccoli.
- Sauté tomatoes and mushrooms in additional butter in frying pan. Layer on pork chops. Pour cream over all.
- Bake at 350° for 45 minutes.
- Serve with hot cooked rice.
- **Yield: 4 servings.**

Helga B. Visscher
Reference Librarian, McClure Education Library
University Libraries

Herb Baked Pork Chops and Rice

4 thick centercut or butterfly pork chops

marjoram

thyme

salt and pepper to taste

8 tablespoons uncooked rice

1 (10½-ounce) can beef consommé

½ bell pepper, sliced

½ onion, sliced

½ tomato, sliced

- Sprinkle pork chops with majoram, thyme, and salt and pepper to taste.
- Place rice in a large casserole dish. Top with pork chops and cover with consommé. Layer vegetables over pork and cover.
- Bake at 350° for 1 hour.
- **Yield: 4 servings.**

Annette Jones Watters '72 '73 '75
Assistant Director, Center for Business and
Economic Research
College of Commerce and Business Adminstration

Oriental Pork and Pasta

1 pound thin spaghetti, broken into thirds

2 cups water

½ cup soy sauce

¼ cup sherry

2½ tablespoons cornstarch

2 pounds ground pork

2 cloves garlic, minced

1 tablespoon minced ginger root

½ teaspoon crushed red pepper

4 ounces green onions, including tops, chopped

- Cook spaghetti according to package directions.
- Combine water, soy sauce, sherry, and cornstarch; set aside.
- In a large skillet over medium heat, cook pork thoroughly with garlic, ginger, and pepper. Add onions, and cook for 2 minutes. Add sauce; cook and stir until mixture bubbles and thickens.
- Pour over spaghetti and toss to mix.
- **Yield: 4 servings.**

Robert W. Halli, Jr.
Associate Professor, Department of English
College of Arts and Sciences

Broccoli Ham Roll-Ups

2 (10-ounce) packages frozen broccoli spears
8 (1-ounce) slices Swiss cheese
8 (6 x 4-inch) slices cooked ham
1 (10¾-ounce) can cream of mushroom soup
½ cup sour cream
2 teaspoons Dijon mustard
2 tablespoons sliced almonds

- Place broccoli in a baking dish and cover tightly with plastic wrap, folding back a small corner to allow steam to escape. Microwave on high for 2 to 3 minutes. Rearrange spears. Cover and microwave for an additional 3-4 minutes. Drain broccoli and set aside.
- Place one slice of cheese on each ham slice. Divide broccoli into 8 portions; arrange a portion on each ham slice, placing stems to the center and flowerets to the outside. Roll up securely, and place seam side down in a greased 12 x 8-inch baking dish.
- Combine soup, sour cream, and mustard; pour over ham rolls. Sprinkle with almonds. Cover with heavy duty plastic wrap, folding back at corner for steam to escape. Microwave on high for 8 to 10 minutes or until casserole is thoroughly heated, giving dish a half turn after 5 minutes.
- **Yield: 8 servings.**

Paige Horn
Wife of Lee Horn '87 '90
Florence, Alabama

Ham Loaf with Horseradish Sauce

2 pounds ground ham
1½ pounds ground pork
⅔ cup bread crumbs
1 (10¾-ounce) can tomato soup, divided
⅔ teaspoon salt
⅔ teaspoon pepper
2 teaspoons onion juice
1½ tablespoons chopped parsley

Sauce:
½ cup whipping cream
½ cup applesauce
½ cup horseradish

- Combine ham, pork, bread crumbs, half of soup, salt, pepper, onion juice, and parsley. Form into loaf.
- Bake at 300° for 1 1/2 hours. Pour remaining soup over top and bake 30 minutes longer.
- For sauce, mix ingredients and serve with ham loaf.
- **Yield: 8 servings.**

Beverly C. Smith
Executive Secretary, New College

Ham Logs

⅔ pound ground ham, smoked
1⅓ pounds lean ground pork
1 cup Italian dry bread crumbs
1 cup milk
¼ teaspoon pepper
2 eggs, beaten
⅓ cup diced onions
16 sausage links
¾ cup brown sugar
1 tablespoon dry mustard
¼ cup vinegar
¼ cup water

- Combine ham, pork, bread crumbs, milk, pepper, eggs, and onions. Mix thoroughly. Roll around sausage links to form 16 logs.
- Combine remaining ingredients in a saucepan and cook for 5 minutes.
- Place logs in a baking dish and bake at 350° for 30 minutes or until done, basting with brown sugar sauce.
- **Yield: 8 servings.**

The sausage links have a slightly red tint even when the ham logs are done.

Judy Bonner '69 '73
Dean, College of Human Environmental Sciences

Nothing but the Best!

Ham and Potato Casserole

2 pounds frozen hash brown potatoes
2 cups grated cheddar cheese
1 teaspoon pepper
1 tablespoon onion flakes
1 (10¾-ounce) can cream of chicken soup
1 (12-ounce) carton lite sour cream
1½ cups cooked ham, diced
1½ cups crushed corn flakes
½ cup margarine, melted

- Preheat oven to 350°.
- Combine all ingredients except cornflakes and margarine. Place in greased 9 x 13-inch pan.
- Toss together cornflakes and margarine. Spread over casserole.
- Bake for 1 hour.
- **Yield: 4 to 6 servings.**

Helen M. Goetz
Professor and Chair Emerita,
Department of Consumer Sciences
School of Home Economics

Christmas Sausage and Rice Casserole

1 cup uncooked rice
2 cups chopped carrots
1 cup chopped green pepper
1 cup chopped celery
1 medium onion, chopped
1 (14-ounce) can chicken broth
¾ cup water
1 pound bulk pork sausage, cooked and
    drained

- Lightly grease a 3-quart casserole dish. Spread rice evenly on bottom of dish.
- Top with carrots, green pepper, celery, and onion.
- Combine broth and water. Pour over vegetables. Top with sausage.
- Cover and bake at 350° for 30 minutes. Stir thoroughly, cover and bake an additional 30 minutes.

Sherry Smart Harvey
Administrative Specialist
Seebeck Computer Center

Jeff Jackson's BBQ Sauce

1 gallon ketchup
½ cup salt
1 cup sugar
1 cup prepared mustard
1 (6-ounce) bottle hot sauce
1 (8-ounce) bottle Worcestershire sauce
1 gallon cider vinegar
1 (1-ounce) can of ground red pepper
1 (1-ounce) can of ground black pepper
juice of 8 lemons
1 pound margarine

- Combine all ingredients except lemon juice and margarine in a large stock pot. Bring to a boil.
- Watch carefully as it comes to a boil, stirring frequently, as it will boil over suddenly because of the sugar. When you can't "stir down" a boil, turn it off.
- Add lemon juice and margarine. After margarine melts, carefully bring back to boil and it's done.
- **Yield: 2¼ gallons.**

From the recipe of Jefferson Davis Jackson, 1869-1971. The son of a slave, Jeff Jackson was Eugene Allen Smith's wagon driver, cook, and general assistant. He is the tall black man in many of the early pictures of the wagon camp. After Smith's death he worked for the late Dr. Walter B. Jones at the Geological Survey for many years. He wrote in a beautiful Spencerian hand, and many of the early labels in the museum were his work. His cooking was fondly remembered by old-time museum and survey employees. This is his BBQ sauce recipe as passed on by Mrs. Walter B. Jones, who admits that "It sure makes a lot!"

Jeff Jackson's BBQ Sauce, Small Batch

(with Walter Gowan's improvements)

46 ounces ketchup
⅛ cup salt
⅓ cup mustard
1 heaping tablespoon black pepper
4 ounces Worcestershire sauce
32 ounces cider vinegar
⅓ cup sugar
1 tablespoon red pepper
3 ounces hot sauce
lemon juice
⅓ pound margarine

- Jeff's orginal sauce, while very good, may be a bit "hot" and "vinegary" for some folks. Walter Gowan, a longtime Museum of Natural History volunteer, has modified a small batch recipe that is milder but still savory.
- **Makes about ¾ gallon. Store what's left over in a large whiskey bottle.**
- **Follow the same procedure as for the large batch.**

John Hall
Assistant Director
Alabama Museum of Natural History

Crab Gumbo

15 fresh crabs
2 tablespoons crab boil
6 tablespoons bacon drippings
4 large onions, chopped
3 cloves garlic, pressed
1 (10-ounce) box frozen cut okra
2 (15-ounce) cans tomatoes
1 (15-ounce) can tomato sauce
1 (8-ounce) can tomato paste
1 teaspoon salt
¾ cup uncooked rice
1 tablespoon Worcestershire sauce
1 pound shrimp, shelled and deveined
½ pint oysters, optional
½ teaspoon filé powder

- Pull pinchers, flippers, and shells away from backs of crabs. Remove "dead man's fingers" and digestive organs from crabs. Wash thoroughly.
- Place the crabs in a stock pot and cover with water. Add crab boil. Boil gently for 15 minutes and then remove from heat. When cool, remove meat from shells.
- Place bacon drippings in a heavy Dutch oven. Add onions, garlic, and okra. Brown lightly for about 30 minutes, stirring constantly.
- Add tomatoes, tomato paste, tomato sauce, and salt. Cook and cover over low heat for 1 hour, thinning occasionally with stock.
- Add rice and Worcestershire sauce, stirring well. Cover and continue cooking slowly for 15 minutes. Add shrimp and cook 15 minutes more. Add crabmeat and oysters, if desired. Continue to cook slowly for another 15 minutes. Remove from heat and add gumbo filé, mixing well.
- **Yield: 10 or more servings.**

Ben Avis Orcutt, '36
Professor Emerita, School of Social Work
Frances Ophelia Albritton, '40

Tasso, Chicken, and Seafood Gumbo

¼ cup oil

3 pounds frozen cut okra

1 large onion, minced

freshly minced garlic

2 fryers, boiled, skinned, and deboned, stock
reserved

½ pound tasso, thinly sliced

¼ pound smoked sausage, thinly sliced

1 quart oysters, with liquid

1 pound can diced stewed tomatoes

½ pint roux

cayenne and black pepper

2 bunches green onions, tops only, chopped

½ bunch fresh parsley, chopped

3 bay leaves

5 pounds shrimp, peeled

cooked white rice

- In heavy skillet, heat oil, add okra, and cook until "slime" is cooked out and okra can be mashed. After okra is cooked down, add onion and garlic. When tender, add tomatoes.
- Put chicken stock in heavy pot; when warm, add tasso, sausage, and oysters. Add roux to stock, stirring occasionally to prevent sticking. Add okra mixture. Rinse out okra skillet with 1 cup of water and add to stock. Add salt and pepper (red and black) to taste. Add hot water as needed, green onion tops, parsley, and bay leaves. Cover and simmer 1½ hours. Take lid half off if mixture begins to boil. Add chicken and shrimp.
- Serve over rice.

Freezes great. If seafood is not available, increase sausage to 1½ pounds. This is an authentic Cajun recipe from friends in Mandeville, Louisiana.

Lisa Horn Pierce '81
Mandeville, Louisiana

Nothing
but the
Best!

Gulf Seafood Gumbo

1 whole chicken

1 clove garlic

2 stalks celery

1 medium onion, chopped

1 carrot

salt and pepper to taste

1 bay leaf

2 cups chopped yellow onion

2 cups chopped celery

6 cups tomatoes, diced, or 2 (15-ounce) cans
    crushed tomatoes

2 cups chopped okra or 2 (16-ounce) bags
    frozen chopped okra

1 pint oysters, including liquid

2 pounds peeled medium shrimp

1 pound bay scallops

salt, pepper, and hot sauce to taste

1 cup cooked rice per person to be served

- Put chicken, garlic, celery, onion, and carrot in a stock pot. Salt and pepper to taste. Bring to a boil, then turn down very low and simmer for hours until chicken falls away from the bone and the liquid is reduced to at least ⅔ of its original depth.
- Remove chicken and vegetables. Reserve chicken for another use. Let broth cool and remove fat. Add bay leaf, onion, celery, tomatoes, and okra. Bring to a boil, then simmer for a couple of hours. In the last 10 minutes of cooking, add oysters, shrimp, and scallops. Do not overcook or seafood will be tough. Let everyone add salt, pepper, and hot sauce to their taste.
- Serve over rice.

This freezes quite well. When heating frozen gumbo, let it thaw in the refrigerator, then warm on stove until it begins to boil.

Jan Pruitt Duvall '77
Associate Director of University Relations

Crabmeat Fried Rice

⅓ cup uncooked rice

⅔ cup water

1 beef bouillon cube

½ cup chopped celery

¼ cup chopped green onions, optional

margarine

1 egg, beaten

½ (8-ounce) can sliced water chestnuts,
    drained*

1 (4-ounce) can sliced mushrooms, drained

6 ounces imitation crabmeat, chopped

2 tablespoons soy sauce

*remaining water chestnuts freeze well in their
  juice

- Cook rice with water and bouillon cube. Set aside.
- Sauté celery and onions in a small amount of margarine in a 12-inch skillet. Push vegetables to one side. Pour egg into skillet and scramble. Chop in small pieces.
- Add all other ingredients. Stir to mix ingredients and heat thoroughly.
- Serve with egg rolls.
- **Yield: 2 main course servings.**

Beth Russell '70
York, Alabama

Courthouse Crab

½ cup chopped celery

½ cup green onions, including tops

½ cup chopped red and green bell peppers

¼ cup butter

1 (8-ounce) package cream cheese

1 (10¾-ounce) can mushroom soup

1 (10¾-ounce) can cream of celery soup

1 (4-ounce) jar pimento, drained, rinsed, and chopped

1 (4-ounce) can mushrooms, drained and sliced

1 tablespoon favorite seafood seasoning

1 tablespoon Worcestershire sauce

¼ teaspoon hot sauce

¼ teaspoon garlic powder

1 tablespoon celery seed

pepper to taste

1 pound white lump crabmeat or 2 (8-ounce) cans of crabmeat

4 tablespoons wine

- Sauté celery, onions, and bell pepper in butter until tender. Set aside to cool.
- Heat cream cheese and soups in a double boiler, stirring until smooth and well-blended. Add remaining ingredients, except crabmeat and wine, to cheese mixture, including sautéed vegetables; blend.
- Carefully fold in crabmeat, then add wine.

Courthouse Crab may be served as hors d'oeuvres in a chafing dish with miniature pastry shells or crackers, or as an entrée over cheese toast with a green salad.

Connie J. Morrow '83
Mobile, Alabama

Deviled Crab

½ clove minced garlic
1 tablespoon chopped onion
3 tablespoons chopped celery
3 tablespoons chopped green pepper
3 tablespoons butter
1 cup crabmeat
2 eggs, beaten
1 cup canned tomatoes
1 tablespoon prepared mustard
1 tablespoon Worcestershire sauce
dash hot sauce
10 saltines, crumbled
¼ cup mayonnaise, preferably homemade
buttered cracker crumbs
grated sharp cheddar cheese

- Sauté garlic, onion, celery, and green pepper in butter; add crabmeat.
- Combine eggs and tomatoes. Add mustard, Worcestershire sauce, and hot sauce; mix with crabmeat mixture. Add crumbled saltines and mayonnaise. Turn into shallow baking dish or pie pan.
- Cover with buttered cracker crumbs and bake at 350° for 20 minutes. Sprinkle grated cheese over top and bake for 15 minutes more.
- **Yield: 4 servings.**

Frances McLean
Assistant Professor Emerita, Department of Clothing,
Textiles, and Interior Design
School of Home Economics

Crab Stuffed Chicken

4 chicken breasts, deboned
4 tablespoons butter, divided
¼ cup flour
¾ cup milk
¾ cup chicken broth
⅓ cup dry white wine
¼ cup chopped onion
1 tablespoon butter
1 (7½-ounce) can crabmeat, drained and flaked
1 (3-ounce) jar mushrooms
½ cup cracker crumbs
2 tablespoons parsley
½ teaspoon salt
dash of pepper
1 cup Swiss cheese
½ teaspoon paprika

- Pound chicken to ⅛-inch thickness.
- Melt 3 tablespoons butter. Blend in flour. Add milk, broth, and wine at once. Cook and stir until sauce bubbles and thickens. Set aside.
- In a skillet, cook onion in remaining butter until tender but not brown. Stir in crabmeat, mushrooms, cracker crumbs, parsley, salt, and pepper. Stir in wine sauce. Spread about ¼ cup sauce on each breast. Fold. Place in baking dish seam side down.
- Bake uncovered at 350° for 1 hour. Uncover, sprinkle with cheese and paprika, and continue baking until cheese is melted.

H. T. Boschung '49 '50 '57
Professor Emeritus, Department of Biological Sciences
College of Arts and Sciences

Creole Fish Orleans

¼ cup butter
1 cup chopped onion
½ cup sliced celery
1 teaspoon minced garlic
1 (16-ounce) can tomatoes
1 bay leaf
1 tablespoon Worcestershire sauce
¼ teaspoon salt
⅛ teaspoon hot pepper sauce
1 cup sliced fresh mushrooms
1½ pound fish fillets
parsley
cooked rice

- In large skillet, melt butter. Sauté onion, celery, and garlic for 3 minutes. Stir in tomatoes, bay leaf, Worcestershire sauce, salt, and pepper sauce. Simmer 15 minutes or until thickened. Add mushrooms.
- Roll fillets, arrange in sauce. Cover and cook 10 minutes longer until fish is done.
- Remove fish to serving platter. Remove bay leaf from sauce and spoon sauce around fish. Garnish with parsley and serve with rice.

Fish may also be baked in the sauce until done, if preferred.

Cindy Bowes
Programmer Analyst, Systems Development

Robert's Favorite Fish

10 fish fillets
juice of 2 medium lemons
½ cup mayonnaise
½ cup sour cream or yogurt
2 tablespoons Cherchie's Lem'n Dill
2 cups plain bread crumbs
1 cup margarine, melted

- Sprinkle fish with lemon juice.
- Combine mayonnaise, sour cream, and Lem'n Dill. Dip fillets in mixture, then in bread crumbs.
- Place fillets in baking dish and top with margarine.
- Bake at 350° for 30 minutes. When the fish is tender, broil to crisp on top.

Sherry Livingston Kirksey '75 '77
Coaling, Alabama

Grilled Orange Roughy with Lemon Soy Marinade

¼ cup freshly squeezed lemon juice

2 tablespoons soy sauce

¼ teaspoon garlic powder

¼ teaspoon pepper

¼ teaspoon hot sauce

¼ cup olive oil

4 (½-inch thick, 6-ounce) fillets of orange
    roughy or trigger fish

- Combine lemon juice, soy sauce, garlic powder, pepper, and hot sauce in the container of an electric blender; process 10 seconds. With motor running, gradually add olive oil in a slow steady stream.
- Place fish in a shallow dish and top with marinade; cover and marinate 1 hour in refrigerator. Remove from marinade, reserving marinade.
- Place fish on grill over medium coals (300-400°). Grill 3 minutes on each side; turn once and brush with reserved marinade.
- **Yield: 4 servings.**

Dennis C. James
Associate Professor, Department of Clothing, Textiles, and
Interior Design
College of Human Environmental Sciences

Mel's Baked Seafood Delight

scamp, grouper, orange roughy, snapper or
    any white flaky fish

lemon or lime juice

Lowry's Seasoned Salt

mayonnaise

lemon slices

almonds, shaved

- Wash and remove skin from fillets. Drain. Sprinkle juice over entire fillet, then sparingly apply Lowry's Seasoned Salt. Let stand for approximately 10 minutes.
- Coat with a thin layer of mayonnaise. Top with lemon slices and shaved almonds.
- Spray broiler pan with non-stick spray. Place aluminum foil over slotted part of broiler pan. Place fish on rack.
- Cook in preheated 375° oven for no longer than 20 minutes. Remove from oven and serve.

This is an old Greek fisherman's recipe that was given to me about 35 years ago.

Melford E. Espey, Jr. was the first mascot for The University of Alabama-1961-1966.

Melford E. Espey, Jr. '67 '70 '72
Director of University Recreation

Seafood Lasagna

½ cup butter

2 cloves garlic, crushed

½ cup all-purpose flour

½ teaspoon salt

2 cups milk

2 cups chicken broth

8 ounces mozzarella cheese, grated

1 teaspoon basil

¼ teaspoon pepper

8 ounces cottage cheese

8 ounces uncooked lasagna noodles

1 (7½-ounce) can crabmeat, drained

1 (4½-ounce) can shrimp, drained

½ cup Parmesan cheese

- Melt butter in 3-quart saucepan; add garlic. Stir in flour and salt. Cook, stirring constantly, until bubbly. Remove from heat. Stir in milk, broth, mozzarella cheese, basil, and pepper. Heat to boiling, stirring constantly, until cheese is melted.
- Spread ¼ of sauce (about 1½ cups) in ungreased 13 x 9-inch baking dish.
- Rinse lasagna noodles with hot water. Place 3 to 4 noodles over sauce. Spread cottage cheese over noodles. Repeat with ¼ of sauce and noodles. Top with seafood, ¼ of sauce, remaining noodles, and sauce. Sprinkle Parmesan cheese over top.
- Bake uncovered at 350° for 35-40 minutes. Let stand 15 minutes before cutting.

Betty Wedgeworth
Secretary, Department of Consumer Sciences
College of Human Environmental Sciences

Crab and Shrimp Casserole

2 onions, chopped

1 green pepper, chopped

¾ cup chopped celery

½ cup butter

1 (10¾-ounce) can cream of mushroom soup

1 (10¾-ounce) can cream of celery soup

1 cup half and half

2 pounds crab meat

1 pound cooked shrimp, shelled and deveined

2 cups cooked white rice

2 cups cooked wild rice

¼ cup slivered almonds

pepper to taste

- Sauté onion, green pepper, and celery in butter until tender.
- Combine with remaining ingredients except almonds and place in greased casserole dish. Top with almonds.
- Bake at 350° until brown.
- **Yield:12 servings.**

Beverly Kellen
Director for Administration
Russell Student Health Center

Nothing but the Best!

Queen Ann Shrimp

¼ cup butter, melted
2 tablespoons minced onion
1 tablespoon green pepper
4 tablespoons flour
½ teaspoon mustard
2 cups milk
1 cup grated cheddar cheese
½ cup sherry, optional
1 (4-ounce) can mushrooms, drained
1 (2-ounce) jar pimento, minced
2 cups cooked, peeled shrimp
cracker crumbs
paprika

- Melt butter in a saucepan. Add onions and green pepper and sauté until tender. Add flour, stirring in a spoonful at a time. Add milk a little at a time to make a smooth sauce.
- When sauce is hot, add cheese, mustard, mushrooms, and pimento. Stir constantly until mixture thickens. Salt and pepper to taste. A half cup of sherry may be added at this time.
- Add shrimp and pour into greased casserole dish. Top with cracker crumbs and sprinkle with paprika.
- Bake in 375° oven until bubbly and brown on top, about 20 minutes.

Sally L. Edwards
Director, Child Development Resources and Services
College of Human Environmental Sciences

Shrimp Creole

½ cup vegetable oil
½ cup flour
4 cloves garlic, chopped
2 stalks celery, chopped
½ cup chopped bell pepper
2 (15-ounce) cans tomato sauce
salt, black pepper, cayenne pepper to taste
1 pound peeled shrimp
cooked rice

- Heat oil in saucepan and add flour. Cook, stirring constantly, to make a dark roux.
- Add garlic, celery, and bell pepper. Cook until tender but not brown.
- Add tomato sauce, and cook 20 minutes. Season to taste with salt, pepper, and cayenne pepper.
- Add shrimp. Let cook slowly until shrimp are tender, about 25 minutes.
- Serve over rice.
- **Yield: 8 servings.**

Debbie Riley
Administrative Secretary, Housing and Residential Life

Shrimp with Angel Hair Pasta

½ cup butter
1½ pounds raw shrimp, peeled and deveined
green onions, chopped
green pepper, chopped
¼ cup white cooking wine, optional
Cavenders All-Purpose Greek Seasoning
Old Bay Seasoning
Tony Chachere's Creole Seasoning
lemon pepper
cayenne pepper
garlic salt
white Worcestershire Sauce
1 package alfredo sauce
angel hair pasta

- Melt butter in a large skillet. Add shrimp, green onions, green peppers, and wine. Sprinkle spices and Worcestershire sauce over shrimp.
- Add alfredo sauce and mix well. Cook until shrimp are done, about 15 minutes.
- Cook pasta according to package directions.
- Serve shrimp over pasta.
- **Yield: 4 servings.**

You may also substitute chicken for shrimp.

Angie Lancaster
Assistant Registrar, College of Engineering

Shrimp with Cream Sauce

10 very large, whole shrimp
Worcestershire sauce
1 tablespoon crushed black pepper
1 tablespoon whole peppercorns
½ lemon, cut and crushed
½ cup butter
1 cup cream
¼ cup white wine

- Place shrimp in sauté pan with ovenproof handle. Sprinkle with Worcestershire sauce and cook over low heat. Add pepper, peppercorns, and lemon. Cook until shrimp begin to turn pink, but remain gray for the most part.
- Add butter and keep over heat until butter melts and begins to thicken.
- Bake in 250 degree oven for 15 minutes. Do not overcook.
- Remove pan from oven and remove shrimp, leaving 3 to 4 tablespoons butter sauce in pan. Over medium heat, deglaze with wine. Add cream and cook until reduced by half, being careful not to boil the cream.
- Pour over shrimp and serve with large pieces of French bread.

Also known in New Orleans as Barbecued Shrimp.

Kenric Minges '72
Client Coordinator, Small Business Development

Shrimp Stroganoff

3 pounds raw shrimp, shelled and deveined

8 tablespoons butter, divided

⅔ cup chopped onion

½ pound mushrooms, sliced

1 clove garlic, crushed

2 tablespoons flour

1 cup chicken broth

1 tablespoon tomato paste

¼ teaspoon Worcestershire sauce

1 tablespoon chopped fresh dill or 1 teaspoon
    dried dill

1½ teaspoons salt

1 cup sour cream

cooked rice

- Sauté shrimp in 6 tablespoons butter for 5 minutes. Remove shrimp and reserve.
- Add remaining butter, onion, mushrooms, and garlic. Sauté 5 minutes.
- Stir in flour, chicken broth, tomato paste, Worcestershire sauce, dill, and salt. Simmer for 2 minutes. Add some of hot sauce to sour cream, then return to pan and mix well. Add shrimp. Heat, but do not boil.
- Serve hot with cooked rice.

H.T. Boschung '49 '50 '57
Professor Emeritus, Department of Biological Sciences
College of Arts and Sciences

Grilled Shrimp

2 pounds jumbo shrimp, shelled and deveined

½ cup peanut oil

juice of one lemon

1 medium onion, sliced

¼ cup chopped parsley

3 garlic cloves, chopped

1 teaspoon dried basil

1 teaspoon dry mustard

1 teaspoon salt

- Place shrimp in bowl and cover with remaining ingredients.
- Marinate, refrigerated, for several hours.
- Cook shrimp on hot grill for about 5 minutes.

Caroline Powell
Director of Corporate and Foundations Relations,
Development Office
Glenn Powell '64 '66
General Counsel, The University of Alabama System

Barbecued Shrimp

3 slices bacon, chopped
1½ cups margarine
3 tablespoons Dijon mustard
¼ teaspoon basil
2 tablespoons minced onion
½ teaspoon oregano
2 tablespoons crab boil
1½ teaspoons chili powder
¼ teaspoon thyme
1 teaspoon fresh-ground black pepper
2 to 3 cloves garlic, crushed
½ teaspoon hot sauce
1½ pounds large shrimp, with shells

- Preheat oven to 350°.
- Cook bacon in skillet until translucent. Add all other ingredients except shrimp. Simmer for 5 minutes.
- Place shrimp in baking dish and cover with sauce. Stir once to coat all the shrimp.
- Bake, uncovered, for 20 minutes, stirring twice during the baking process.
- Serve hot and at once with a good French bread to soak up the wonderful sauce.

You may peel these shrimp before eating, but NOT before cooking. You can also eat them shell and all, leaving only a pile of tails on the plate, as many people in New Orleans do. Have a towel ready for each guest, for this most delicious dish is very messy.

Barbara J. Hill
Secretary, Department of Mineral Engineering
College of Engineering

Gail's Shrimp and Tortellini

1 (9-ounce) package fresh tortellini with
    cheese filling
1 pound medium fresh shrimp, peeled and
    deveined
⅓ cup butter
1 shallot, minced
2 tablespoons chopped fresh basil or 2
    teaspoons dried basil
½ cup grated Parmesan cheese
fresh basil for garnish

- Cook pasta according to package directions; drain and set aside.
- Melt butter in large skillet over medium-high heat. Add shrimp, shallot, and basil. Cook 5 minutes, stirring constantly.
- Add pasta and Parmesan cheese. Toss gently. Garnish with additional basil.
- **Yield: 4 servings.**

Angie Webb, '61
Birmingham, Alabama

Nothing but the Best!

Spaghettini with Shrimp, Scallops, and Sun-Dried Tomatoes

6 ounces spaghettini pasta

3 tablespoon olive oil, divided

3 tablespoons unsalted butter

4 garlic cloves, diced

⅓ pound uncooked medium shrimp, peeled and deveined

⅓ pound scallops

½ cup bottled clam juice

⅓ cup sun-dried tomatoes

¼ cup minced fresh parsley

lemon peel

salt and pepper

- Cook pasta in large pot of boiling salted water until just tender but still firm to bite, stirring occasionally to prevent sticking. Drain pasta thoroughly. Toss with one tablespoon olive oil.
- Melt butter with remaining olive oil in heavy large skillet over low heat. Add garlic and sauté until tender, about three minutes.
- Increase heat to medium-high. Add shrimp and scallops. Sauté until shrimp turns pink and scallops are almost cooked, about two minutes.
- Add clam juice and pasta to skillet. Increase heat to high. Cook, tossing mixture with tongs, until pasta has absorbed most of the liquid and mixture is heated, about three minutes.
- Add tomatoes, parsley, and lemon peel to pasta and toss gently. Season with salt and pepper. Serve immediately.
- **Yield: 8 servings.**

Cheryl Parker
Secretary, Department of Advertising and Public Relations
College of Communication

Shrimp and Spinach Alfredo

1 cup mayonnaise

2 (8-ounce) cartons sour cream

1 (10¾-ounce) can cream of mushroom soup

¼ cup olive oil

¼ cup red wine vinegar

¼ cup white wine

2 pounds shrimp, cooked, peeled, and deveined

1 package spinach fettucini, cooked and drained

3 cups grated sharp cheese

- Combine mayonnaise, sour cream, soup, olive oil, vinegar, and wine.
- Toss together shrimp and pasta. Top with sauce and stir to coat. Place in a 9 x 12-inch casserole dish.
- Sprinkle with cheese and bake at 350° until cheese bubbles.

Mayonnaise, sour cream, and soup may be light or fat-free. It still tastes great! Crabmeat or chicken may be used instead of shrimp.

Cherry Bryant '66
Tuscaloosa, Alabama

Greek Pasta with Shrimp and Olives

¾ pound tomatoes, chopped

1 large red bell pepper, seeded and chopped

4 ounces feta cheese, crumbled

½ cup olive oil

½ cup chopped pitted black olives (preferably brine-cured)

¼ cup fresh lemon juice

2 tablespoons dry vermouth or dry white wine

1 tablespoon dried thyme

6 green onions, chopped

¾ pound linguine, freshly cooked and drained

¾ pound cooked bay shrimp

- Mix all ingredients except linguine and shrimp in large bowl.
- Add linguine and shrimp and toss to blend. Season salad to taste with salt and pepper.
- Can be prepared 30 minutes ahead. Let stand at room temperature.

Jan Brakefield, '75 '77
Coordinator of College Relations
College of Human Environmental Sciences

Crawfish Ètouffée

1¼ cups margarine

2 medium onions, finely chopped

1 bell pepper, finely chopped

4 ribs celery, finely chopped

1 (10-ounce) can Rotel tomatoes with peppers

juice of ½ large lemon

dash of Worcestershire sauce

10 fresh mushrooms, sliced

⅓ cup chopped parsley

2 garlic cloves, minced

1 (10¾-ounce) can cream of mushroom soup

3 pounds cooked, peeled crawfish

rice

hot pepper sauce

- Melt margarine in saucepan. Sauté onion, bell pepper, celery, and tomatoes for about 4 minutes, covered, stirring occasionally.
- Add lemon juice, Worcestershire sauce, mushrooms, parsley, garlic, and mushroom soup. Heat.
- Add crawfish and cook until crawfish are heated, about 10 to 15 minutes.
- Serve over rice and pass the hot sauce.
- **Yield: 6 generous servings.**
- **Variation**: For Shrimp Ètouffée, substitute 3 pounds peeled, uncooked shrimp for crawfish.

Barbara J. Hill
Secretary, Department of Mineral Engineering
College of Engineering

Nothing but the Best!

Black Beans and Rice

1 pound black beans
1 large onion, chopped
3 large green peppers, chopped
1 clove garlic
½ cup olive oil
ham bone
3 bay leaves
1 tablespoon salt
1 tomato, chopped
¼ teaspoon oregano
dash of hot sauce
cooked rice
chopped green onions

- Rinse beans. Cover with water and soak overnight. Do not drain.
- Add additional water to cover by 1 inch. Add remaining ingredients except rice and green onions. Cook for several hours until beans are soft.
- Serve over rice and garnish with green onions.

Ernestine Jackson '64
Director Emerita, Coordinated Program in Dietetics
School of Home Economics

Red Beans and Rice

1 pound dried red beans
water
1 (8-ounce) can tomato sauce
2 teaspoons garlic powder
¼ teaspoon hot sauce
1 teaspoon Worcestershire sauce
1 pound Kielbasa sausage, smoked or spicy
    hot
½ cup chopped celery
1 cup chopped onion
3 large cloves garlic, pressed
2 bay leaves
salt and pepper to taste
2 cups cooked rice

- In large pot, soak beans in cold water for at least 2 hours. Drain.
- Add 8 to 10 cups water, tomato sauce, garlic powder, hot pepper sauce, and Worcestershire sauce. Cook, uncovered, over low heat.
- In a skillet, sauté sausage until grease is rendered. Transfer to bean pot.
- Sauté celery and onion in sausage grease until soft. Add garlic and stir several times. Pour into bean pot. Add bay leaves and salt and pepper.
- Continue cooking 2 to 2½ hours, until beans are soft and creamy. Remove bay leaves.
- Serve the beans over rice and with garlic bread as an accompaniment.
- **Yield: 6 to 8 servings.**

Lynne S. April '76
Director, Accounting and Reporting, Financial Affairs

 Meatless

Pasta Primavera

2 tablespoons olive oil
1 cup sliced zucchini, ¼-inch thick
1 cup sliced yellow squash, ¼-inch thick
½ cup chopped onion
½ cup chopped green bell pepper
½ cup sliced mushrooms
1 teaspoon minced garlic
1 cup water
1 (6-ounce) can tomato paste
1 tablespoon chopped parsley
2 teaspoons sugar
1 teaspoon Italian seasoning
¼ teaspoon pepper
½ pound pasta, cooked and drained
grated Parmesan cheese

- In skillet, heat oil and sauté zucchini, squash, onion, bell pepper, mushrooms, and garlic until tender.
- Stir in remaining ingredients except pasta and Parmesan cheese. Bring to boil, reduce heat and simmer 10 minutes.
- Serve over pasta, sprinkled with Parmesan cheese.
- **Yield: 4 servings**

Veronica Purcell
Secretary, External Degree Program
New College

Fettuccine with Fresh Tomato Sauce

1½ tablespoons red-wine vinegar
3 tablespoons olive oil
salt
pepper
1 pound tomatoes, peeled, seeded, and
    chopped
¼ cup thinly sliced green onions
¼ cup thinly sliced stuffed green olives
¼ pound fettuccine, cooked and drained

- In a bowl, whisk together vinegar, oil, salt, and pepper to taste. Stir in tomatoes, green onions, and olives.
- Place pasta in a bowl, add sauce, and toss.
- **Yield: 2 servings.**

Leatha A. Darden '62 '64
Associate Professor, Department of Clothing,
Textiles, and Interior Design
College of Human Environmental Sciences

Three Pepper Pasta

1 (8-ounce) package mostaccioli or penne
   macaroni
3½ teaspoons salt, divided
1 large red pepper, cut into ½-inch strips
1 large yellow pepper, cut into ½-inch strips
1 large green pepper, cut into ½-inch strips
1 large onion, cut into ½-inch strips
3 tablespoons olive or salad oil
1 tablespoon sugar
3 tablespoons balsamic or red wine vinegar
¾ teaspoon dried basil leaves
½ teaspoon cracked black pepper
fresh basil sprig

- In a Dutch oven or large saucepot, prepare the pasta according to package directions, using 2 teaspoons salt. Drain pasta and return to pot.
- In a 12-inch skillet, heat oil until hot over medium-high heat. Cook peppers, onion, and remaining salt until vegetables are tender and browned, about 15 minutes.
- Stir in sugar, vinegar, basil, and pepper. Heat mixture through.
- Toss pasta with vegetable mixture.
- To serve, spoon pasta onto a large platter and garnish with a sprig of fresh basil.
- **Yield: 4 servings.**

Angie Webb, '61
Birmingham, Alabama

John's Favorite Pasta

½ cup olive oil
1 tablespoon sliced garlic, unpeeled
1½ teaspoons seeds from dried hot pepper
   (found at Asian grocer)
spaghetti, cooked and drained
grated Parmesan cheese

- Combine oil, garlic, and pepper seeds in heavy duty nonmetal saucepan. Cover. Cook at just below a simmer, approximately 30 to 45 minutes. Do not cook too fast!
- Strain oil and toss with hot spaghetti.
- Serve with grated Parmesan cheese.
- **Yield: 4 servings.**

John Formby
Hayes Professor of Economics
Department of Economics, Finance, and Legal Studies
College of Commerce and Business Administration

Garden Fresh Lasagna

1 eggplant, peeled
1 teaspoon Kosher (coarse) salt
8 tablespoons olive oil, divided
1 green bell pepper, julienned
1 red bell pepper, julienned
1 large onion, thinly sliced
8 ounces fresh mushrooms, thinly sliced
1 (10-ounce) package fresh spinach, cleaned
¼ cup unbleached all-purpose flour
8 ounces lasagna noodles
New Basic Tomato Sauce (see facing page)
Bechamel Sauce (see facing page)
¼ cup freshly grated Parmesan cheese
8 ounces low-fat ricotta cheese
½ cup slivered fresh basil leaves
8 ounces mozzarella cheese, grated

- Slice eggplant into ¼-inch rounds. Sprinkle with coarse salt and let drain in a colander for one hour. Wipe off salt and pat dry.
- Heat 2 tablespoons olive oil in a large skillet. Sauté bell pepper and onion over low heat until soft but not brown. Remove from skillet with a slotted spoon.
- Add 1 tablespoon olive oil and sauté mushrooms until cooked. Remove from skillet.
- Dredge eggplant with flour, shaking off excess, and lightly brown on both sides over medium-low heat, adding more olive oil as needed. Transfer cooked eggplant to paper towels.
- Preheat oven to 350°.
- Boil spinach in a small amount of water until cooked. Drain and chop.
- Cook noodles in boiling water until just tender. Drain, rinse under cold water and drain again.
- Spread a small amount of tomato sauce in a 13 x 9-inch baking dish. Layer lasagna noodles, half of peppers, onion, mushrooms, and all of eggplant.
- Add Parmesan cheese to the Bechamel Sauce and spoon half over vegetables. Sprinkle with half of basil.
- Again layer tomato sauce and noodles. Cover with spinach and ricotta cheese. Add tomato sauce and final layer of lasagna noodles. Spread with the remaining Bechamel Sauce and basil. Top with remaining tomato sauce and sprinkle with mozzarella cheese.
- Cover dish with aluminum foil and bake for 30 minutes. Uncover and bake until brown and bubbly, about 15 minutes more.
- **Yield: 12 servings.**

Marly Dukes Thomas
Wife of former UA President, Dr. Joab Thomas

Nothing but the Best!

New Basic Tomato Sauce

4 (14½-ounce) cans plum tomatoes
1 cup chopped onion
½ cup finely chopped carrots
2 cloves finely chopped garlic
3 tablespoons olive oil
¼ cup dry red wine
2 tablespoons tomato paste
½ cup chopped fresh parsley
1 tablespoon dried oregano
2 tablespoons dried basil
½ teaspoon ground nutmeg
½ teaspoon freshly ground black pepper
salt to taste
pinch of dried red pepper flakes, optional

- Drain and chop tomatoes, reserving 1 cup of the juice.
- Sauté onions, carrots, and garlic in olive oil, stirring until wilted.
- Add tomatoes, reserved juice, wine, tomato paste, and remaining ingredients. Cover and cook over medium heat for 15 minutes, stirring once.
- Remove cover and simmer another 45 minutes, stirring occasionally.

Marly Dukes Thomas
Wife of former UA President, Dr. Joab Thomas

Bechamel Sauce

4 tablespoons unsalted butter
3 tablespoon unbleached all-purpose flour
1½ cups milk
pinch of paprika
pinch of ground nutmeg
¼ teaspoon salt
⅛ teaspoon white pepper

- Melt butter in a heavy saucepan. Add flour and cook, stirring constantly, over low heat for 3 minutes.
- Raise heat to medium and slowly add milk, stirring with wire whisk. Cook until sauce thickens, about 5 minutes.
- Add paprika, nutmeg, salt, and pepper. Stir well and remove from heat.

Marly Dukes Thomas
Wife of former UA President, Dr. Joab Thomas

Zucchini Pizza

3½ cups coarsely grated zucchini

2 eggs, beaten

2 cups shredded mozzarella cheese, divided

½ cup grated Parmesan cheese

⅓ cup all-purpose flour

1 tablespoon olive oil

1 cup spaghetti sauce

⅛ teaspoon crushed red pepper

1 teaspoon oregano

- Press zucchini between paper towels to remove excess moisture.
- Combine zucchini, eggs, 1 cup of mozzarella cheese, Parmesan, and flour in a medium bowl; stir well. Press into a greased 9 x 13 inch pan.
- Bake uncovered at 350° for 20 to 25 minutes. Remove from oven and brush with oil.
- Broil 5½ inches from heat for 5 minutes. Remove from oven.
- Top with spaghetti sauce, remaining cheese, red pepper, and oregano. Bake for an additional 20 minutes.
- **Optional**: Top with your favorite pizza toppings.

Tracey Eason '87
Tuscaloosa, Alabama

Desserts

Desserts

Angel Food Cake

1 cup sifted cake flour
1¼ cups sugar, divided
10 egg whites
1 teaspoon cream of tartar
¼ teaspoon salt
1 teaspoon vanilla extract
¼ teaspoon almond extract

- Preheat oven to 350°.
- Sift flour 3 times with ½ cup sugar.
- Beat egg whites until foamy. Add cream of tartar and salt and beat until stiff, but not dry. Whip in remaining sugar, 2 tablespoons at a time. Add vanilla and almond extracts.
- Sift about ¼ cup of flour mixture at a time over the egg whites. Fold in until no flour shows.
- Turn into an ungreased 10-inch tube pan and bake for 45 minutes.
- Let cake cool thoroughly in pan.
- **Yield: 10 servings.**

Carolyn Mobley
Admissions, Capstone Medical Center
College of Community Health Sciences

Coffee Angel Food Cake

Cake:
1 angel food cake mix
1 teaspoon vanilla or ½ teaspoon almond
  extract and ½ teaspoon vanilla
1 tablespoon very finely ground gourmet-
  flavored coffee or powdered instant coffee

Icing:
½ cup butter, softened
¼ teaspoon salt
2½ cups sifted confectioners sugar
3 to 4 tablespoons milk
1 teaspoon vanilla or ½ teaspoon almond
  and ½ teaspoon vanilla extract
2 tablespoons very finely ground gourmet-
  flavored coffee or powdered instant coffee
slivered almonds
butter
salt

- Prepare cake mix according to package directions, folding in extracts and coffee granules. Bake according to package directions.
- For icing: Cream butter and salt. Add sugar gradually, beating well after each addition.
- Add 3 tablespoons milk gradually. Add extracts and coffee granules. Beat until light and fluffy, adding remaining milk if needed.
- Spread almonds on a cookie sheet. Dot with butter and sprinkle with salt. Bake at 375° until almonds are golden, checking frequently.
- When cake has cooled completely, spread with icing and cover with almonds.

Sidney Lynn Hennessey '85
Staff Assistant and Conference Housing Specialist
Housing and Residential Life

Apple Kuchen

1 egg, slightly beaten
milk
1½ cups sugar, divided
2 tablespoons butter, softened
2 cups unsifted all-purpose flour
2 teaspoons baking powder
pinch of salt
2 cups peeled and sliced apples
4 tablespoons flour
1 teaspoon cinnamon

- Place egg in an 8-ounce measuring cup and fill with milk.
- In a mixing bowl, combine ¾ cup sugar, butter, 2 cups flour, baking powder, and salt. Spread in 8-inch square baking pan.
- Layer apples over batter.
- In a separate bowl, combine remaining sugar, flour, and cinnamon. Mix with fork until crumbs form. Sprinkle over apples.
- Bake at 350° for 1 hour. Reduce heat to 325° if using a glass baking dish.

Jennifer Thompson
Library Clerk, Health Sciences Library
College of Community Health Sciences

Apple Pecan Cake

1½ cups oil
2 eggs
2 cups sugar
¼ cup orange juice
2½ cups all-purpose flour
2 teaspoons baking powder
1 teaspoon baking soda
1 teaspoon salt
1 teaspoon vanilla extract
3½ cups chopped apples
1 cup chopped pecans

- Combine oil, eggs, sugar, and orange juice in mixing bowl. Beat until creamy.
- Sift flour, baking powder, soda, and salt together. Add to egg mixture gradually, mixing well after each addition.
- Add vanilla, apples, and pecans; mix well.
- Spoon into greased 9 x 13-inch cake pan.
- Bake at 350° for 1 hour and 10 minutes or until a wooden toothpick inserted in center comes out clean.
- **Yield: 12 servings.**

Broxie C. Stuckey '55
Gordo, Alabama

Mrs. Deal's Apple Cake

2 cups sugar

1 cup oil

3 eggs

3 cups all-purpose flour

1 teaspoon salt

1 teaspoon baking soda

3 tart apples, peeled and chopped

1 cup chopped pecans or walnuts

1 teaspoon vanilla

Frosting:

1 (8-ounce) package cream cheese

½ cup butter

1 (16-ounce) box powdered sugar

1 teaspoon vanilla

¾ cup chopped pecans

- Cream sugar and oil. Beat in eggs one at a time.
- Sift flour, salt, and soda together. Add half to sugar mixture and beat with mixer until combined. Add remaining flour mixture and beat again.
- Add apples, nuts, and vanilla. Mix well.
- Pour into three greased and floured 8-inch round pans or two 9-inch pans.
- Bake at 325° for 45 to 50 minutes or until a wooden toothpick inserted in center comes out clean. Cool 15 to 20 minutes before removing from pans.
- For frosting: Mix cream cheese and butter until creamy.
- Add sugar gradually and combine thoroughly.
- Add vanilla and nuts.
- Frost cake after it is thoroughly cooled.

It is best to make frosting while cake is baking. Refrigerate until cake has cooled.

Beverly A. Kissinger
Assistant Professor, Department of Clothing,
Textiles, and Interior Design
College of Human Environmental Sciences

Jim's Apple Cake

1 1/2 cups vegetable oil

2 cups sugar

3 eggs

2 teaspoons vanilla

3 cups all-purpose flour

2 teaspoons cinnamon

1/2 teaspoon salt

1 teaspoon baking soda

1/2 teaspoon nutmeg

3 cups Rome apples, peeled and diced

1 cup chopped pecans

Glaze:

2 tablespoons butter

2 tablespoons firmly packed brown sugar

2 tablespoons sugar

2 teaspoons milk

1/4 teaspoon vanilla

- Combine oil and sugar in a large bowl. Blend very well. Add vanilla.
- Add eggs, one at a time, beating after each addition.
- Sift dry ingredients into oil mixture. Add apples and pecans.
- Pour into greased tube pan. Batter will be very stiff.
- Bake at 325° for 1 hour and 15 minutes or until a wooden toothpick inserted in center comes out clean. Let cake rest while mixing the glaze.
- For glaze: Melt butter and sugars. Add milk and vanilla. Boil 1 minute.
- Spoon over warm cake. Let cool before remodeling.

Bill Alford '70
Tuscaloosa, Alabama

Dried Apple Cake

4 cups all-purpose flour

1 teaspoon cinnamon

1 teaspoon ground cloves

1 teaspoon allspice

4 teaspoons baking soda

2 cups sugar

1 cup butter, melted

2 1/2 cups dried apples, cooked

1/4 cup buttermilk

1 cup chopped pecans or raisins or 1/2 cup
   pecans and 1/2 cup raisins

2 teaspoons vanilla

- Sift flour, spices, and soda together.
- Cream sugar and butter. Add apples.
- Add flour mixture and buttermilk alternately to apple mixture. Mixture will be very thick.
- Stir in pecans and vanilla.
- Pour into a greased and floured tube or bundt pan.
- Bake at 350° 1 hour to 1 hour and 15 minutes or until a wooden toothpick inserted in center comes out clean.

Dianne Denese Housh Burt '75
Fayette, Alabama

Nothing but the Best!

Blueberry Cake

1 cup margarine, softened

2 cups sugar

4 eggs

1 teaspoon vanilla

3 cups all-purpose flour, divided

½ teaspoon salt

1 teaspoon baking soda

2 cups blueberries

sugar

- Cream margarine and sugar.
- Add eggs one at a time, beating until light and fluffy. Add vanilla.
- Dredge blueberries with 1 cup flour.
- Sift together remaining flour, salt, and baking soda. Fold into batter. Add blueberries.
- Pour into greased tube pan which has been dusted with sugar.
- Bake at 350° for 45 minutes or until a wooden toothpick inserted in center comes out clean. Cool for 15 minutes before removing from pan.

Lynn Wilson
Accountant, Financial Accounting

Quick and Easy Blueberry Cake

1 (18¼-ounce) box yellow cake mix

1 (8-ounce) package cream cheese, softened

½ cup oil

3 eggs

1 (15-ounce) can blueberries, drained

2 teaspoons vanilla

- Combine all ingredients and mix well.
- Pour into greased and floured tube pan.
- Bake at 350° for 45 minutes or until done.

Annette Sanderson
Wife of Former Head Basketball Coach Wimp Sanderson

Country Pound Cake

2 cups sugar

2 cups self-rising flour

1 cup vegetable oil

6 eggs

1½ tablespoons vanilla

- Combine all ingredients except vanilla in a large mixing bowl. Beat with mixer for 10 minutes.
- Add vanilla and stir.
- Pour into floured and greased bundt pan. Bake at 350° for 50 to 60 minutes or until a wooden toothpick inserted in center comes out clean.
- Serve with fruit.

Kim H. Jones
Sales Clerk, University Supply Store

 Cakes

Buttered Rum Pound Cake

1 cup butter, softened

3 cups sugar, divided

6 eggs, separated

3 cups all-purpose flour

¼ teaspoon baking soda

1 (8-ounce) carton sour cream

1 teaspoon vanilla extract

1 teaspoon lemon extract

Buttered Rum Glaze:

6 tablespoons butter

3 tablespoons rum

¾ cup sugar

3 tablespoons water

½ cup chopped walnuts

- Cream butter. Gradually beat in 2½ cups sugar.
- Add egg yolks, one at a time, beating well after each addition.
- Sift together flour and baking soda. Add to creamed mixture alternately with sour cream, beginning and ending with flour mixture.
- Stir in extracts.
- Beat room temperature egg whites until foamy. Gradually add remaining sugar, 1 tablespoon at a time, beating until stiff peaks form.
- Fold into batter.
- Pour into a greased and floured 10-inch tube pan.
- Bake at 325° for 1½ hours or until a wooden toothpick inserted in center comes out clean.
- Cool in pan 10 to 15 minutes. Remove from pan to a serving plate.
- While warm, prick cake surface at 1-inch intervals with a wooden pick or meat fork; pour warm glaze over cake. Let cake stand overnight before serving.
- For glaze: combine all ingredients except nuts in a small saucepan. Bring to a boil and boil, stirring constantly, 3 minutes.
- Remove from heat, and stir in nuts.

Margaret Balentine
Associate Professor, Home Economics Education
College of Human Environmental Sciences

Five Flavor Pound Cake

1 cup margarine
½ cup shortening
2½ cups sugar
5 eggs, beaten
3 cups all-purpose flour, sifted
1 teaspoon baking powder
1 cup milk
1 teaspoon vanilla flavoring
1 teaspoon lemon flavoring
1 teaspoon rum flavoring
1 teaspoon coconut flavoring
1 teaspoon butter flavoring

Glaze:

1 cup sugar
½ cup water
1 teaspoon vanilla flavoring
1 teaspoon lemon flavoring
1 teaspoon rum flavoring
1 teaspoon coconut flavoring
1 teaspoon butter flavoring

- Cream margarine and shortening together. Add sugar and beat until light and fluffy. Add eggs.
- Sift together flour and baking powder. Add to creamed mixture alternately with milk.
- Add the flavorings. Beat well.
- Pour into a greased and floured tube pan and bake at 325° for 1½ hours, or until a wooden toothpick inserted in center comes out clean.
- For glaze: combine sugar and water in a saucepan. Bring to a boil and boil, stirring constantly, until mixture begins to thicken. Remove from heat and add flavorings.
- Pour a little glaze over cake while it is still in pan.
- After cake has cooled a little, remove it to a serving dish. Pour remaining glaze over warm cake.

Annette Sanderson
Wife of Former Head Basketball Coach Wimp Sanderson

Old Fashioned Pound Cake

1 cup butter
½ cup shortening
3 cups sugar
5 eggs, beaten
3 cups sifted all-purpose flour
½ teaspoon baking powder
½ teaspoon salt
1 cup milk
2 tablespoons lemon extract

- Cream together butter, shortening, and sugar. Mix well.
- Add eggs one at a time, beating well after each addition.
- Add flour, baking powder, salt, milk, and lemon extract. Mix well.
- Pour into a greased tube pan and bake at 325° for 1½ hours or until a wooden toothpick inserted in center comes out clean.

Skeet Hobbs
Wife of Head Basketball Coach David Hobbs

Sour Cream Pound Cake

1 cup margarine, softened

3 cups sugar

6 eggs

3 cups all-purpose flour

¼ teaspoon baking soda

½ teaspoon salt

1 cup sour cream

1 tablespoon almond, rum, or lemon
   flavoring

1 tablespoon vanilla flavoring

- Preheat oven to 300°.
- Cream butter and sugar together. Add eggs, one at a time, beating after each addition.
- Combine flour, soda, and salt. Add to creamed mixture.
- Stir in sour cream and flavorings.
- Pour into a greased and floured bundt pan and bake for 1½ hours or until a wooden toothpick inserted in center comes out clean.

Jade Abernathy
Program Assistant, Department of Advertising
and Public Relations
College of Communication

White Wine Pound Cake

1 (18¼-ounce) box yellow cake mix

1 (3½-ounce) box instant vanilla pudding
   mix

½ cup white wine

4 eggs, beaten

½ cup corn oil

½ cup milk

½ cup chopped nuts

Glaze:

1 cup sugar

½ cup margarine

¼ cup white wine

- Preheat oven to 325°.
- Mix all ingredients in mixer on low speed until combined. Beat on medium speed for two minutes longer.
- Pour into prepared bundt cake pan and bake for one hour or until a wooden toothpick inserted in center comes out clean.
- Remove from oven but leave in pan. While cake is cooling slightly, prepare glaze.
- For glaze: Combine sugar, margarine, and wine in a saucepan. Cook on low until sugar is dissolved.
- Spread glaze over warm cake in pan. Allow to set for 30 minutes before removing to a serving plate. Do not wait more than 30 minutes or it may stick.

Keeps well and freezes well.

Katie Roycroft
Retired Secretary, Department of Art
College of Arts and Sciences

Carrot Cake

2 cups all-purpose flour

2 cups sugar

2 teaspoons baking soda

3 teaspoons cinnamon

1 teaspoon salt

1½ cups corn oil

4 eggs, beaten

3 cups grated carrots

Icing:

1 (8-ounce) package cream cheese, softened

½ cup margarine, softened

1 (16-ounce) box confectioners sugar

1 cup chopped nuts

2 teaspoons vanilla

- Combine flour, sugar, baking soda, cinnamon, and salt in a large mixing bowl.
- Add oil, eggs, and carrots. Blend well.
- Pour batter into greased and floured cake pans and bake at 350° for 35 to 40 minutes or until a wooden toothpick inserted in center comes out clean.
- Remove from oven and cool.
- For icing: Beat cream cheese and margarine until light and fluffy. Gradually add sugar and mix until smooth. Stir in nuts and vanilla.
- Spread over cooled cake.

Frances Hansford '78
Wife of Nathaniel Hansford,
William A. Rose Professor of Law
and former Dean, School of Law

Chewy Cake

½ cup butter, softened

1 (16-ounce) box light brown sugar

2 eggs

2 cups self-rising flour

1 teaspoon vanilla

2 cups pecans

- All mixing should be done by hand.
- Combine butter and brown sugar. Add eggs one at a time, stirring after each addition.
- Add flour and vanilla and mix well. Add pecans and stir until well mixed. Batter will be very stiff.
- Pour into a well greased 13 x 9-inch pan.
- Bake at 350° for 25 to 30 minutes.

Teresa Gilstrap Pruett
Office Assistant, Division of Environmental
and Industrial Programs
College of Continuing Studies

Chocolate, Chocolate, Chocolate Rum Cake

1 (18¾-ounce) package devil's food cake mix

1 (3½-ounce) package instant chocolate pudding mix

1 (8-ounce) carton nonfat yogurt

1 large egg or 3 egg whites

½ cup rum

¾ cup chopped walnuts

1 (6-ounce) bag chocolate chips

1 teaspoon vanilla

Glaze:

¼ cup cocoa

¾ cup confectioners sugar

rum

- Combine all cake ingredients in a large bowl; mix well.
- Pour into greased and floured bundt cake pan.
- Bake at 350° for 30 to 45 minutes, or until toothpick comes out clean.
- Cool on wire rack.
- For glaze: mix cocoa and sugar with small amounts of rum until mixture is thin enough to drizzle over cooled cake.

Alex Snider
Wife of John Snider, Dean
College of Continuing Studies

Chocolate Puddin' Cake

1 cup all-purpose flour, sifted

1½ teaspoons baking powder

½ teaspoon salt

¼ cup butter, softened

⅔ cup sugar

½ cup milk

1 square unsweetened chocolate, melted, or 3 tablespoons cocoa

1 teaspoon vanilla

Topping:

½ cup brown sugar

½ cup sugar

3 tablespoons cocoa

¼ teaspoon salt

1½ cups boiling water

- Preheat oven to 350°.
- Sift together flour, baking powder, and salt.
- With spoon, cream butter with sugar until light and fluffy.
- Add flour mixture and milk, stirring just enough to blend.
- Add chocolate and vanilla.
- Pour into a greased 8 x 8 x 2-inch pan.
- For topping: Combine brown sugar, sugar, cocoa, and salt. Sprinkle over batter.
- Pour boiling water over top. Do not stir.
- Bake for one hour. Cool slightly in pan.
- Cut cake into squares. Serve warm with sauce from pan spooned over each serving.
- **Yield: 9 servings.**

Voni B. Wyatt '81
Personnel Officer
University Libraries

Nothing but the Best!

German Chocolate Upside Down Cake

1 cup shredded coconut
1 cup chopped pecans
1 (18½-ounce) box German chocolate cake
   mix
½ cup margarine
1 (8-ounce) package cream cheese, softened
1 (16-ounce) box confectioners sugar

- Combine coconut and nuts. Spread in a greased 13 x 9-inch pan.
- Prepare cake mix according to package directions. Pour over coconut-pecan mixture.
- Place margarine and cream cheese in a saucepan and heat until warm. Stir in confectioners sugar. Continue stirring over low heat until sugar is free of lumps.
- Spoon over top of batter.
- Bake at 350° for 35 to 40 minutes. Remove from oven and cool. Do not cut until cool.

Note: In spite of the name, this cake should not be inverted onto a platter because the sticky bottom that makes it delicious also makes it stick to the pan. However, individual servings can be inverted.

Betty Hutchins
Library Assistant, Law School Library
School of Law

Toffee Bar Cake

1 (18½-ounce) package German chocolate
   cake mix
6 toffee candy bars
1 (14-ounce) can sweetened condensed milk

- Prepare cake according to package directions.
- Cook in an oblong pan according to directions.
- While cake is cooking, crush candy bars while still in packages and pour into a small bowl.
- Remove cake from oven and punch holes all over the top with the end of a large wooden spoon.
- Pour milk over cake. Add crushed candy and cover immediately with aluminum foil.

Linda Southern
Program Assistant
Alumni Affairs

Cakes

Madolyn's Chocolate Cake

2 cups sugar

2 cups all-purpose flour

1 cup margarine

4 tablespoons cocoa

1 cup water

½ cup buttermilk

1 teaspoon baking soda

2 eggs, slightly beaten

1 teaspoon vanilla

Icing:

½ cup margarine

4 tablespoons cocoa

⅓ cup milk

1 (16-ounce) box confectioners sugar

1 cup chopped nuts

1 teaspoon vanilla

- Preheat oven to 400°.
- Sift sugar and flour together in a large bowl.
- Combine margarine, cocoa, and water in a saucepan. Bring to a rapid boil and pour over flour mixture. Mix well, but do not beat!
- Add buttermilk, soda, eggs, and vanilla. Mix well.
- Pour into a greased baking pan. Bake for 20 minutes or until toothpick inserted in center comes out clean. Leave cake in pan.
- For icing: Bring to a boil butter, cocoa, and milk. Remove from heat and add sugar, nuts, and vanilla. Stir until smooth.
- Spread icing on warm cake.

Mrs. William Clipson '61
Retired Associate Professor, Department of Business Education
College of Education

Swiss Chocolate Cake

1 (18¼-ounce) box Swiss chocolate cake mix

1 (3½-ounce) package instant vanilla pudding

3 eggs

¾ cup oil

1½ cups milk

Icing:

1 (8-ounce) package cream cheese, softened

1 cup confectioners sugar

½ cup sugar

1 (12-ounce) container frozen whipped topping, thawed

½ cup chopped pecans

2 plain chocolate bars, chilled and coarsely chopped

- Combine all cake ingredients.
- Pour into 3 greased and floured cake pans.
- Bake at 350° for 25 minutes or until a wooden toothpick inserted in center comes out clean.
- For icing: Mix cream cheese and sugars. Fold in whipped topping, pecans, and candy.
- Spread between cooled cake layers and over top.

Kay Branyon
Secretary, Department of American Studies
College of Arts and Sciences

Black Bottom Cupcakes

1 ½ cups sifted flour
¼ cup unsweetened cocoa
½ teaspoon salt
1 teaspoon baking soda
⅓ cup cooking oil
1 teaspoon vanilla
1 tablespoon vinegar
1 cup sugar
1 cup water

Filling:

1 (8-ounce) package cream cheese, softened
1 egg, beaten
⅓ cup sugar
⅛ teaspoon salt
1 cup chocolate pieces
chopped almonds

- Sift flour, cocoa, salt, and baking soda together. Add remaining ingredients. Beat until well-blended.
- Pour into greased cupcake tins.
- For filling: Combine cream cheese, egg, sugar, and salt. Beat well with wooden spoon. Stir in chocolate pieces.
- Spread over batter in tins. Top with almonds. Bake at 350° for 30 minutes or until wooden toothpick inserted in center comes out clean.

When my husband and I were in law school and we had been through a long studying spell, it was fun to make these cupcakes. They were great spirit-lifters and were easy to share.

Jenelle Mims Marsh
Assistant Dean for Student/Academic Affairs, Dean's Office
Law School
Gene Marsh
Professor of Law
Law School

Italian Coconut Cream Cake

½ cup butter
½ cup shortening
2 cups sugar
5 eggs, separated
2 cups all-purpose flour
1 teaspoon baking soda
1 cup buttermilk
1 teaspoon vanilla
1 (3½-ounce) can coconut
½ cup chopped pecans

Icing:
¼ cup margarine, softened
1 (8-ounce) package cream cheese
1 (16-ounce) box confectioners sugar
1 teaspoon vanilla
pecans

- Cream butter, shortening, and sugar. Add egg yolks and blend well.
- Add flour, baking soda, and buttermilk. Stir in vanilla, coconut, and pecans.
- Beat egg whites until stiff but not dry. Fold into batter.
- Pour into 2 greased and floured cake pans.
- Bake at 325° for 35 minutes or until a wooden toothpick inserted in center comes out clean. Cool.
- For icing: Blend margarine and cream cheese. Gradually add sugar and beat until smooth. Mix together the ingredients until creamy. Stir in vanilla.
- Spread over cooled cake. Top with pecans.

Sara Bryant
Wife of Jennings Bryant, Reagan Chair of Broadcasting
College of Communication

Nothing but the Best!

Cranberry Upside Down Cake

½ cup margarine

1 cup brown sugar

3 cups raw cranberries, divided

2 cups all-purpose flour

1 tablespoon baking powder

⅛ teaspoon salt

½ cup margarine, softened

1 cup sugar

1 egg

1 tablespoon vanilla

1 cup milk

whipped cream

- Melt margarine in bottoms of two 8-inch pie pans. Add brown sugar and stir until melted.
- Layer half of cranberries in each pie pan, completely covering bottoms.
- In a large bowl, sift together flour, baking powder, and salt.
- In another bowl, beat margarine until creamy. Add sugar and beat well until light and fluffy.
- Add egg and beat. Add vanilla and beat well. Stir in dry ingredients alternately with milk, mixing well after each addition.
- Pour batter over cranberries.
- Bake at 350° for 35 to 45 minutes until cake springs back when touched lightly.
- Serve warm or cold with whipped cream.
- **Yield: 12 servings.**

Madeleine Gregg
Assistant Professor, Teacher Education
College of Education

Date Cake

1 cup boiling water

8 ounces chopped dates

1 teaspoon baking soda

1 cup sugar

1 tablespoon butter

1 egg

½ teaspoon baking powder

1⅓ cups all-purpose flour

Topping:

8 ounces pecan halves

8 ounces chopped dates

1 cup cold water

1 cup sugar

- Pour boiling water over dates and soda. Set aside to cool.
- Mix sugar, butter, and egg; add dates and soda mixture. Stir in baking powder and flour.
- Pour into greased pan and bake at 325° for 45 to 60 minutes.
- For topping: Combine all ingredients in a saucepan. Bring to a boil, reduce heat, and cook, stirring, until thickened.
- Spread hot topping over cake as soon as it comes out of the oven. Reheat topping if necessary.

Margaret Wright

Winnie Kay's Fig Preserve Cake with Caramel Icing

1½ cups sugar

½ cup margarine, softened

3 eggs

2 cups all-purpose flour

1 teaspoon baking soda

1 teaspoon allspice

½ teaspoon salt

1 cup buttermilk

1 cup drained and chopped fig preserves

Caramel Icing:

½ cup buttermilk

1 cup sugar

½ teaspoon baking soda

⅓ cup margarine

- Cream sugar and margarine in a mixing bowl. Add eggs one at a time, beating well after each addition.
- Sift together flour, baking soda, allspice, and salt. Add to creamed mixture alternately with buttermilk. Stir in preserves.
- Pour into a greased and floured tube pan or two loaf pans.
- Bake at 350° for 1 hour in tube pan or 30 minutes in loaf pans, or until a wooden toothpick inserted in center comes out clean.
- For icing: Combine all ingredients in a saucepan. Cook slowly, stirring continuously.
- Cook until it forms a soft ball. Cool for 5 minutes.
- Beat with wire whisk or wooden spoon until icing changes color and begins to stiffen. Spread over cooled cake.

Hint: If candy thermometer is unavailable, pour a small spoonful of syrup over ice. When it forms a soft ball, it is ready.

WynnDee Turberville

Very Berry Lemon Cake with Blueberry Sauce

1 (15-ounce) can blueberries in heavy syrup
1 (18¼-ounce) box lemon butter cake mix
1 (8-ounce) carton plain yogurt
4 eggs
confectioners sugar
whipped cream

Blueberry Sauce:
¼ cup sugar
1 tablespoon cornstarch
1 cup reserved blueberry syrup

- Drain blueberries and reserve 1 cup of syrup for sauce. Rinse and drain berries.
- In a large mixer bowl, combine cake mix, yogurt, and eggs. Blend 1 minute at low speed, scraping bowl occasionally. Fold in berries.
- Pour batter into well-greased and lightly floured 10-inch bundt or tube pan.
- Bake at 350° for 35 to 45 minutes or until a wooden toothpick inserted in center comes out clean.
- Cool on cake rack 15 minutes before removing from pan. Cool completely. Sprinkle with confectioners sugar. Serve with sauce and whipped cream.
- For blueberry sauce: In a small saucepan, combine sugar and cornstarch. Gradually stir in reserved blueberry syrup. Stir constantly over medium heat until sauce is thickened and clear.
- Serve over cake.

Connie M. Mobley
Office Assistant, Business Office
University Libraries

Mandarin Orange Cake

1 (18½-ounce) box yellow cake mix
1 (11-ounce) can mandarin oranges plus
   juice
4 eggs
½ cup oil

Icing:
1 (3¾-ounce) box vanilla instant pudding
   mix
1 (15¼-ounce) can crushed pineapple,
   drained
1 (9-ounce) frozen whipped topping, thawed

- Combine cake mix, oranges, juice, eggs, and oil in a large bowl. Beat 2 minutes at high speed with electric mixer. Reduce speed to low and beat 1 minute.
- Pour batter into 3 greased and floured 9-inch cake pans.
- Bake at 350° for 20 to 25 minutes or until a wooden pick inserted in center comes out clean.
- Cool in pans 10 minutes. Remove from pans and cool completely.
- For icing: Combine all ingredients. Beat 2 minutes at medium speed with electric mixer.
- Let stand for 5 minutes or until mixture reaches spreading consistency.
- Spread icing on cake layers.
- Refrigerate for at least 2 hours before serving. Store in refrigerator.

Rhonda S. Doty
Clerical Assistant, Central Receiving and Property Control

Orange Cake

2 cups flour
1 teaspoon baking powder
1 teaspoon baking soda
1 cup butter, softened
1½ cups sugar, divided
3 eggs, separated
1 cup sour cream
1 tablespoon grated orange rind
½ cup chopped pecans
¼ cup orange juice
⅓ cup orange-flavored liqueur
2 tablespoons chopped pecans

- Sift flour, baking powder, and baking soda together.
- Cream butter, 1 cup sugar, and egg yolks in a large bowl until light and fluffy.
- Add flour mixture alternately with sour cream, beginning and ending with flour. Stir in orange rind and nuts.
- Beat egg whites in a small bowl with electric mixer until stiff but not dry. Fold into batter.
- Spoon batter into a greased 9-inch tube pan. Bake at 350° for 50 minutes or until a wooden pick inserted in center comes out clean.
- Combine orange juice and remaining sugar in a small saucepan. Heat, stirring constantly at low heat until sugar is dissolved.
- Remove from heat and stir in liqueur. Spoon mixture over hot cake.
- Cool in pan on wire rack 15 minutes; loosen around edge of pan with knife. Turn onto wire rack and sprinkle with pecans. Cool completely.

Lucinda Roff
Dean, School of Social Work

Dump Cake

1 (21-ounce) can pie filling, any flavor
1 (20-ounce) can crushed pineapple, drained
1 (18¼-ounce) box yellow cake mix, dry
1 cup margarine, cut into pats
1 cup chopped pecans

- Layer all ingredients in a 13 x 9-inch pan in the order given.
- Bake at 350° for 35 to 40 minutes.

Great served hot with ice cream.

Ann Smith Brasher
Accounting Specialist
School of Mines and Energy Development

Punch Bowl Cake

1 (18¼-ounce) box yellow cake mix or a
   prepared angel food cake
1 (3½-ounce) box vanilla instant pudding
   mix
12 ounces fresh or frozen strawberries, with
   juice
1 (20-ounce) can crushed pineapple, with
   juice
1 (12-ounce) bag coconut
1 (16-ounce) container frozen whipped
   topping, thawed
pecans, optional
cherries, optional

- Prepare cake mix and instant pudding mix
  according to package directions.
- Bake cake according to package directions and
  cool.
- Crumble half in a large glass bowl. Layer with
  strawberries, pudding, pineapple, coconut, and
  whipped topping. Repeat layers.
- Top with pecans and cherries if desired.

Anna Marie Turner

University Fruit Cake

4 cups flour, divided
8 teaspoons nutmeg
1 teaspoon baking powder
1½ pounds raisins
3 cups pecans
½ pound citron
1½ cups margarine
2 cups sugar
pinch of salt
7 eggs
1 cup grape juice

- Sift 3 cups flour, nutmeg, and baking powder
  together.
- Dredge raisins, pecans, and citron in remaining
  flour.
- Cream margarine, sugar, and salt in a large bowl
  until light and fluffy. Add eggs one at a time,
  beating after each addition.
- Add sifted ingredients and grape juice
  alternately. Stir in fruit and nuts.
- Grease and flour 4 loaf pans or 2 tube cake pans.
  Fill pans ⅔ full.
- Bake at 250° for 1 to 1½ hours or until a wooden
  toothpick inserted in center comes out clean.

*This recipe was given to Milla Boschung's great aunt in a
university foods lab in 1927. Their family has always
referred to it as the University Fruit Cake.*

*Milla Dailey Boschung '70 '73 '95
Assistant Dean and Head, Department of Consumer Sciences
College of Human Environmental Sciences*

Granny's Raisin Cake

1 (15-ounce) box raisins
2 cups sugar
1 cup butter
2 cups boiling water
1 teaspoon allspice
1 teaspoon cinnamon
1 teaspoon nutmeg
2 teaspoons baking soda
4 cups all-purpose flour
½ teaspoon salt
1 cup chopped nuts

- Combine raisins, sugar, butter, water, and spices in a saucepan. Bring to a boil and add baking soda.
- Remove from heat and let cool completely.
- After mixture has cooled, add flour, salt, and nuts.
- Pour into a greased and floured tube pan and bake at 350° for approximately 1 to 1½ hours or until a wooden toothpick inserted in center comes out clean.

Judy Williams
Secretary, Career Services Office
School of Law

Crimson Cake

1 (18¼-ounce) box white cake mix
1 cup chopped fresh or frozen strawberries
4 eggs, beaten
1 (3-ounce) box strawberry-flavored gelatin
½ cup cooking oil

Icing:
½ cup butter, softened
1 (16-ounce) box confectioners sugar
1 cup chopped strawberries

- Combine all cake ingredients. If mixture seems too dry, stir in ½ cup water.
- Pour into three greased and floured cake pans.
- Bake at 325° for 30 to 35 minutes or until a wooden toothpick inserted in center comes out clean. Cool.
- For icing: Mix all ingredients well and spread between layers and on top and sides of cooled cake.

Kate Hodges
Athens, Alabama

Four Layered Strawberry Cream Cheese Cake

1 (18¼-ounce) box butter recipe cake mix

½ cup margarine, softened

⅔ cup water

3 eggs, beaten

Topping:

1 (8-ounce) package cream cheese, softened

1 cup sugar

1 teaspoon fresh lemon juice

1 (12-ounce) container frozen whipped topping, thawed

1 (21-ounce) can strawberry pie filling

- In a large bowl, mix together cake mix and butter until grainy. Add water and eggs. Combine well.
- Pour into 2 greased and floured cake pans.
- Bake at 350° for 30 to 35 minutes or until golden brown.
- Let cool. When completely cool, cut each layer in half horizontally to make a total of 4 layers.
- For topping: Place cream cheese in a large bowl. Slowly beat in sugar and mix until creamy. Stir in lemon juice. Fold in whipped topping.
- Spread a layer of cream cheese mixture over first layer of cake. Top with one-quarter of pie filling. Continue on remaining layers.
- Spread remaining cream cheese topping on sides and top of cake. Spread remaining filling over top of cake.

Cake can be stored in refrigerator for up to a week.

Rosalie A. Hubbert
Secretary, Office of Undergraduate Admissions

Molasses Cake with Vinegar Sauce

½ cup milk

2 tablespoons vinegar

¼ cup butter

1 tablespoon brown sugar

⅔ cup molasses

2 cups flour

1 teaspoon baking soda

Vinegar Sauce:

¾ cup sugar

1 tablespoon all-purpose flour

1½ cups water

1 tablespoon vinegar

¼ teaspoon nutmeg

1 tablespoon butter

- Combine milk and vinegar in a measuring cup and set aside to sour.
- Cream butter and brown sugar. Add molasses and mix well.
- Sift together flour and baking soda. Add flour mixture to the batter alternately with the soured milk in 3 additions, beginning and ending with flour.
- Bake in a greased and floured 8 or 9-inch square pan at 350° for 35 to 40 minutes or until cake springs back when touched in the center.
- Serve warm or cool with vinegar sauce.
- For sauce: Combine sugar and flour in a saucepan. Slowly add water, stirring constantly with a wire whisk. Bring to a boil and cook over medium heat for 10 minutes.
- Stir in remaining ingredients.

The Vinegar Sauce is also good with gingerbread and plain puddings.

The Steward's records from the University held in the W.S. Hoole Special Collections of the University Library show that on December 7, 1873, the students were served molasses cake and sauce for dessert following their noon dinner of beef, corn bread, sweet potatoes, rice, biscuits, bacon, and turnips. I do not know if this is the recipe Horace the Cook used, but it is adapted from a cookbook of the period.

Rae K. Eighmey
Wife of John Eighmey, Professor,
Department of Advertising and Public Relations
College of Communication

Nusstorte (Graham Cracker Cake)

2 cups graham cracker crumbs

2 tablespoons all-purpose flour

2 teaspoons baking powder

¼ teaspoon salt

½ cup unsalted butter, softened

1 cup sugar

3 eggs, separated

1 cup milk

1 teaspoon vanilla

pinch of cream of tartar

Icing:

1 cup heavy cream, well-chilled

1 teaspoon sugar

⅓ cup semi-sweet chocolate

- Preheat oven to 350°.
- Line 2 buttered 9-inch round cake pans with wax paper. Butter the paper, and dust with flour, knocking out excess.
- In a bowl, stir together graham cracker crumbs, flour, baking powder, and salt.
- In a large bowl, cream together butter and sugar with an electric mixer until light and fluffy. Beat in egg yolks one at a time, beating well after each addition.
- Stir the crumb mixture into butter mixture in batches alternately with milk. Stir in vanilla.
- In a bowl, beat egg whites with cream of tartar until they hold a stiff peak. Stir one-quarter of egg whites into batter. Fold remaining egg whites in gently but thoroughly.
- Divide batter between prepared pans and bake on the middle rack of oven at 350° for 20 minutes or until tester comes out clean .
- Invert on a cooling rack, remove wax paper, and let cool.
- For icing: In a bowl, beat cream with sugar until it holds a stiff peak. Fold in chocolate.
- Frost cake and let chill for 1 hour before serving.

Sherry Smart Harvey
Administrative Specialist
Seebeck Computer Center

Oatmeal Cake

1½ cups boiling water
1 cup instant oatmeal
½ cup shortening
1 cup brown sugar
1 cup sugar
2 eggs
1⅓ cups all-purpose flour
1 teaspoon baking soda
½ teaspoon salt

- Pour boiling water over instant oatmeal and let stand for 20 minutes.
- Cream remaining ingredients. Add oatmeal and mix well.
- Pour batter into greased and floured bundt pan or 2 loaf pans.
- Bake at 350° for 45 minutes for bundt pan or 35 minutes for loaf pans.

Linda Campbell Price '63 '65
Systems Coordinator
Financial Affairs

Peanut Butter Cake

1 (18¼-ounce) box white cake mix
½ cup peanut butter

Icing:
½ cup peanut butter
1½ teaspoons vanilla
1 (16-ounce) box confectioners sugar
3 tablespoons milk

- Prepare cake mix according to package directions. Stir in peanut butter.
- Pour into a 13 x 9-inch pan and bake according to directions. Cool completely.
- For icing: Combine all ingredients and spread over cake.

Sandra Perkins
Advisor/Contract Coordinator, External Degree
New College

Red Velvet Cake

½ cup margarine, softened

1½ cups sugar

2 eggs

1 teaspoon vanilla

2 ounces red food coloring

2¼ cups all-purpose flour

3 tablespoons cocoa

¾ teaspoon salt

1 cup buttermilk

1 teaspoon baking soda

1 teaspoon vinegar

Icing:

3 tablespoons all-purpose flour

1 cup milk, divided

½ cup shortening

½ cup margarine, softened

1 cup sugar

1 teaspoon vanilla

- Cream margarine, sugar, eggs, vanilla, and food coloring.
- In another bowl, mix flour, cocoa, and salt. Add buttermilk alternately with flour mixture to creamed mixture.
- Mix soda and vinegar. Beat into batter.
- Pour into three greased and floured 8-inch cake pans.
- Bake at 350° for 25 to 30 minutes or until a wooden toothpick inserted in center comes out clean.
- Cool on rack before icing.
- For icing: Mix flour with ½ cup milk in blender until smooth. Add remaining milk.
- Place in a double boiler and cook, stirring constantly, until fairly thick. Cool completely.
- Cream together shortening and margarine. Add sugar and vanilla. Beat until light and fluffy, about 10 to 15 minutes.
- Add milk mixture and blend thoroughly.
- Spread icing between layers, and on top and sides of cooled cake.

Lisa C. Summerford '86
Hartselle, Alabama

Smash Cake

1 (18¼-ounce) box yellow cake mix

3 eggs

½ cup margarine, softened

1 cup finely chopped nuts

1 (8-ounce) package cream cheese, softened

1 (16-ounce) box confectioners sugar

1 teaspoon vanilla

whipped cream or vanilla ice cream

- Preheat oven to 350°.
- Combine cake mix, 1 egg, margarine, and nuts. Press into a 13 x 9-inch glass baking dish.
- Combine 2 eggs, cream cheese, confectioners sugar, and vanilla. Beat until smooth. Pour over cake mixture.
- Bake for 30 minutes or until brown.
- Serve warm with whipped cream or vanilla ice cream.

Sarah S. Pate
Academic Coordinator
Student Support Services

Nothing but the Best!

Sour Cream Coffee Cake

¾ cup butter, softened

1½ cups sugar

3 eggs

1½ teaspoons vanilla

3 cups flour

1½ teaspoons baking powder

1½ teaspoons baking soda

¼ teaspoon salt

1½ cups sour cream

½ cup brown sugar

½ cup chopped nuts

1½ teaspoons cinnamon

- Preheat oven to 350°.
- Cream butter and sugar until light and fluffy. Add eggs one at a time, beating well after each addition. Add vanilla.
- Sift flour, baking powder, baking soda, and salt together. Add flour mixture to butter mixture alternately with sour cream.
- Combine brown sugar, nuts, and cinnamon.
- Spread one-third of batter in a greased tube pan. Top with one-third of nut mixture. Repeat twice.
- Bake for 60 minutes. Cool for 15 minutes before removing from pan.
- Freezes well. Warm in microwave for serving.

You may mix any fruit into batter and sprinkle with filling mixture. Apples, raisins, nuts, chocolate chips—use your imagination. Anything goes!

Susan and Marshall Ginsburg '59
Reston, Virginia

Divinity Icing

2½ cups sugar
½ cup water
½ cup light corn syrup
2 egg whites
pinch of salt
1 teaspoon vanilla
almond extract, optional

- Combine sugar, water, and corn syrup in a saucepan. Bring to a boil. As soon as it begins to boil, remove ¼ cup and reserve it.
- Let remaining syrup cook to hard ball stage.
- Remove from heat and add reserved syrup.
- Beat egg whites. Slowly pour syrup into whites, beating constantly.
- Add flavorings. Continue beating until thick.
- **Yield: Icing for 2 cakes.**

Allison M. MacDonald '88
Randall M. MacDonald '83

Caramel Icing

2¼ cups sugar, divided
¾ cup margarine
1 small can evaporated milk plus enough
   water to equal ¾ cup
¾ cup confectioners sugar
1½ teaspoons vanilla

- Place ¼ cup sugar in a saucepan. Cook over low heat, stirring constantly, until brown.
- Add margarine and melt.
- Add 1 cup sugar and milk. Bring to a boil. Add remaining sugar. Stir until sugar is dissolved.
- Reduce heat to low. Place a candy thermometer into mixture and let cook to a soft ball.
- Remove from heat.
- Beat with mixer. Gradually add confectioners sugar and continue beating until of spreading consistency. Stir in vanilla.

Jean Bonner

Nothing but the Best!

Frosted Brownies

2 cups sugar

1 cup corn oil

4 eggs, beaten

1 cup flour

½ cup cocoa

¼ teaspoon salt

1 teaspoon vanilla

½ cup chopped pecans

Frosting:

3 cups sugar

2 tablespoons corn syrup

3 ounces unsweetened chocolate

½ cup margarine

1 cup milk

1 teaspoon vanilla

- Combine sugar and oil. Add eggs, flour, cocoa, salt, and vanilla. Blend well. Fold in nuts.
- Pour into greased 13 x 9-inch pan. Bake at 325° for 20 minutes. Remove from oven. Let cool and frost.
- For frosting: Combine sugar, corn syrup, chocolate, margarine, and milk in heavy saucepan. Stir until sugar melts and mixture comes to a boil. Boil 3 to 4 minutes, without stirring. In rainy weather, boil 5 minutes .
- Cool and beat until frosting begins to lose its gloss. Add vanilla and spread over brownies.
- When cool, cut into squares.
- **Yield: 8 to 10 servings.**

May be frozen.

Lou Bevill
Wife of U.S. Representative Tom Bevill '43 '48 '81

Chocolate Syrup Brownies

½ cup margarine, softened

1 cup sugar

1 (8-ounce) can chocolate syrup

4 eggs, beaten

1 cup self-rising flour

½ cup chopped nuts

Icing:

1½ cups sugar

6 tablespoons margarine

6 tablespoons milk

1 cup chocolate chips

chopped nuts

- Combine margarine, sugar, syrup, eggs, flour, and nuts. Blend well.
- Pour into greased 8 or 9-inch square pan and bake at 375° for 45 minutes. Cool.
- For icing: Combine sugar, margarine, and milk in medium saucepan. Bring to a boil for 30 seconds. Remove from heat and add chocolate chips. Stir until melted.
- Pour over cooled brownies. Sprinkle with chopped nuts and allow icing to set.

Tamara Hamner
Northport, Alabama

Graham Brownies

2 cups crushed graham crackers
1 (6-ounce) package chocolate or
    butterscotch chips
1 cup chopped pecans
1 (14-ounce) can sweetened condensed milk

- Mix all ingredients and press into a greased pan.
- Bake at 350° for 20 to 30 minutes.

Camille W. Cook '45 '48
Professor Emerita of Law
School of Law

Butterscotch Cheesecake Bars

1 (12-ounce) package butterscotch chips
⅓ cup margarine
2 cups graham cracker crumbs
1 cup chopped nuts
1 (8-ounce) package cream cheese, softened
1 (14-ounce) can sweetened condensed milk
1 teaspoon vanilla
1 egg

- Preheat oven to 350°.
- Melt chips and margarine together in a saucepan. Stir in graham cracker crumbs and nuts.
- Press half of mixture firmly onto bottom of a greased 13 x 9-inch pan.
- In large mixing bowl, beat cream cheese until fluffy. Add condensed milk, vanilla, and egg. Mix well.
- Pour over crust. Top with remaining crumb mixture.
- Bake 25 to 30 minutes or until toothpick inserted near center comes out clean.
- Cool to room temperature; then chill before cutting into bars.
- Refrigerate leftovers.
- **Yield: 24 bars.**

Lisa Parker
Administrative Specialist, Dean's Office
College of Human Environmental Sciences

Nothing but the Best!

Country Squares

1 (9-ounce) package condensed mincemeat
¾ cup water
2 cups graham cracker crumbs
1 (15-ounce) can sweetened condensed milk

- Crumble mincemeat into a small saucepan. Stir in water. Place over medium heat and bring to a boil, stirring constantly. Boil 1 minute. Remove from heat.
- Blend graham cracker crumbs, mincemeat, and condensed milk.
- Pour into a well greased 13 x 9-inch pan.
- Bake at 350° for 30 minutes or until lightly browned. Let cool in pan before cutting.
- **Yield: 24 squares.**

Judith Reeves
Executive Secretary
The Interim Program

Vienna Squares

1 cup butter, softened
1½ cups sugar, divided
2 egg yolks
2½ cups flour
1 (1-ounce) jar raspberry jelly or apricot
    preserves
1 cup semi-sweet chocolate chips
4 egg whites
¼ teaspoon salt
2 cups finely chopped nuts

- Cream butter, ½ cup sugar, and egg yolks.
- Add flour and knead with fingers until combined.
- Pat dough out on a greased cookie sheet to ⅜-inch thickness.
- Bake for 15 to 20 minutes at 350°, until lightly browned.
- Remove from oven. Spread with jelly and top with chocolate chips.
- Beat egg whites with salt until stiff. Fold in remaining sugar and nuts. Gently spread on top of jelly and chocolate.
- Bake for an additional 25 minutes at 350°.
- Cut into squares or bars.

Betsy Barrett
Former Instructor, Department of Human Nutrition and
Hospitality Management
College of Human Environmental Sciences

Peanut Butter Squares

2 cups butter
1¾ cups graham cracker crumbs
2 cups peanut butter
24 ounces confectioners sugar

Icing:
½ cup butter
¼ cup cocoa
6 tablespoons buttermilk
1 (16-ounce) box confectioners sugar
1 teaspoon vanilla

- Melt butter in large saucepan. Stir in peanut butter and heat until melted. Add graham cracker crumbs and confectioners sugar. Mix well.
- Press into a 13 x 9-inch pan.
- For icing: Melt butter in mixing bowl in microwave. Stir in cocoa and buttermilk. Bring to a boil in microwave.
- Gradually add confectioners sugar to butter mixture. Beat with electric mixer until smooth. Add vanilla and blend well.
- Pour icing over peanut butter mixture. Let icing harden for several hours or overnight.

Lynne S. April '76
Director, Accounting and Reporting, Financial Affairs

Big Al's Cookies

⅔ cup vegetable shortening
¾ cup sugar
1 egg
2 teaspoons red food coloring
1 teaspoon red wine vinegar
2¼ cups self-rising flour
2 teaspoons cinnamon

- Whip shortening in mixing bowl at high speed until fluffy. Add sugar and continue beating until smooth. Add egg, food coloring, and vinegar. Continue beating at high speed until evenly blended.
- Combine flour and cinnamon. Add to shortening mixture, beating with mixer or spoon until smooth.
- Cover and place in refrigerator for 2 to 3 hours, or until dough stiffens.
- Roll out on floured surface to ⅛-inch thickness. Cut into elephant shapes and place on an ungreased cookie sheet ½-inch apart.
- Bake at 375° for 8 to 10 minutes.
- **Yield: 3 to 4 dozen.**

Ralph Lane
Professor, Department of Human Nutrition
and Hospitality Management
College of Human Environmental Sciences

Nothing but the Best!

Chocolate Macaroons

1 small bag chocolate chips
2 egg whites
½ cup sugar
½ teaspoon salt
½ teaspoon vanilla
1 (3½-ounce) can coconut

- Melt chocolate chips in double boiler and let cool.
- Beat egg whites until peaks form. Add sugar gradually and continue beating until stiff but not dry. Stir in salt and vanilla.
- Fold in melted chocolate and coconut.
- Drop on ungreased cookie sheet by teaspoonfuls.
- Bake 15 to 20 minutes in 325° oven.

Allison M. MacDonald '88 and
Randall M. MacDonald '83

Chocolate, Chocolate Chip Cookies

1 cup butter, softened
1 cup sugar
½ cup brown sugar
4 ounces Nestle's ChocoBake
2 eggs
1 teaspoon vanilla
1 teaspoon baking soda
½ teaspoon salt
2 cups flour
1 (11½-ounce) bag milk chocolate chips

- Cream together butter, sugars, and ChocoBake. Mix in the eggs, vanilla, soda, salt, and flour until completely blended. Stir in chocolate chips.
- Chill dough at least 2 hours.
- Drop dough by teaspoonfuls onto ungreased baking sheet.
- Bake at 375° for about 8 minutes, until puffed and set, but not hard. Remove from baking sheet when cookies unpuff.
- **Yield: 6 dozen.**

Rona Donahoe
Associate Professor, Department of Geology
College of Arts and Sciences

Cow Chip Cookies

1 cup margarine
1 cup shortening
2 cups sugar
2 cups light brown sugar
4 eggs
2 teaspoons vanilla
½ teaspoon salt
2 teaspoons baking soda
2 teaspoons baking powder
4 cups all-purpose flour
1 cup coconut
2 cups oatmeal
2 cups cornflakes
1 cup chopped nuts
1 (12-ounce) package chocolate chips

- Melt margarine and shortening in a saucepan. Blend in sugars. Add eggs one at a time and mix well after each addition. Add remaining ingredients and blend well.
- Use ¼ cup batter per cookie. Place on lightly greased cookie sheet. Flatten slightly if thinner cookies are desired.
- Bake at 350° until brown.

Lisa Parker
Administrative Specialist, Dean's Office
College of Human Environmental Sciences

Chocolate Drops

2 eggs
½ cup salad oil
1 teaspoon vanilla
1¾ cups all-purpose flour, sifted
½ teaspoon baking soda
½ teaspoon baking powder
½ teaspoon salt
2 ounces unsweetened chocolate, melted
½ cup chopped nuts, optional

- Beat eggs. Add oil and vanilla and continue beating until blended. Add sugar, mixing well.
- Sift together dry ingredients and add to egg mixture.
- Stir in cooled chocolate. Add nuts, if desired.
- Drop by teaspoonfuls on ungreased cookie sheet.
- Bake at 375° for 8 to 10 minutes.
- **Yield: 4 dozen.**

Kathy H. Rice
Secretary, Culverhouse School of Accountancy
College of Commerce and Business Administration

Nothing but the Best!

Gingersnaps

¾ cup butter, softened
1 cup sugar
1 egg
¼ cup molasses
2 cups flour
2 teaspoons baking soda
1 teaspoon ground ginger
1 teaspoon cinnamon
1 teaspoon ground cloves
additional sugar

- Cream butter and sugar, beating until light and fluffy. Add egg and molasses and beat well.
- Sift together flour, soda, and spices. Add to creamed mixture, beating until smooth.
- Chill 2 hours.
- Shape dough into ¾-inch balls and roll in sugar to coat well. Place 2 inches apart on greased baking sheets.
- Bake at 350° for 11 to 12 minutes. Cookies will puff up and then flatten. Cool slightly on cookie sheets, then remove to wire racks to cool completely.

If making gingerbread men, roll dough onto floured board and cut with cookie cutter. Add additional flour if dough is too sticky. Decorate gingerbread men with raisins and sprinkle with sugar.

Martha Mayhall
Hamilton, Alabama

Lace Cookies

½ cup sugar
½ cup butter, melted
1 cup crushed almonds
2 tablespoons flour
2 tablespoons milk

- Preheat oven to 350°.
- Mix sugar and butter together. Add almonds and stir until smooth. Add flour and milk.
- Butter and flour several cookie sheets. Place ½ teaspoon of batter on sheets; leave enough space for cookies to spread.
- Bake 8 to 10 minutes. Let rest 1 minute. Place on rack and cool.

Officers' Dining Room
First Alabama Bank, Birmingham
Mary Bolt Lloyd '42, Manager
1981-1985

Eugenia's Oatmeal Cookies

1 cup sugar

1 cup margarine or ½ cup margarine plus
    ½ cup shortening

2 eggs, beaten

¼ cup milk

1 teaspoon vanilla

2 cups all-purpose flour

2 cups regular oatmeal

¾ teaspoon baking soda

½ teaspoon salt

1 teaspoon cinnamon

1 cup raisins

1 cup chopped nuts

- Cream sugar and margarine until light and fluffy. Add eggs, milk, and vanilla. Mix well.
- Sift together flour, soda, salt, and cinnamon. Stir in oatmeal. Combine dry ingredients with creamed mixture. Stir in raisins and nuts.
- Chill overnight.
- Drop by teaspoonfuls on lightly greased baking sheet.
- Bake at 350° approximately 15 minutes until lightly browned.
- Cool and store in an airtight container.
- **Yield: 9 dozen cookies.**

Mrs. Eugenia Pugh was a competent and delightful secretary in the School of Home Economics Dean's Office until her retirement. She shared these cookies at Christmas and on special occasions.

Mary A. Crenshaw
Dean and Professor Emerita of the School of Home Economics

Oatmeal Cookies

¾ cup flour

½ teaspoon baking soda

½ teaspoon salt

½ cup shortening

6 tablespoons white sugar

6 tablespoons brown sugar

½ teaspoon vanilla

1 egg

1 cup oatmeal

½ cup chopped nuts

- Sift together flour, soda, and salt. Blend in shortening, sugars, vanilla, and egg. Add oatmeal and nuts.
- Drop by teaspoonfuls onto a greased or nonstick cookie sheet.
- Bake at 375° for 10 to 12 minutes.
- **Yield: 5 dozen cookies.**

Ernestine Jackson
Assistant Professor Emerita, Department of Human Nutrition and Hospitality Management and Director of the Coordinated Program in Dietetics School of Home Economics

Governor Lurleen Wallace's Christmas Cookies

¾ cup butter

1 cup sugar

1 egg, separated

3 ounces candied cherries, chopped

1 slice each candied red and green pineapple,
    chopped

1 cup chopped nuts

1 cup flour

⅛ teaspoon salt

- Cream butter, sugar, and egg yolk. Fold in chopped fruit and nuts. Add flour and salt.
- Beat egg white until stiff. Add fruit mixture to it.
- Drop by teaspoonfuls on a lightly greased cookie sheet.
- Bake in 300° oven until light brown. Remove from pan while still warm.

When I was a high school student, I compiled a cookbook of Alabama celebrities. Then-Governor Lurleen Wallace kindly sent this recipe to be included in my book.

Sharan Huffman Grey
Centreville, Alabama

Lizzie's Fruitcake Cookies

1 pound golden raisins

½ cup bourbon

¼ cup margarine, softened

½ cup light brown sugar

2 eggs

1½ cups all-purpose flour

1½ teaspoons baking soda

1½ teaspoons cinnamon

½ teaspoon nutmeg

½ teaspoon cloves

1 pound pecan halves

½ pound candied pineapple, coarsely
    chopped

1 pound candied cherries, coarsely chopped

- Cover raisins with bourbon and soak until plump, at least 1 hour.
- Cream margarine and sugar until light and fluffy. Add eggs one at a time, beating well after each addition.
- Sift flour, baking soda, and spices together. Add to creamed mixture. Add soaked raisins, fruit, and nuts.
- Drop batter by tablespoonfuls onto greased cookie sheet.
- Bake at 325° for 15 minutes.
- Cool and store in airtight containers.
- **Yield: 100 cookies.**

Debbie Riley
Administrative Secretary
Housing and Residential Life

Mama's Tea Cakes

1 cup butter, softened

2 cups sugar

3 eggs

1 teaspoon baking soda

1 teaspoon baking powder

5 to 7 cups flour, sifted

½ cup buttermilk

1 teaspoon vanilla

- Cream butter and sugar until light and fluffy. Add eggs, soda, and baking powder. Add 5 cups flour and buttermilk alternately. Gradually add up to 2 additional cups of flour, until dough is stiff. Stir in vanilla.
- Chill in refrigerator to make dough easier to handle. Remove a portion of dough at a time. Roll out and cut with a cookie cutter.
- Bake at 400° for 10 minutes.
- Store in a tin box so they will retain their crispness.

Officers' Dining Room
First Alabama Bank, Birmingham
Mary Bolt Lloyd '42, Manager
1981-1985

Molasses Cookies

2 teaspoons baking soda

2 teaspoons cinnamon

1 teaspoon cloves

1 teaspoon ginger

¼ teaspoon salt

2 cups all-purpose flour

¾ cup shortening

1 cup sugar

1 egg

¼ cup molasses

- Preheat oven to 350°.
- Sift together soda, cinnamon, cloves, ginger, and salt. Mix thoroughly with flour. Add shortening, sugar, egg, and molasses.
- Drop by teaspoonfuls on ungreased cookie sheet.
- Bake 10 to 12 minutes. Do not brown.
- Cool on newspaper.

For chewier cookies, substitute oil for shortening.

A Paul "Bear" Bryant family recipe.

Cherry H. Bryant '66
Tuscaloosa, Alabama

Nothing but the Best!

Thumbprint Cookies

1 cup margarine, softened

⅔ cup sugar

2 egg yolks

½ teaspoon vanilla

2¼ cups all-purpose flour

¼ teaspoon salt

Chocolate Frosting:

1 cup sugar

¼ cup cocoa

¼ cup milk

¼ cup margarine

½ teaspoon vanilla

Vanilla Glaze:

2 cups confectioners sugar, sifted

3 to 4 tablespoons milk

½ teaspoon vanilla

- Cream margarine. Gradually add sugar, beating at medium speed of an electric mixer until light and fluffy. Add egg yolks, one at a time, beating well after each addition. Stir in vanilla.
- Sift flour and salt together. Add to creamed mixture, mixing well.
- Chill dough at least 1 hour.
- Shape dough into 1-inch balls. Place about 2 inches apart on ungreased cookie sheets. Press thumb in center of each cookie to make an indentation.
- Bake at 300° for 20 to 25 minutes. Do not brown!
- Cool on wire rack. Fill thumbprints with chocolate frosting or vanilla glaze.
- For chocolate frosting: Combine sugar, cocoa, and milk in a saucepan. Bring to a boil. Boil 1½ to 2 minutes, stirring constantly.
- Remove from heat. Stir in margarine and vanilla. Beat until mixture cools slightly.
- For vanilla glaze: Combine all ingredients and stir until smooth.

Kathy H. Rice
Secretary, Culverhouse School of Accountancy
College of Commerce and Business Administration

Toffee Cookies

2¼ cups flour
1 teaspoon baking soda
½ teaspoon salt
½ cup butter
¾ cup sugar
¾ cup packed light brown sugar
1 teaspoon vanilla
2 eggs
1 (10-ounce) package toffee bits

- Stir together flour, soda, and salt.
- In a large bowl, cream butter, sugars, and vanilla until well blended. Add eggs and mix well. Slowly add flour to mixture. Stir in toffee bits.
- Drop by teaspoonfuls on lightly greased cookie sheet.
- Bake at 350° for 9 to 11 minutes. Cool slightly then remove from sheet to wire rack to cool completely. Bake longer for crisper cookies.

Skeet Hobbs
Wife of Head Basketball Coach David Hobbs

Snickerdoodles

½ cup sugar
½ cup firmly packed brown sugar
1 cup shortening
1 egg
1 teaspoon vanilla
2 cups flour
1 teaspoon baking soda
1 teaspoon cream of tartar
½ teaspoon salt
½ teaspoon cinnamon
4 tablespoons sugar

- Cream sugars and shortening until light and fluffy. Add egg and vanilla. Beat well.
- Stir together flour, soda, cream of tartar, and salt. Gradually blend into creamed mixture.
- Combine cinnamon and sugar.
- Shape dough into walnut-size balls. Roll in sugar mixture.
- Bake on ungreased cookie sheet in 350° oven approximately 12 minutes. Let cool 5 minutes before removing from pan.
- **Yield: 3 to 4 dozen.**

Jill F. Jones '92
Assistant Law Librarian, Assistant Lecturer/Cataloging
School of Law

Sand Tarts

1¼ cups butter, softened
2¼ cups sugar
1 teaspoon grated lemon rind
4 cups flour
2 medium eggs, slightly beaten
sugar
cinnamon

- Cream butter and sugar until fluffy. Add lemon rind. Add flour and eggs alternately. Beat until well blended.
- Refrigerate dough overnight in a covered bowl.
- Roll out small portions of dough and cut into desired shapes. Keep unused dough in refrigerator.
- Place on ungreased cookie sheet. Sprinkle with a mixture of sugar and cinnamon.
- Bake at 350° until lightly browned.
- **Yield: 5 to 6 dozen cookies.**

Helen M. Goetz
Professor Emerita of Consumer Sciences
School of Home Economics

Plum-Delicious Cookies

1 cup butter, softened
4½ teaspoons sugar
1 teaspoon vanilla
3 cups all-purpose flour
plum jelly

- Cream butter and sugar until light and fluffy. Add vanilla and flour, mixing well.
- Roll out dough on lightly floured surface. Cut cookies with doughnut cutter center.
- Place cookies on cookie sheet. Make an indentation in center of each cookie and fill with jelly.
- Bake at 350° approximately 10 minutes, until lightly browned.

Mila Key Johnston '68
Greensboro, Alabama

Birmingham Blueberry Pie

2 (8-ounce) packages cream cheese, softened
1¾ cups sugar
1 (16-ounce) container frozen whipped
   topping, thawed
2 small packages walnuts
2 graham cracker pie crusts
blueberry pie filling

- Blend cream cheese and sugar until smooth. Fold in whipped topping and walnuts.
- Pour into crusts. Top with pie filling.
- Chill before serving.

Sherry Dillard
Decatur, Alabama

Cherry Cream Pie

1 (8-ounce) package cream cheese, softened
1 (16-ounce) box confectioners sugar
1 (8-ounce) container frozen whipped
   topping, thawed
1 (21-ounce) can cherry pie filling
2 baked pie crusts, regular or graham cracker

- Blend cream cheese and confectioners sugar until smooth. Fold in whipped topping.
- Pour into crusts. Top with pie filling.
- Chill overnight.

Kathy H. Rice
Secretary, Culverhouse School of Accountancy
College of Commerce and Business Administration

Cherry Pie

1¼ cups sugar
5 tablespoons flour
¼ teaspoon salt
1 tablespoon margarine, softened
3 cups drained canned pitted tart red cherries,
    juice reserved
¼ teaspoon red food coloring, optional
10 drops almond extract
crust for double crust pie
butter, optional
cinnamon, optional

- Combine sugar, flour, and salt. Stir in butter, ½ cup reserved cherry juice, food coloring, if desired, and almond extract. Fold in cherries.
- Line 9-inch pie pan with pastry. Fill with cherry mixture. If desired, dot with butter and sprinkle with cinnamon. Cover with crust or a lattice top.
- Cut a 2½-inch strip of foil and fold it loosely around edge of pie.
- Bake in 425° oven for 30 minutes. Remove foil and bake an additonal 10 minutes.
- Cool before serving.
- **Yield: 10 servings.**

Beverly Smith
Executive Secretary, Dean's Office
New College

Chocolate Chess Pie

½ cup butter
1½ cups sugar
1 tablespoon flour
2 tablespoons cocoa
3 eggs
1 teaspoon vanilla
¼ cup milk
1 unbaked (9-inch) pie shell

- Melt butter in a saucepan.
- Combine sugar, flour, and cocoa. Stir into butter and blend well.
- Add eggs, one at a time, and stir after each addition. Add milk and vanilla.
- Pour into unbaked pie shell.
- Bake at 350° for 40 minutes.

Betty Joyce Cain Mills '50
Birmingham, Alabama

Chocolate Layer Pie

1 cup flour
1 cup chopped pecans
½ cup butter, melted
1 (8-ounce) package cream cheese, softened
1 cup confectioners sugar
2 cups whipped topping
2 (3½-ounce) packages instant chocolate
    pudding
3 cups milk
whipped topping
chopped pecans

- Toss flour, nuts, and butter together in a bowl.
- Spread in a 13 x 9-inch pan, and bake at 350° for 15 to 20 minutes, until lightly browned. Cool.
- Combine cream cheese and confectioners sugar. Fold in whipped topping. Spread over cooled pecan mixture.
- Mix pudding and milk. Spread over cream cheese layer.
- Cover with additional whipped topping and sprinkle with pecans.
- Chill before serving.

Diane W. Freeman '86
Library Assistant Senior, Acquisitions/Serials
University Libraries

Chocolate Marshmallow Pie

20 large marshmallows
¾ cup milk
2 tablespoons cocoa
pinch of salt
1 teaspoon vanilla
1 cup heavy cream, whipped
1 (8-inch) pie shell, baked
whipped cream
pecans

- Combine marshmallows, milk, cocoa, and salt in a double boiler. Heat, stirring, until marshmallows melt.
- Remove from heat and cool.
- Stir in vanilla. Fold in cream.
- Pour into prepared pie shell and chill.
- Garnish with additional whipped cream and pecans.
- **Variation**: For Coffee Pie, add 2 tablespoons instant coffee. Garnish with toasted slivered almonds.

Broxie C. Stuckey '55
Gordo, Alabama

Chocolate Pecan Pie

¾ cup sugar
1 cup dark corn syrup
½ teaspoon salt
2 tablespoons flour
3 eggs, beaten
2 tablespoons butter
3 ounces unsweetened baking chocolate
1½ teaspoons vanilla
1 cup pecan halves
1 unbaked (9-inch) pie crust

- Preheat oven to 300°.
- Combine sugar, corn syrup, salt, flour, and eggs.
- Melt butter and chocolate together. Add to corn syrup mixture. Stir in vanilla.
- Cover bottom of pie shell with pecans. Pour chocolate mixture on top.
- Bake for 1 hour or until set.

Judy Mayer
Wife of Morris Mayer,
Bruno Professor Emeritus of Marketing
College of Commerce and Business Administration

Fudge Brownie Pie

⅓ cup cocoa
1 cup sugar
½ cup butter
2 eggs, beaten
1 teaspoon vanilla extract
½ cup chopped nuts
2 tablespoons all-purpose flour
ice cream

- Combine cocoa, sugar, and butter in a saucepan. Cook over low heat, stirring, until smooth. Remove from heat.
- Add eggs, vanilla, nuts, and flour. Stir until smooth.
- Pour into greased pie pan.
- Place in cold oven. Set oven to 325° and bake for 25 minutes.
- Serve topped with ice cream.

Thomas C. Ford '78
Director, Athletic Department
Intercollegiate Athletics

Creamy Peanut Butter Pie with Fudge Topping

Crust:

14 Oreo cookies

½ cup unsalted butter, melted

3 tablespoons roasted and finely chopped
  peanuts

Filling:

1 (8-ounce) package cream cheese, softened

1 cup sugar

2 teaspoons vanilla

¾ cup plus 2 tablespoons creamy peanut
  butter

¼ cup roasted and finely chopped peanuts

1 cup chilled whipping cream

Topping:

½ cup whipping cream

½ cup sugar

¼ cup unsalted butter

2 ounces unsweetened chocolate, chopped

½ teaspoon vanilla

- For crust: Preheat oven to 375°.
- Line 9-inch metal pie pan with aluminum foil.
- Finely grind cookies in processor. Add butter and peanuts. Blend until moist crumbs form.
- Press mixture firmly onto bottom and sides of lined pie pan.
- Bake 5 minutes, then place in freezer for 30 minutes.
- Invert pan to release crust. Gently peel off foil and return crust to pie dish. Refrigerate.
- For filling: Using electric mixer, beat cream cheese in large bowl until smooth. Beat in sugar and vanilla. Gradually beat in peanut butter. Mix in nuts.
- In another bowl, beat chilled whipping cream to stiff peaks. Fold cream into peanut butter mixture in four additions.
- Transfer filling to crust, mounding slightly. Refrigerate at least 6 hours or overnight.
- For topping: Stir whipping cream and sugar in heavy saucepan over medium heat until sugar dissolves.
- Simmer without stirring until reduced to ⅔ cup, about 6 minutes. Add butter, chocolate, and vanilla. Stir until melted and smooth.
- Let topping stand until cool but still pourable, about 15 minutes. Spoon over pie, covering completely.
- Refrigerate until set, at least 4 hours.
- To serve, slice pie with warm knife.
- **Yield: 8 servings.**

Tommie Jean Hamner
Associate Professor Emerita, Department of Human
Development and Family Studies
College of Human Environmental Sciences

Nothing but the Best!

Smoky Mountain Apple Pie

6 baking apples, peeled and sliced
cinnamon to taste
5 slices white bread, crusts removed
1 egg, beaten
1 ½ cups sugar
1 cup margarine, melted
1 teaspoon vanilla
ice cream

- Coat a 13 x 9-inch baking dish with cooking spray.
- Layer apples in dish and sprinkle with cinnamon.
- Slice bread into fingers. Layer over apples.
- In a mixing bowl, combine egg and sugar. Stir in margarine. Add vanilla.
- Pour egg mixture over bread, completely covering bread.
- Bake at 350° for 30 minutes or until golden brown and bubbly.
- Eat it up while it's hot. Don't forget the ice cream on top!

Carol Olive
Administrative Secretary, Department of Journalism
College of Communication

Coconut-Pineapple Custard Pie

4 eggs, beaten
2 cups sugar
1 tablespoon cornmeal
1 tablespoon flour
½ cup margarine, softened
1 tablespoon vanilla
1 (12-ounce) can crushed pineapple,
    undrained
1 (3½-ounce) small can coconut
2 unbaked (9-inch) pie crusts

- Combine all ingredients except crusts in mixing bowl
- Pour into crusts.
- Bake at 350° for 45 minutes or until brown and firm.

Lisa Parker
Administrative Specialist, Dean's Office
College of Human Environmental Sciences

Makes Its Own Crust Coconut Pie

4 eggs
1¾ cups sugar
½ cup self-rising flour
½ teaspoon baking powder
2 cups milk
1 teaspoon vanilla
dash of salt
¼ cup margarine, melted
2 (3½-ounce) cans coconut

- Preheat oven to 350°.
- In a large bowl, beat eggs until light. Add sugar, flour, milk, and vanilla. Beat well. Stir in margarine and coconut.
- Pour into 2 well-greased and floured 9-inch pie pans.
- Bake for 40 minutes until golden brown. Crust will form as it bakes.

Mable Adams
Beloved Faculty Member and Assistant Dean, 1944-70
School of Home Economics

Lemon Chess Pie

2 cups sugar
1 tablespoon flour
1 tablespoon cornmeal
4 eggs, beaten
¼ cup butter, melted
¼ cup milk
grated rind of two lemons
¼ cup lemon juice
1 (9-inch) pie shell, unbaked

- Toss sugar, flour, and cornmeal together lightly with a fork.
- Add eggs, butter, milk, lemon rind, and juice. Beat with mixer until smooth and thoroughly blended.
- Pour into unbaked pie shell.
- Bake at 375° for 35 to 45 minutes or until top is golden brown.

Tommie Jean Hamner
Associate Professor Emerita, Department of Human Development and Family Studies
College of Human Environmental Sciences

Mandarin Orange Pie

2 (6-ounce) cans mandarin oranges, divided
1 (16-ounce) carton frozen whipped topping, thawed
1 (14-ounce) can sweetened condensed milk
1 (6-ounce) can frozen orange juice concentrate, thawed
1 cup chopped pecans
2 (8-inch) graham cracker pie crusts

- Drain and chop one can of mandarin oranges.
- Combine with whipped topping, condensed milk, orange juice, and pecans in a large bowl. Mix thoroughly.
- Pour into pie crusts. Garnish with remaining oranges. Chill before serving.

Deborah Hamilton
Assistant Director, Center for Business and Economic Research
College of Commerce and Business Administration

Nothing but the Best!

Easy Orange Chiffon Pie

¾ cup orange-flavored breakfast drink mix

1 (14-ounce) can sweetened condensed milk

1 (8-ounce) carton sour cream

1 cup whipped topping

1 graham cracker pie crust

- Dissolve drink mix in condensed milk. Fold in sour cream and whipped topping.
- Pour into pie crust.
- Chill overnight in refrigerator.
- **Yield: 8 servings.**

Carolyn Elaine Stewart '95
Acquisitions
University Libraries

Peach and Berry Pie

4½ cups peeled and sliced fresh peaches

¾ cup blueberries or blackberries

½ cup sugar

¼ cup firmly packed brown sugar

3 tablespoons flour

¼ teaspoon cinnamon

¼ teaspoon almond extract

1 tablespoon butter

pastry for 9-inch double crust deep dish pie

- Preheat oven to 400°.
- Place peaches and berries in a large bowl.
- Combine sugar, flour, and cinnamon. Sprinkle over fruit. Add almond extract and toss lightly.
- Fill pie crust with fruit mixture. Dot with butter. Place top crust on filling and press outside edge together to seal. Cut 1-inch slits in top of crust.
- Place in center of oven. Bake 45 to 50 minutes or until top is golden brown.

Marian Loftin '58
Regional Director, Economic and Community Affairs
Dothan, Alabama

Mila's Peach Pie

1 cup sugar

2 tablespoons cornstarch

1 cup water

¼ cup peach-flavored gelatin mix

1½ cups fresh peach slices

1 (9-inch) deep-dish pie shell, baked

1 (12-ounce) carton whipped cream or lite non-dairy whipped topping, optional

- Combine sugar, cornstarch, and water in medium saucepan. Cook over medium heat until thick and clear, stirring constantly.
- Remove from heat, and add gelatin. Stir well to dissolve gelatin. Cool briefly.
- Add peaches, stirring to coat completely.
- Pour fruit into pie shell. Refrigerate several hours or overnight.
- Garnish with whipped cream or non-dairy topping, if desired.

Mila Key Johnson '68
Greensboro, Alabama

Jeanne's Strawberry Pie

4 egg whites

1 cup sugar

20 round crackers, crushed

1 cup chopped nuts

3 (10-ounce) boxes frozen strawberries, thawed and drained

1 (16-ounce) carton frozen whipped topping, thawed

- Beat egg whites and sugar until stiff. Fold in cracker crumbs and nuts.
- Spread over bottom and sides of a greased 9-inch pie pan.
- Bake at 350° for 30 minutes. Cool.
- Fold strawberries into whipped topping. Fill cooled crust.

A delicious pie with the perfect colors for a Crimson Tide gathering!

Betsy Barrett
Former Instructor, Department of Human Nutrition and Hospitality Management
College of Human Environmental Sciences

Cream Cheese Pie

Crust:

vanilla wafers, finely crushed

¼ cup butter, melted

¼ cup sugar

Filling:

3 (8-ounce) packages cream cheese, softened

¾ cup sugar

1 tablespoon flour

¼ teaspoon salt

2 eggs, separated

2 teaspoons vanilla

½ cup evaporated milk

pinch of salt

- For crust: Toss wafer crumbs with butter and sugar and press into greased deep dish pie pan.
- For filling: Beat cream cheese with electric mixer until light and fluffy.
- Combine sugar, flour, and salt. Mix thoroughly. Add to cream cheese and beat until smooth. Add egg yolks and vanilla. Beat until well blended. Add evaporated milk and mix.
- Beat egg whites with a pinch of salt until soft peaks form. Fold into cream cheese mixture.
- Fill crust. Place on cookie sheet and bake at 325° for 45 minutes.
- Serve warm. Refrigerate any leftovers.

Judy Mayer
Wife of Morris Mayer, Bruno Professor Emeritus of Marketing
College of Commerce and Business Administration

Nothing but the Best!

Pumpkin Praline Pie

Crust:

⅓ cup finely chopped pecans

⅓ cup firmly packed brown sugar

3 tablespoons butter, softened

1 (9-inch) pie shell, unbaked

Pie filling:

3 eggs, slightly beaten

½ cup sugar

½ cup firmly packed brown sugar

2 tablespoons flour

¾ teaspoon salt

¾ teaspoon cinnamon

½ teaspoon ginger

¼ teaspoon cloves

1½ cups mashed pumpkin, cooked or canned

1½ cups half and half

- For crust: Toss together pecans, brown sugar, and butter. Press into bottom of unbaked pie shell. Prick sides with fork.
- Bake at 450° for 10 minutes. Cool 2 minutes.
- For pie filling: Combine all ingredients except pumpkin and half and half in a mixing bowl. Add pumpkin and mix.
- Heat half and half and gradually stir into pumpkin mixture. Blend well.
- Pour into pie shell.
- Bake at 350° for 50 to 60 minutes or until a knife inserted halfway between center and edge of filling comes out clean. Cool.
- **Yield: 10 servings.**

Beverly Smith
Executive Secretary, Dean's Office
New College

Surprise Angel Pecan Pie

3 egg whites, room temperature
⅛ teaspoon salt
1 cup sugar
1 teaspoon vanilla
¾ cup chopped pecans
¾ cup crushed soda crackers
1 teaspoon baking powder

Topping:
1 cup whipping cream
2 tablespoons sugar
1 teaspoon vanilla

- Preheat oven to 350°.
- Grease a 9-inch pie pan. Line with foil and grease foil.
- Beat egg whites and salt with mixer at high speed until soft peaks form. Gradually add sugar, 2 tablespoons at a time, beating well after each addition. Continue beating until stiff, glossy peaks form. Add vanilla.
- Fold pecans, crackers, and baking powder into egg white mixture. Spread evenly in prepared pie pan.
- Bake 35 minutes or until light golden, but not brown.
- Cool on wire rack for 2 hours. Using foil, lift pie from pan; refrigerate until well chilled, at least 1 hour or overnight.
- For Topping: In small bowl, with mixer at medium speed, beat whipping cream with sugar and vanilla until stiff peaks form.
- Remove foil from crust and place pie on plate. Spread with whipped cream.
- **Yield: 8 servings.**

Mary Catherine Beasley
Professor Emerita, Department of Consumer Sciences
School of Home Economics

Walnut Pie

½ cup light corn syrup
1 cup sugar
¼ cup butter, melted
3 eggs, well beaten
1 cup chopped English walnuts
1 (9-inch) pie shell, unbaked

- Combine syrup, sugar, and melted butter. Add eggs and walnuts and mix well.
- Pour into pie shell and bake at 300° for 45 minutes.

Isabel Vartanian, R.D '57
Hopewell, Virginia

Egg Custard Pie

6 eggs

1 cup sugar

1 teaspoon vanilla

2 tablespoons butter, melted

2 cups milk

1 (9-inch) deep dish pie shell, baked lightly

- Beat eggs. Add sugar and beat well. Add vanilla and melted butter. Blend well. Add milk and beat lightly.
- Pour in pie shell and bake at 350° for 1 hour or until it does not shake in the middle.

Penny Calhoun Gilsen
Reference Librarian, Law School Library
School of Law

Pie Crust

For 6-inch double, 8 or 9-inch single:

½ cup shortening

½ teaspoon salt

1⅓ cups sifted flour

¼ cup plus 2 tablespoons water

For 8 or 9-inch double, 10-inch single:

¾ cup shortening

1 teaspoon salt

2 cups sifted flour

½ cup water

For 10-inch double:

1 cup plus 2 tablespoons shortening

1½ teaspoons salt

3 cups sifted flour

¾ cup water

- Cut shortening into salt and flour with pastry blender. Add water while tossing with a fork and blend just until dough forms.
- Turn out onto heavily floured cloth and knead slightly just to cover with flour.
- Roll out and sprinkle more flour on dough as needed to keep it from sticking.

Beverly C. Smith
Executive Secretary, Dean's Office
New College

Judy's Apple Cobbler

1½ cups self-rising flour
½ cup shortening
⅓ cup milk
2 cups finely chopped apples
1 teaspoon apple pie spice or cinnamon
½ cup butter
2 cups sugar
3 cups water

- Preheat oven to 350°.
- Cut shortening into flour until particles resemble fine crumbs. Add milk and stir with a fork just until dough leaves the side of the bowl.
- Turn onto a lightly floured board. Knead just enough—do not overwork the dough. Roll dough into a large rectangle ½-inch thick. Dust liberally with flour.
- Sprinkle apples evenly over dough. Roll up jellyroll-style. Slice into ½-inch thick slices.
- Place in a 13 x 9 x 2-inch pan.
- Combine sugar, spice, butter, and water in a saucepan. Heat, stirring, until sugar melts.
- Pour carefully around rolls. (This looks like too much liquid, but the crust will absorb it.)
- Bake for 55 to 60 minutes.

This cobbler may be made with other fruit—fresh, frozen, or canned such as blackberries, cherries, or peaches. If using peaches, add ½ teaspoon almond extract and 1 teaspoon vanilla to the sugar mixture.

Judith Reeves
Executive Secretary
The Interim Program

Granny's Peach Cobbler

1 cup milk
1 cup self-rising flour
1 cup sugar
½ cup butter, melted
1 (20-ounce) can peaches, drained
ice cream

- Preheat oven to 350°.
- Mix milk, flour, and sugar. Stir well.
- Pour butter into sugar mixture. Spoon in peaches. If too thick, add a little juice from peaches.
- Pour into greased baking dish.
- Bake for 30 minutes until golden brown.
- Serve topped with ice cream.

Teresa Gilstrap Pruett
Office Assistant, Division of Environmental and Industrial
Programs
College of Continuing Studies

Quick and Easy Peach Cobbler

4 (12-ounce) cans sliced peaches
1 (18¼-ounce) box yellow cake mix
½ cup butter

- Layer peaches in a 13 x 9-inch pan.
- Pour cake mix over peaches, spreading out evenly and crumbling up any lumps.
- Top with butter sliced into thin enough pieces to cover entire surface.
- Bake at 350° for one hour or longer, until golden brown on top.
- Serve hot.

Melinda Sue Foster
Administrative Secretary, Engineering Student Services
College of Engineering

Rhubarb Crunch

2 cups diced rhubarb
1¼ cups flour, divided
¾ cup sugar
1 cup firmly packed brown sugar
1 cup oatmeal
¼ teaspoon salt
½ cup margarine, softened

- Arrange rhubarb in greased 9 x 9-inch baking dish.
- Combine ¼ cup flour and sugar. Sprinkle over rhubarb.
- Blend together remaining ingredients and sprinkle over rhubarb mixture.
- Bake at 325° for 40 minutes or until topping is brown.
- **Yield: 8 servings.**

Kay Culton
Director, Freshman Writing Lab Center
for Athletic Student Services

Crimson Roll

3 eggs

1 cup sugar

1 (1-ounce) bottle red food coloring

1 teaspoon white vinegar

⅔ cup applesauce

1 teaspoon lemon juice

¾ cup flour

1 teaspoon baking powder

2 teaspoons cinnamon

1 teaspoon ginger

1 teaspoon nutmeg

½ teaspoon salt

1 teaspoon vanilla

1 cup chopped pecans

Filling:

1 (8-ounce) package cream cheese, softened

3 cups powdered sugar

6 tablespoons butter, softened

1 teaspoon vanilla

- Beat eggs on high speed of mixer for 5 minutes. Gradually beat in sugar. Stir in food coloring and vinegar; mix well. Stir in applesauce and lemon juice.
- Sift together flour, baking powder, spices, and salt. Fold into applesauce mixture
- Spread batter in a greased and floured jelly roll pan. Top with chopped pecans.
- Bake at 375° for 15 minutes or until done. Turn out on a towel sprinkled with powdered sugar.
- Starting at narrow end, roll towel and cake together. Nuts should be on outside. Cool.
- For filling: Combine all ingredients and blend well. Chill.
- Unroll cooled roll and spread filling over cake. Roll and freeze.

This is elegant and delicious.

Beth Gibbs '84 '86
Computer Coordinator
College of Human Environmental Sciences

Cheesecake

1 cup graham cracker crumbs

¼ cup butter, melted

½ cup plus 1 tablespoon sugar, divided

2 (8-ounce) packages cream cheese, softened

1 egg, beaten

½ cup milk

2 teaspoons vanilla

1 (8-ounce) carton sour cream

- Combine cracker crumbs, butter, and 1 teaspoon sugar thoroughly. Press firmly into buttered 8-inch springform pan.
- Bake at 400° for 10 minutes. Remove from oven and reduce temperature to 350°.
- Beat cream cheese on high speed of mixer until light and fluffy. Add egg, ½ cup sugar, milk, and 1 teaspoon vanilla. Blend well. Spread evenly on cooled crust.
- Bake 20 minutes. Remove from oven and cool. Increase oven temperature to 450°.
- Combine sour cream, remaining sugar, and vanilla. Blend well. Pour over cooled filling and bake an additional five minutes.
- Chill before serving.
- **Yield: 6 servings.**

Yvonne Houben '87
Business Coordinator, University Recreation

Caramel-Brownie Cheesecake

1¾ cups vanilla wafer crumbs

¼ cup plus 1 tablespoon butter, melted

1 (14-ounce) package caramels

1 (5-ounce) can evaporated milk

2 cups coarsely crumbled unfrosted
  brownies*

3 (8-ounce) packages cream cheese, softened

1 cup firmly packed brown sugar

3 large eggs

1 (8-ounce) carton sour cream

2 teaspoons vanilla

whipped cream, optional

chocolate-lined wafer roll cookies, optional

*Note: Buy prepackaged unfrosted brownies from
a bakery, or prepare your favorite mix; let cool
and crumble enough to yield 2 cups.

- Combine vanilla wafer crumbs and butter, stirring well. Press mixture firmly in bottom and 2 inches up sides of a 9-inch springform pan.
- Bake at 350° for 5 minutes. Let cool completely on a wire rack.
- Combine caramels and milk in a small heavy saucepan. Cook over low heat, stirring often, until caramels melt.
- Pour caramel mixture over crust. Sprinkle crumbled brownies over caramel.
- Beat cream cheese at medium speed of an electric mixer 2 minutes or until light and fluffy. Gradually add sugar, mixing well. Add eggs, one at a time, beating just until blended. Stir in sour cream and vanilla.
- Pour batter over brownie crumbs.
- Bake at 350° for 50 to 60 minutes or until cheesecake is almost set.
- Remove from oven, and let cool to room temperature on a wire rack.
- Cover and chill at least 4 hours. Remove sides of springform pan. Garnish with whipped cream and cookies, if desired.

Janice Faulkner '88
Tuscaloosa, Alabama

Nothing but the Best!

Chocolate Caramel Pecan Cheesecake

1 ¼ cups graham cracker crumbs

¼ cup butter, melted

1 (14-ounce) package caramels

1 (5-ounce) can evaporated milk

1 cup toasted and chopped pecans

2 (8-ounce) packages cream cheese, softened

½ cup sugar

2 eggs

1 teaspoon vanilla

¾ cup semisweet chocolate morsels, melted

pecan halves

- Combine crumbs and butter, stirring well.
- Press mixture evenly onto bottom and 1 inch up sides of a 9-inch springform pan.
- Bake at 350° for 6 to 8 minutes. Cool.
- Combine caramels and milk in a heavy saucepan. Cook over low heat until melted, stirring often.
- Pour over graham cracker crust. Sprinkle pecans evenly over caramel layer and set aside.
- Beat cream cheese at medium speed of an electric mixer until light and fluffy. Gradually add sugar, mixing well. Add eggs, one at a time, beating well after each addition. Stir in vanilla and chocolate. Beat until blended. Spoon over pecan layer.
- Bake at 350° for 30 minutes. Remove from oven, and run knife around edge of pan to release sides.
- Let cool to room temperature on a wire rack. Cover and chill at least 8 hours.
- When ready to serve, remove cheesecake from pan. Arrange pecan halves around top edge of cheesecake.

Leigh Ann Danner Summerford '80
Tuscaloosa, Alabama

Italian Ricotta Cheesecake

unbaked pie crust

1 pound whole milk ricotta cheese

5 tablespoons sugar, divided

3 eggs, separated

3 tablespoons all-purpose flour

1 tablespoon rum

3 tablespoons cream

2 tablespoons vanilla extract

rind of one lemon, plus 1 tablespoon lemon
  juice

¼ cup chopped candied fruit

2 tablespoons sugar

- Line an 8-inch round cake pan (not a pie pan) with pie crust. With fingers, press the dough evenly in the pan and up to the top rim of the pan.
- Preheat oven to 425°.
- Beat ricotta cheese well with 3 tablespoons sugar, egg yolks, flour, rum, cream, vanilla, lemon rind, and lemon juice.
- Add fruit and mix well.
- In a separate bowl, beat egg whites with remaining sugar until stiff. Fold beaten whites carefully but thoroughly into the cheese batter.
- Pour into crust and bake 10 minutes. Reduce temperature to 350° and bake for an additional 50 minutes. Turn off oven, open door slightly, and leave for 15 minutes more.
- Remove from oven and allow to cool on a rack.

Michael P. Cava
Ramsay Professor, Chemistry Department
College of Arts and Sciences

Joe Namath's Favorite Almond Torte

1¼ cups sugar

8 ounces almond paste

1¼ cups butter, softened

1 teaspoon vanilla

6 eggs, room temperature

1 cup flour

1½ teaspoons baking powder

¼ teaspoon salt

- Preheat oven to 325°.
- Beat sugar with almond paste at high speed of electric mixer, until paste is in fine pieces, or pulverize in food processor.
- Add butter and vanilla. Cream mixture until it is light and fluffy. Beat in eggs, one at a time, mixing well after each addition.
- Combine flour and baking powder. Add to sugar mixture. Blend well.
- Pour into a buttered and floured 9-inch springform pan. Smooth top with a spatula.
- Bake for 1 to 1¼ hours, or until toothpick comes out clean and center feels springy when touched gently.

Joe Namath '63
New York, New York

Fruit Pizza

Crust:

1 (16-ounce) roll refrigerated sugar cookie
  dough

Filling:

1 (8-ounce) package cream cheese, softened

½ cup sugar

1 teaspoon vanilla

fruit: oranges, peaches, pears, grapes,
  strawberries, bananas, kiwi

Topping:

¼ cup lemon juice

1 cup orange juice

3 tablespoons cornstarch

1 cup sugar

¾ cup water

- For crust: Cut dough into thin slices. Layer on a pizza pan, leaving ¼-inch space between slices.
- Bake at 350° for 15 to 18 minutes. Let cool at least 15 minutes.
- For filling: Combine cream cheese, sugar, and vanilla. Mix until well blended. Spread over cooled crust.
- Slice fruit and arrange on filling.
- For topping: Combine all ingredients in a saucepan. Cook over medium heat until liquid is thick and clear, stirring often. Pour over fruit.
- Refrigerate until ready to serve.

Penny Calhoun Gibson '83 '89
Reference Librarian, Law School Library
School of Law

All Shook Up Vanilla Ice Cream

pint-size plastic bag
½ cup milk
1 tablespoon sugar
¼ teaspoon vanilla
gallon-size plastic bag
6 tablespoons salt

- In a pint-size bag, mix milk, sugar, and vanilla. Seal.
- Fill gallon-size bag half full of ice and salt. Put sealed small bag into the ice. Seal large bag.
- Shake bag about 5 minutes until it becomes ice cream. Remove small bag from ice. Wipe off.
- Open and dig in!

Joan Smithson '71
Tuscaloosa, Alabama

Fresh Peach Ice Cream

6 cups pureed fresh peaches
3 cups sugar
4 cups half and half

- Puree fresh peaches in blender or food chopper.
- Mix thoroughly with sugar and cream.
- Freeze in ice cream freezer.

This ice cream is rich and delicious, but does not keep well in freezer. Many former students majoring in food and nutrition will remember going to Dr. Stitt's home for this ice cream.

Kathleen Stitt '46 '55
Professor Emerita, Department of Human Nutrition and
Hospitality Management
College of Human Environmental Sciences

"No Cook" Chocolate Ice Cream

2 (3-ounce) packages chocolate instant
  pudding
2 (14-ounce) cans sweetened condensed milk
½ gallon milk

- Combine all ingredients. Freeze in ice cream freezer.

Sandra Perkins '84
Advisor/Contract Coordinator, External Degree
New College

Nothing but the Best!

Homemade Low-Fat Ice Cream

3 cups sugar
1 carton Egg Beaters (equivalent to 4 eggs)
1 teaspoon vanilla
dash of salt substitute
2 (12-ounce) cans light evaporated milk
skim milk

- Combine all ingredients except skim milk. Mix well.
- Pour into ice cream maker. Fill to line with skim milk.
- Freeze according to manufacturer's directions.
- **Yield: 1 gallon.**

It's GREAT!

Linda Southern
Program Assistant
Alumni Affairs

Frozen Coconut Cream Dessert

Crust:
1 cup all-purpose flour
½ cup margarine, melted
1 cup chopped pecans

Filling:
¼ cup margarine
1 (7-ounce) can flaked coconut
½ cup chopped pecans
1 (8-ounce) package cream cheese, softened
1 (14-ounce) can sweetened condensed milk
1 (12-ounce) container frozen whipped topping, thawed
1 (12-ounce) jar caramel sauce

- For crust: Combine all ingredients. Pat into 9 x 13-inch pan. Bake at 350° for 20 minutes. Cool.
- For filling: Cook margarine, coconut, and pecans over low heat until coconut is browned, stirring to avoid burning. Cool.
- Beat cream cheese until smooth. Add condensed milk. Mix well. Fold in whipped topping.
- Layer half of cream cheese mixture over cooled crust. Top with half of coconut mixture. Drizzle half of caramel sauce over this. Repeat.
- Freeze.

Karen Greenlee Conner '72
Birmingham, Alabama

Frozen Banana Orange Treats

3 bananas, peeled and mashed
2 cups orange juice
3 tablespoons lemon juice
½ cup sugar

- Mix all ingredients. Freeze in ice cube trays or small containers.

This recipe has been in the Paul "Bear" Bryant family for generations. It is enjoyed by children of all ages.

Cherry H. Bryant '66
Tuscaloosa, Alabama

Rich Banana Pudding

1 (6-ounce) large package instant vanilla pudding
2½ cups cold milk
1 (14-ounce) can sweetened condensed milk
1 (16-ounce) container whipped topping, thawed
sliced bananas
vanilla wafers

- Mix pudding and milk. Add condensed milk and blend. Fold in half the whipped topping.
- Alternate layers of custard, bananas, and vanilla wafers. Top with remaining whipped topping.
- Refrigerate overnight before serving.

Fresh, ripe peaches or strawberries in place of bananas are great! Beautiful in footed, glass trifle bowl, which is also the perfect size.

Ann Smith Brasher
Accounting Specialist, School of Mines and Energy
Development

Bread Pudding with Bourbon Sauce

6 eggs
2½ cups sugar
1 tablespoon cinnamon
1 tablespoon nutmeg
1 tablespoon vanilla
½ cup margarine, melted
1 quart milk
6 cups French bread crumbs
1 cup chopped pecans
1 cup raisins

Bourbon Sauce:
⅔ cup sugar
1 egg
½ cup butter, melted
1 teaspoon fresh lemon juice
nutmeg
⅓ cup bourbon

- Whip eggs until frothy. Add sugar, spices, vanilla, and margarine. Mix well.
- Add milk and bread crumbs. Mix and let soak for 15 minutes. Stir in nuts and raisins.
- Pour into greased 3-quart baking dish. Bake at 350° for 45 minutes or until set.
- For bourbon sauce: Combine sugar and egg in small bowl and beat with mixer until blended. Stir in melted butter.
- Cook on top of double boiler over simmering water, whisking constantly, until sugar is dissolved and sauce has thickened.
- Remove from heat and add lemon, nutmeg, and bourbon.
- Pour warm sauce over pudding.

Becky Strickland
Adjunct Faculty, Department of Consumer Sciences
College of Human Environmental Sciences

Nothing but the Best!

Janie Darden's Chocolate Bread Pudding

2 cups biscuit crumbs
1 quart milk
¼ cup margarine
2 eggs, beaten
6 tablespoons cocoa
1½ cups sugar
1 teaspoon vanilla

- Preheat oven to 350°.
- Crumble biscuits into milk in a saucepan. Add margarine. Cook over low heat until margarine melts and biscuits are soft.
- Add eggs, cocoa, sugar, and vanilla. Beat well.
- Pour into 2 buttered medium baking dishes. Set in pan containing an inch of hot water.
- Bake at 350° for 1 hour or until firm.

Leatha Darden
Associate Professor, Department of Clothing,
Textiles, and Interior Design
College of Human Environmental Sciences

The "Bear's" Crimson and White Dessert

1 angel food cake
1 (6-ounce) package instant vanilla pudding
1 (20-ounce) can crushed pineapple, drained
1 (21-ounce) can strawberry pie filling
1 (8-ounce) container frozen whipped
    topping, thawed
chopped nuts, optional
fresh strawberries, optional

- Tear cake into bite-size pieces. Layer one-third in a trifle bowl.
- Mix pudding according to package directions. Spread half of pudding over cake. Top with half of pineapple, half of pie filling, and one-third of whipped topping.
- Repeat layering. For final layer, use remaining cake and spread with remaining topping.
- Garnish with nuts and strawberries, if desired.

Linda Letson

Death By Chocolate

1 (18¾-ounce) box devil's food lite cake mix
½ cup Kahlua
2 (3½- ounce) boxes chocolate mousse mix
1 (12-ounce) container lite whipped topping
4 toffee candy bars

- Bake cake mix as directed on box. Cool and crumble.
- Put half into a large trifle bowl. Sprinkle ¼ cup Kahlua over cake.
- Mix mousse as directed on box. Spread half over cake. Top with half of whipped topping.
- Crush candy bars and sprinkle half over whipped topping.
- Repeat all layers.

Karen Greenlee Conner '72
Birmingham, Alabama

Desserts

Oreo Cookie Ice Cream Cake

1 (16-ounce) can chocolate syrup
1 (14-ounce) can sweetened condensed milk
½ cup butter
30 Oreo cookies, crushed
¼ cup butter, melted
½ gallon vanilla ice cream, softened
1 (8-ounce) carton frozen whipped topping, thawed
shaved chocolate, optional
chopped nuts, optional

- Combine syrup, condensed milk, and butter in saucepan. Bring to a boil, then simmer for 5 minutes. Remove from heat, and let cool.
- Cover bottom of 13 x 9-inch pan with cookie crumbs. Drizzle with melted butter. Stir and pat down. Freeze for 30 minutes.
- Spread softened ice cream over cookie mixture and freeze for 30 minutes.
- Spread cooled chocolate mixture over ice cream and freeze for 30 minutes.
- Top with whipped topping and sprinkle with chocolate shaving and nuts, if desired.

Shelby Chandler
Program Assistant, Department of Criminal Justice
College of Arts and Sciences

Super Sweet Chocolate Dessert

4 ounces German sweet chocolate
¼ cup margarine
1 (14-ounce) can evaporated milk
1½ cups sugar
3 tablespoons cornstarch
⅛ teaspoon salt
2 eggs, beaten
1 teaspoon vanilla
1½ cups flake coconut
½ cup chopped nuts
whipped topping, whipped cream, or ice cream, optional

- Melt chocolate and margarine over low heat in a heavy saucepan. Add milk. Beat well with beater to blend ingredients. Set aside to cool.
- Combine sugar, cornstarch, and salt. Mix well. Add eggs and vanilla. Beat until well blended.
- Gradually add cooled chocolate mixture. Beat until well blended.
- Pour into a greased 8-inch square baking pan. Sprinkle with coconut and nuts.
- Bake at 375° for 45 to 50 minutes. Cut into squares to serve.
- Garnish with whipped topping, whipped cream or ice cream, if desired.
- **Yield: 8 to 12 servings.**

Freezes well.

Mary A. Crenshaw
Dean and Professor Emerita
School of Home Economics

Nothing but the Best!

Apricot-Chocolate Truffles

1 (10-ounce) package premium-quality
   bittersweet chocolate, finely chopped
½ cup whipping cream
2 tablespoons powdered sugar
2 beaten egg yolks or 3 tablespoons egg
   substitute
2 tablespoons Kirschwasser liqueur
½ cup finely chopped dried apricots
1 (12-ounce) box chocolate cookie wafers,
   finely chopped

- Finely chop chocolate in food processor, being careful not to melt it.
- Combine cream and sugar in medium saucepan. Cook over low heat, stirring continuously. Remove from heat when boiling begins.
- Quickly stir in chocolate until melted. Stir in Kirschwasser, eggs, and apricots until smooth.
- Store mixture in saucepan in refrigerator 6 to 8 hours.
- Spread cookie crumbs on waxed paper. Shape apricot mixture into 1½-inch truffles. Roll in cookie crumbs.
- Keep refrigerated in decorative tin or muffin tin.
- **Yield: 30-36 truffles.**

Dr. John F. Schmitt
Assistant Dean, The Graduate School
Professor of Communicative Disorders
College of Arts and Sciences

Divinity

4 egg whites
4 cups granulated sugar
½ cup corn syrup
1 cup water
¼ teaspoon salt
1 teaspoon vanilla
pecan halves

- Beat egg whites until stiff.
- Cook sugar, corn syrup, water, and salt in a heavy saucepan to 240° on a candy thermometer.
- Pour ½ cup hot syrup over egg whites, beating constantly. Add vanilla and continue beating.
- Continue cooking remaining syrup to 260°. Pour over egg white mixture slowly, beating until the divinity holds peaks.
- Spoon onto buttered wax paper. Decorate with pecan half on each piece.
- **Yield: 60 large pieces.**

Studying food and nutrition at The University of Alabama is a family tradition. Mrs. Pacey's daughter, Susan Pacey Harvison, and her granddaughter, Kim Pacey, are also graduates. Mrs. Pacey owns the famous Punta Clara Kitchen in Point Clear, Alabama.

Dorothy Broadbeck Pacey '42
Point Clear, Alabama

Punta Clara Pralines

3½ cups sugar, divided
1½ cups water
¼ teaspoon salt
1 tablespoon corn syrup
1 tablespoon margarine
1 teaspoon butter maple flavoring
1 cup pecans

- Cook 1 cup sugar in heavy saucepan, stirring continuously, until golden brown. Add water and salt. Stir until no lumps of sugar are on spoon or bottom of pan.
- Add syrup, margarine, and remaining sugar. Cook to 238° on candy thermometer and remove from heat.
- Cool to 180°. Add flavoring and pecans. Beat until candy thickens.
- Spoon out onto buttered wax paper.
- **Yield: 30 2-inch pralines.**

Dorothy Broadbeck Pacey '42
Point Clear, Alabama

Sugar Bowl Pralines

1 cup buttermilk
2 cups sugar
2 tablespoons butter
1 tablespoon baking soda
⅛ teaspoon salt
2½ cups chopped pecans

- Mix buttermilk, sugar, butter, soda, and salt in a heavy saucepan. Cook over high heat for 4 to 6 minutes.
- Remove from heat and add pecans. Beat until creamy.
- Drop spoonfuls onto wax paper and allow to cool.

May also be served warm as a sauce over vanilla ice cream.

Adam Hodges
Athens, Alabama

Chocolate Logs

1 (16-ounce) box confectioners sugar
1 cup flake coconut
1 cup chopped pecans
1 teaspoon vanilla
1 cup graham cracker crumbs
½ cup crunchy peanut butter
1 cup butter, melted
½ block paraffin
1 (6-ounce) package semi-sweet chocolate chips

- Thoroughly mix sugar, coconut, pecans, vanilla, and graham cracker crumbs into peanut butter. Pour butter over mixture and blend well.
- Shape into 2 x 2½-inch logs.
- Melt paraffin and chocolate chips together over boiling water.
- Leave chocolate mixture over hot water in double boiler. With a fork, dip and roll each log in chocolate until well coated, working quickly.
- Place on wax paper to dry.

Deborah F. Davis
Capstone Medical Center

Rocky Road Candy Squares

1 (12-ounce) package semi-sweet chocolate
    morsels
1 (14-ounce) can sweetened condensed milk
2 tablespoons butter
1 (10-ounce) package miniature
    marshmallows
2 cups dry toasted peanuts

- Combine chocolate, condensed milk, and butter in top of double boiler. Heat over boiling water until chocolate is melted.
- In a large mixing bowl, combine marshmallows and nuts. Add chocolate mixture and stir until marshmallows and nuts are coated.
- Pour into a buttered 12 x 9-inch glass dish.
- Chill at least 2 hours or until firm enough to cut smoothly. Cut into small squares.
- May be kept at room temperature in air-tight container.

Note: At holiday time, garnish with thinly sliced red cherries.

Jade Abernathy
Program Assistant, Department of Advertising
and Public Relations
College of Communication

Strawberry Shaped Treats

¼ cup margarine
½ cup sugar
1 (8-ounce) package pitted dates, chopped
½ cup canned coconut
pinch of salt
1½ cup rice cereal
½ cup chopped pecans
1 egg, beaten
1 teaspoon vanilla
1 (1¼-ounce) jar fine, red sugar crystals
1 (12-ounce) can green decorator frosting

- Place margarine and sugar in skillet. Stir over low heat until sugar is dissolved. Add dates and coconut. Continue cooking over low heat, stirring constantly, until mixture bubbles and thickens. Add salt and remove from heat.
- Stir in cereal, pecans, egg, and vanilla. Let cool 8 to 10 minutes or until it can be handled.
- Shape into strawberries. Roll in red sugar crystals until well coated. Let cool completely.
- Make stems for strawberries with green frosting.

Toppy Ezell '67 '69 '74
Associate Professor Emerita,
Department of Management and Marketing
College of Commerce and Business Administration

Sherried Pecans

½ cup cream sherry
1½ cups sugar
1 teaspoon water
½ teaspoon cinnamon
dash salt
2½ cups pecan halves

- Combine sherry, sugar, and water in a saucepan. Bring to a boil and cook to soft ball stage.
- Remove from heat. Add cinnamon and salt. Add pecan halves and stir gently until cloudy looking.
- Quickly spread on wax paper, separating nuts.

Ruth H. Paulk '56
Lexington, Kentucky

Grandmother's Homemade Christmas Candy

2 cups sugar
½ cup light corn syrup
¼ cup margarine
½ cup milk
4 heaping tablespoons cocoa
pinch of salt
½ teaspoon vanilla
2 cups peanuts, parched and ground

- Place all ingredients except ground peanuts, in a large saucepan. Cook over medium heat, stirring, until sugar dissolves.
- Continue cooking, without stirring, until mixture reaches a soft ball stage when tested in cold water.
- Remove from heat and let cool 3 minutes.
- Beat until mixture begins to thicken. Add peanuts and stir well.
- Pour into buttered pan. When firm, cut in 1-inch squares.
- **Variation**: For caramel candy, use brown sugar and omit cocoa.

Olivia Kendrick
Associate Professor, Department of Human Nutrition and
Hospitality Management
College of Human Environmental Sciences

Chocolate Party Mix

4 cups Captain Crunch Cereal
4 cups Rice Krispies
2 cups salted roasted peanuts
2 (24-ounce) packages chocolate almond bark

- Toss cereals and peanuts together in a large bowl.
- Melt chocolate and pour over cereal mixture.
- Spread in thin layer on wax paper. When completely set, break into pieces.

Patricia Powell '59
Hoover, Alabama

Nothing but the Best!

Oleta's Butterscotch Crunch Squares

1 cup flour
½ cup instant oatmeal
¼ cup firmly packed brown sugar
½ cup butter, melted
½ cup chopped pecans
1 (12-ounce) jar butterscotch or caramel ice
    cream topping
1 quart vanilla ice cream, softened

- Combine flour, oatmeal, and brown sugar. Stir in butter. Mix well until mixture resembles coarse crumbs. Stir in pecans and pat mixture into a 9-inch square baking pan.
- Bake at 400° until browned. Stir while warm so a crumbly mixture is formed. Let cool.
- Pat three-quarters of crumb mixture in bottom of 9-inch square pan. Drizzle half of topping over crumbs in pan. Spoon softened ice cream over topping mixture. Sprinkle with remaining crumb mixture. Freeze.
- Cut into squares to serve.

Lisa Parker
Administrative Specialist, Dean's Office
College of Human Environmental Sciences

Chocolate Sauce

1½ squares unsweetened baking chocolate
2 tablespoons water
½ cup sugar
½ teaspoon salt
1½ tablespoons light corn syrup
½ cup evaporated milk
½ teaspoon vanilla

- Melt chocolate over hot water. Add water, sugar, salt, and syrup.
- Cook over direct heat until a soft ball is formed when dropped in cold water. Remove from heat.
- Add milk and vanilla and stir until smooth.

From the University Club cookbook published in the early 1960s.

Lydia Roper
Associate Professor, Department of Clothing, Textiles, and
Interior Design
College of Human Environmental Sciences

Index

College of Human Environmental Sciences
Box 870158
The University of Alabama
Tuscaloosa, Alabama 35487-0158

Please send _____ copies of *Nothing but the Best!* @ $24.95 each $ _____

Postage and Handling @ $ 4.00 each _____

Alabama residents add 8% sales tax _____

Name _____

Address _____

City _____ State _____ Zip _____

Make checks payable to The University of Alabama

College of Human Environmental Sciences
Box 870158
The University of Alabama
Tuscaloosa, Alabama 35487-0158

Please send _____ copies of *Nothing but the Best!* @ $24.95 each $ _____

Postage and Handling @ $ 4.00 each _____

Alabama residents add 8% sales tax _____

Name _____

Address _____

City _____ State _____ Zip _____

Make checks payable to The University of Alabama

College of Human Environmental Sciences
Box 870158
The University of Alabama
Tuscaloosa, Alabama 35487-0158

Please send _____ copies of *Nothing but the Best!* @ $24.95 each $ _____

Postage and Handling @ $ 4.00 each _____

Alabama residents add 8% sales tax _____

Name _____

Address _____

City _____ State _____ Zip _____

Make checks payable to The University of Alabama